Jethro K. Lieberman, a graduate of Yale, held a Felix Frankfurter Scholarship at the Harvard Law School, where he was also editor of *Harvard Legal Commentary*. Mr. Lieberman has served on the Washington staffs of United States Senators William Proxmire and Kenneth B. Keating. A member of the New York and Washington, D.C., Bars, he is on leave from *Business Week* magazine, where he was a staff writer specializing in law, to serve on active duty in the Judge Advocate General's Corps, United States Naval Reserve.

UNDERSTANDING
OUR CONSTITUTION

Jethro K. Lieberman

A FAWCETT PREMIER BOOK

Fawcett Publications, Inc., Greenwich, Conn.
Member of American Book Publishers Council, Inc.

for my wife, Susan Eileen

A Fawcett Premier Book published by arrangement with
Walker and Company

Library of Congress Catalog Card Number: 67-13236

First Premier printing, May 1968

Published by Fawcett World Library
67 West 44th Street
New York, New York 10036

Printed in the U.S.A.

ACKNOWLEDGMENTS

A short book on the Constitution involves so many possible errors that I would be seriously remiss were I to fail to acknowledge with many thanks the help of all those who cut down that possibility:

For his help in structuring the book and his characteristic willingness to give so freely of his time, my former teacher, the late Professor Mark DeWolfe Howe of Harvard Law School.

For their help through initial discussions, Kenneth F. Hadermann, Division Director, history teacher, former chairman of the department (and also my former teacher), at White Plains High School, White Plains, New York; Anthony Zanezzi, history teacher at White Plains; John Lindsey, chairman of the history department, Wayland High School, Wayland, Massachusetts; and the 11th grade history classes at Wayland during 1966-1967 who reacted to part of it in lecture form.

For their critical readings of the manuscript and copious suggestions, Professor Alpheus T. Mason of Princeton University and Wayne A. Frederick, instructor in history at Phillips Academy, Andover, Massachusetts.

For her help with the index, for her comments and suggestions, and her willingness to hold dinner that extra minute while another sentence was typed, my wife, herself a history teacher.

For the help that authors alone can appreciate, Edward L. Burlingame and the other editors at Walker and Company.

For any errors of fact or interpretation which remain, the blame must lie entirely with me.

J.K.L.

Cambridge, Massachusetts
April 1967

PREFACE

Learned Hand, one of America's eminent jurists, spoke of law at one time, of liberty on another occasion. He believed that the best law was a product of reason; he said, "the spirit of liberty is the spirit which is not too sure that it is right." These two concepts, law and liberty, provide the theme for the present work, *Understanding Our Constitution*. To understand our Constitution, according to Jethro Lieberman, is to recognize that the American experience has been a constant attempt to equate individual freedom with a society of law. What the Constitution means today is found in its words, these words which are designed to insure liberty, but not license; to provide a social order without despotism. Today's Constitution is largely the opinion of the Supreme Court, the final arbiter; a group of men without power to enforce any decisions; a group whose power is only to pronounce a judgment.

Thus, the emphasis of this volume is the work of the Supreme Court as it defines, codifies, and extends the meaning of the Constitution to solve the problems created by an ever-expanding and increasingly complex society of free men. If the student is to begin to understand the present interpretations of those words written as early as 1787, his best chance is through the study of cases which have led the Court to rule. That Mr. Lieberman believes this is clearly evident by his careful and discriminating choice in selecting cases that reflect this most important role of the Supreme Court.

A word of caution to the prospective student is necessary. This text is not designed as a history of the Supreme Court or the evolution of our present laws. Although it contains much that is historical, its approach is from the functional point of view; its orientation is for the present. How the federal system operates today and how the Constitution is interpreted today are the questions to which Mr. Lieberman addresses himself. In the meaning of "necessary and proper" was defined in 1819, as it was, then you find a discussion of *McCulloch v. Maryland;* if "to regulate commerce . . . among the several states" is contested in 1964 because Congress used this delegated power to insure constitutional rights to Negroes, you find an analysis of *Heart of Atlanta Motel, Inc. v. United States.*

The organization of this volume is provided by the Constitution itself. A clause by clause analysis from the first word of Article I to the last word of the recently adopted Twenty-fifth Amendment is included. The first chapter sets up the Eighteenth-Century European influence of enlightened rationalism as well as the American scene before the Philadelphia Convention; it sets forth the five basic principles on which the Constitution is designed and introduces the role of the Supreme Court as the instrument for change.

Seldom in the history of the United States has the citizen been as acutely aware as he is today of the Supreme Court's decisions; rulings that have directly affected his daily living patterns; rulings that have become press headlines; opinions that have provoked editorial debate. These decisions have been significant because they deal with the constitutionality of contested laws that were enacted to prevent old practices or to promote new ones in the daily life of our society. If the Supreme Court decides that a law is constitutional, the average citizen, even though he does not understand the law or the opinion, accepts the execution of the law. He does so largely as an act of faith which is conditioned by a strong tradition that long ago established the Supreme Court as the people's guardian of the Constitution.

Consequently, the best way for the able initiate to study the Constitution is to analyze the rulings and opinions of the Supreme Court. Herein lies the significance of this text. Although the entire document is at hand, emphasis is placed on the meaningful interpretations that have reaffirmed the way of life so many came to find in America. "The Rights of the People," Part II, analyzes sharply significant rulings which determine current lawful practices. What do the following phrases mean: legal equality, free speech, proportional representation, religious freedom and fair trials? These are today's questions. The Supreme Court's answers are found in Chapters Six, Seven, Eight, Nine and Eleven. For each significant case that has shaped today's answers, Mr. Lieberman presents the facts of the case, the points of law on which it was argued, the Court's ruling and the reasoning of the judges that produced the ruling. Clearly and concisely the logic and the pragmatic meaning of the law are set forth.

Nor does the author overlook the federal system as to its design and functions. Certainly, most of the structure and power problems arose in the early years of America, but to know and understand the operations of the government in Washington, D.C., today is to appreciate the definitions of constitutional concepts as determined largely by Nineteenth-Century judicial interpretations. However, there have been significant Twentieth-Century changes, part of which came through the amending process; the rest, through judicial review. "The Powers and Structure of Government," Part I, coupled with Chapters Ten, Twelve and Thirteen, explain the organization and functions of the separate branches of government. Significant clauses are emphasized; obsolete or evident ones are only noted. For example, this section will make the critical student aware that the commerce power has more relevance to America today than does the territorial power.

Of utmost importance to the student's comprehension of structure and function in our federal government today is the role of the "independent" commissions. Mr. Lieberman's insight into the significance of judicial review is witnessed when he says, "From Marshall's decision in *McCulloch,* the 'necessary and proper clause' has become one of the most important in the Constitution. From it, in fact, has evolved a 'fourth branch' of government, nowhere mentioned in the Constitution itself." There follows a clear analysis of how the federal government has been able to meet new problems by extending its responsibilities through expanding the Executive department. The discussion emphasizes that Congress uses its delegated authority to establish commissions with the expertise necessary to administer laws too complex and specialized for ordinary execution. Certainly, the discussion of the National Labor Relations Board, with its executive, legislative, and judicial functions, will give the discerning student a clear example of the extended dimensions of our federal government.

The final chapter lends perspective to the entire volume. Understanding the Constitution today is to realize the "inevitability of change"; therefore, the critical student should sense that new problems will evoke new solutions under our Constitution, the meaning of which will continue to live through judicial review.

The primary value of this work is found in its sound scholarship. However, its organization and inclusive coverage only serve to increase its value. These aspects of the volume lead to multiple uses. It can be a valuable reference for courses in American history, contemporary problems, and American government. Of course, its basic design is to serve as a text for a purposeful, discrete unit in any curriculum which is structured for the able, interested student of the Constitution of the United States. Not to be overlooked is the "Table of Cases," a valuable reference aid as a supplement to the text and as a guide to the official sources.

In writing *Understanding Our Constitution*, Mr. Lieberman has provided a thoughtful study which will challenge the serious student to comprehend better the meaning of individual liberty and social responsibility as they exist today in America.

Wayne A. Frederick
Phillips Academy
Andover, Massachusetts

CONTENTS

Preface by Wayne A. Frederick

PART ONE

THE POWERS AND STRUCTURE
OF GOVERNMENT

1   The Inevitability of Change

That well-known Vice President of the United States, George M. Dallas (after whom Dallas, Texas, was named in 1846), once defended our highest law with these words: "The Constitution in its words is plain and intelligible, and it is meant for the homebred, unsophisticated understandings of our fellow citizens."

Yet a full half-century of squabbling by some of the most sophisticated men in America over what the words of the Constitution meant preceded his defense. Nor has that squabbling stopped today. Nearly every day the newspapers bring us reports that someone thinks something that somebody else did is unconstitutional and that that somebody else is equally convinced that what he did was entirely within the meaning of the Constitution.

The truth is that often the Constitution is very difficult to understand and apply. Consider the 7th Amendment to the Constitution, a seemingly straightforward provision:

In suits at common law, where the value of the controversy shall exceed twenty dollars, the right of *trial by jury* shall be preserved . . .

Suppose your neighbor plays with dynamite, that he has succeeded in blowing up the house on the other side of you, and that your house is next on his agenda. Suppose further that your house is worth more than $20. Afraid that your house will be destroyed, you go to court, asking that your neighbor be ordered to get rid of his explosives. Your neighbor responds by asking for a jury trial in order to determine whether his hobby is really dangerous. How should the judge rule?

Suspense is unnecessary. The answer is that neither in the state courts nor in the federal courts would a jury be allowed; the judge alone would decide the case. A lawsuit which seeks to stop someone from doing something is NOT a "suit at common law."

Does this sound unintelligible? Here is a case in which the Constitution is easy to apply but difficult to understand. The explanation lies in a tradition which began in England some five centuries ago, a tradition which is still vitally important today and which we will explore in Chapter 4 (see pp. 105–6, 191–2).

The plain fact is that the Constitution of the United States is in parts completely meaningless on its face. In order to understand the Constitution we must look to American history, for our history and the Constitution have shaped each other.

In 1687, around the time of the Massachusetts witchcraft trials and exactly one century before the Constitution was written, Sir Isaac Newton published a book outlining a theory of the physics of the heavens, a theory which with modifications by Einstein is still studied in physics courses today. That theory swept across the intellectual world; it was the last blow to the medieval view of the universe. No longer was the earth regarded as motionless in space like the center of a lazy Susan; the heavens were alive—not with witches—but with orderly movement. The Newtonian view held that the planets behaved according to precise, mathematical laws. Newton's equations were the logic of the universe.

Newton's theories had effects far beyond the world of physics. During the next century they wound their way into theology, political philosophy, and social thought. The political and social thinking which emerged—that reason and logic could solve man's problems, that man and society were perfectible, that human progress was inevitable—had a profound effect on the educated leaders of the colonies at the time of the Revolution—James

Madison, Thomas Jefferson, Benjamin Franklin, John Adams, Alexander Hamilton, and others.

For a century and a half the American colonies had been governed by countries across the ocean. Yet unless the colonists could control their own lives and direct their own fortunes, progress—in their view—was impossible. So a revolution against a distant despot was fought and won.

But the attempt at self-government following the Revolution was nearly disastrous. The Constitution was a reaction to the unpopular government which flourished in many of the states after the war. Some state legislatures openly passed laws in violation of provisions contained in their state constitutions, declaring jury trials invalid, taking property, sentencing men to death without a trial, destroying newspapers, reversing judgments of courts, and behaving often as arrogantly as the king who had been overthrown.

The Constitution was also a response to the inability of the states to get along among themselves. Because the people had successfully overthrown the heavy-handed rule of King and Parliament, they were wary of establishing a central government which could control them from a national capital. So from 1781, when the war ended, until 1789, when the Constitution went into effect, the states governed themselves in a loose federation under the Articles of Confederation. These articles gave very few powers to the national Congress and no significant ones; it could not raise revenues, it could not regulate commerce between the states, laws could not be passed without the agreement of three-quarters of the thirteen states, and worse yet, even when laws were passed, the national Congress had no power to enforce them. The people of each state, meanwhile, were jealous of the commerce and progress of compatriots in the other states, and fierce competition threatened to ruin the economies of the smaller states and destroy what union there was.

By 1787, the situation had become intolerable to many. The British had begun to smile again, sure that the American effort at self-government was a pitiful exercise in futility. The overriding national concern had been how to pay off the war debt, amounting to $42,000,000. The Congress could not compel the states to pay, and some were unwilling. In 1786, Daniel Shays led a rebellion in Massachusetts. He and his fellow farmers had been hard-hit by the debt and they refused to pay, defying the authority of courts, attacking an arsenal, calling for paper money to help them out. For months a virtual state of war existed in the state. By then it was clear to most of the national leaders in all states (except Rhode Island, which took no part in drafting the Constitution) that something had to be done. On February 21, 1787, the Confederation Congress approved a proposal to call a convention to reform the Articles of Confederation.

Even before the Convention began in Philadelphia on May 25, 1787, many of the fifty-five men who were to attend realized that an entirely new Constitution would have to be written. During the four months in which the Convention met, the Articles of Confederation were abandoned and the new Constitution slowly and painfully drafted.

The fundamental problem which the Convention had to solve was, how could the power to control the actions of people *itself* be controlled? The power of the states was so disruptive that the stability of the union was threatened. Very well, the states must be controlled by a national government. But how? And who would control it?

These were the questions the Constitution was designed to answer. Like Newton, the Convention delegates used some notions of fundamental forces to construct and describe an orderly, working system. They had five basic principles:

1. *Federalism.* Since the states had too much power, they created a national "federal" government to moderate and control their activities. Two basic governments over every square inch of land instead of one. Give certain powers to each and deny certain powers to each. Make each dependent in part on the other so that each can check the power of the other.

2. *Separation of Powers.* Since an all-purpose federal government run by one group of men would be able to

crush anyone who opposed it, the delegates created three organs with different powers. Let a Congress pass laws, let a President see that they are carried out, and let a Supreme Court resolve disputes when they arise.

3. *Checks and Balances.* Since any one of these branches might try to destroy the others, the Convention gave each of them power to check the others' actions. Let the President have power to veto the laws of Congress. But let the Senate have power to disapprove the President's treaties and to keep out of office people the President chooses. Let the President have power to appoint the judges, but let the judges have power to decide in certain cases when the President and his assistants are acting unlawfully. Delegate certain powers to Congress and let the judges decide when Congress goes beyond its delegated authority.

4. *Rule by Majority.* Since a government responsible to no one is usually responsive to no one, the people are empowered to elect their representatives by a majority vote. Let the members of Congress pass laws only when a majority agree, and let a similar majority prevail in the cases decided by judges. Hold elections frequently so that the people can say whether or not they like what their officials are doing. If the members of Congress and the President know they can be voted out of office, perhaps they will govern *for* the people and not simply dominate them.

5. *Unalienable Rights.* Since majority rule can be oppressive if a minority is disliked, those who drafted the Constitution made sure that a minority cannot be dealt with unjustly simply because a majority wishes to do so. Let the Constitution be the highest law and let it declare that certain unalienable rights are guaranteed to all, no matter what color, no matter what religion, no matter what language they speak. Let judges hold office for a lifetime, so that they need not fear the wrath of the majority when they rule that the "right to life, liberty, and the pursuit of happiness" cannot arbitrarily be taken from anyone.

These were the principles the delegates to the Philadelphia Convention considered in order to solve the problems of exercise and control of power. The Constitution was supposed to contain the solution to these problems.

No great sigh of relief or applause greeted the delegates when the Convention adjourned. Compromise always brings dissatisfaction—the Constitution was not perfect. *The Federalist Papers,* written by Madison, Hamilton, and Jay, brilliantly argued the case for the Constitution. Others found strong reasons against it. But the fear of too little power to stop the collapse of the country outweighed the fear that the new government would have too much. And the knowledge that Washington and Franklin favored the new Constitution did more than a little to help, since they above all others were universally esteemed and admired.

"I confess that there are several parts of this Constitution which I do not at present approve," Franklin said in a speech delivered to the Convention by his fellow delegate from Pennsylvania, James Wilson. Not strong enough to speak to the assembly at the age of eighty-one, Franklin pointed the way to approval when he said, "But I am not sure I shall never approve them. For having lived long, I have experienced many instances of being obliged by better information or fuller consideration, to change opinions . . . which I once thought right, but found to be otherwise. . . . Thus I consent, Sir, to this Constitution because I expect no better, and because I am not sure that it is not the best."

It was this kind of thinking—that the proposed Constitution was, if not perfect, at least a good compromise and one which should be given a chance to prove itself—that led to its ratification. By the summer of 1788, all but North Carolina and Rhode Island had agreed to the Constitution, and the Confederation Congress proclaimed it in effect the following March.

Thus it was the failure of the Articles of Confederation to meet the responsibilities of the United States that made the Constitution *necessary*. Power clustered in thirteen state centers was tearing the Union apart. But it was the willingness of the former colonists to experiment, to seek the new, their sense of compromise and optimism, and their belief that problems could be solved by human reason, that made the Constitution *possible*.

For a fundamental characteristic of the American people was their willingness to try change. Their very presence in the New World signified that fact—else why would they be here? Indeed, America was to be a severe drain on all parts of the world, taking from abroad so many who were daring, open-minded, and ready to experiment.

In the Constitution, the Founding Fathers attempted to create a form of government which would be stable yet allow for change. This was the basic tension in America, and still is: a yearning for democratic stability and peace, but a dedication to constant, ceaseless change.

The Constitution was to be the chief written instrument to control and channel the change. How could it provide stability? If the Constitution had been a long, tightly written code, spelling out in detail every minute aspect of how power should be exercised and controlled it could not have survived. To be permanent, to lay down a guideline and philosophy for free government, the Constitution had to be written in broad language. The delegates to the Constitutional Convention were interested in a basic framework to endure for all time. This meant that 18th century concepts, grammar, and vocabulary had to be broad enough and strong enough to reach out and talk to the future. It meant that though the centuries would bring changes so startling the Framers would not recognize the America that is today, the Constitution could nevertheless contain that change within its fundamental principles.

So the Constitution which emerged from the Philadelphia Convention was short, broadly phrased, and in parts, due to political compromise, terribly ambiguous. The original Constitution—now a fading yellow document on public display in the National Archives in Washington, D.C.—is only 4,000 words long, more or less. (The twenty-five Amendments have added approximately 2,500 more words.)

Had it been the product of pure logic, the Constitution would have failed. But like Newton's laws, it was founded on a mature observation of the facts. Although it is in many ways an extraordinary document, the Constitution was not suddenly invented by those fifty-five men. It came from the experience of the states in the decades before. Many of its clauses are to be found word for word in the constitutions of the states in the 1780's. The experience of the states grew in turn from the long centuries of English legal tradition which had preceded. Some of the Constitutional phrases were taken verbatim from the Articles of Confederation. The Constitution came from the past and looked to the future.

In looking to the future it is not necessary to resolve with clarity what later years and generations can decide case by case, as disputes arise. Thus the meaning of many of the words in the Constitution was not fixed, nor could it be. This quality of the Constitution's words—that they can change meaning as circumstances change—makes them unlike most other words. They are *alive*. This quality makes the Constitution a document apart from nonlegal documents: it is a storehouse of *living* words. This life cannot be entrusted to the hands of the private dictionary makers. It is not for the publisher to say what "due process of law" means (a phrase which appears twice in the Constitution) or what is included within the meaning of "equal protection of the laws."

Judges, not publishers, define the meaning of the words. The definitional process, if complex, is not mysterious: the Constitution is defined through lawsuits. And the ultimate interpreters are the nine Justices of the Supreme Court. "We are not final because we are infallible, but we are infallible only because we are final," wrote Mr. Justice Jackson. Subsequent rulings of the Supreme Court, and Amendments to the Constitution, show that not even the Supreme Court is final. Nothing is final when men want change.

The most important limitation on the Supreme Court's power to pass on the constitutionality of laws—whether of Congress or of state legislatures—is that it can make legal pronouncements only when deciding a lawsuit and even then, only when the interpretation is necessary to the correct decision in the specific case.

Should Congress pass a law abolishing the right to jury

trials in federal criminal cases, for instance, the Supreme Court would be powerless to strike down the obviously unconstitutional law (see 6th Amendment, p. 180). The Court must wait until someone, during the course of a regular trial in a lower court, was refused a jury on the grounds that Congress had abolished it. If the loser protested the trial judge's ruling, he could appeal the case to a higher court, urging reversal of the judgment on the grounds that his right to jury trial had been unconstitutionally taken away. From the decision in that court an appeal could be made to the Supreme Court—the government arguing that the Congressional law abolishing juries was constitutional, the private citizen arguing that it was not. Then, and only then, in the course of deciding the case in favor of the private citizen, could the Court declare the law unconstitutional because it conflicted with the 6th Amendment. Nor would this be the end of the case: the Supreme Court would "remand" or return the case to the trial court and order it to start all over, this time with a jury. Thus, it is only within the context of a specific dispute that the Court interprets the Constitution. This power of "judicial review," as it is called, is one of the many ways in which one branch of the federal government can check the unlawful actions taken by another.

The Supreme Court, too, is limited in power, for there is no way by which the Court can make sure its judgments are carried out. In 1832, John Marshall, the great Chief Justice, set forth the Court's ruling that the treaty ceding land within Georgia to the Cherokee Indians was federal law and that the state of Georgia had no right to exercise authority over such lands.[169] * But President Andrew Jackson was not willing to carry out the Court's decision in this and related cases. "John Marshall has made his decision," he reportedly said; "now let him enforce it." Marshall had no means at his disposal, nor could anyone help the Indians without the backing of the Presi-

---

* Footnote numbers throughout the text refer to cases in the alphabetical Table of Cases, p. 250ff. Whenever the name of a case is omitted in the text, the reader will be referred to a more complete description of the case in the Table. Cases named in the text are not footnoted: the reader will find the case in its alphabetical place in the Table. For more detailed explanation of the Table, see p. 249.

dent. In the end, the United States Army forced the Cherokee out of Georgia.

That episode proved that the Court's voice is a legal one but its power a moral one only. Even if the Supreme Court can eventually protect the constitutional rights of those persecuted, it cannot nip the persecution in the budding. It can take years to fight a case through the lower courts in order to ask that highest court in Washington to take the appeal. By then, the litigant may have lost his job, his friends, his savings, his land. Prosecutors, goaded by the impassioned mob of the moment, can bring a person to trial to harass him, even in the face of his constitutional rights.

Getting through the lower courts is no guarantee that the Supreme Court will agree to review a case. The Court can refuse even to consider a case in all but the following five circumstances: (1) when a lower federal court has ruled that a state law is unconstitutional; (2) when the highest state court rules that a federal statute or treaty is unconstitutional; (3) when the highest state court rules that a state law is constitutional and the losing party thinks not; (4) when a federal court holds a federal law unconstitutional in a suit to which the United States is a party; and (5) when a federal court grants or denies an injunction against enforcement of a state law or Act of Congress. In these instances, the Supreme Court must agree to decide the case, if one of the parties insists. (Law in the United States is based on the "adversary system," and courts do not ask parties to appeal. Parties to suits are pitted against each other. They are responsible for going to court, gathering evidence, presenting it in the proper fashion, proving their cases. Courts do not initiate lawsuits; they wait for individual litigants to come to them. And in criminal cases, it is the executive branch of the government, not the court, that brings the case and prosecutes the defendant.)

Suppose a federal court rules that a law is *constitutional*. This is not one of the three circumstances in which the Court must agree to review, and it may and often does refuse to hear such cases. Nevertheless, Congress has given the Court jurisdiction to take the appeal if it wants to, by issuing a "writ of certiorari" to the lower court. This simply means that at least four of the nine Justices thought the case important enough to consider. The Court does not "grant cert" for trivial cases, but when a conflict occurs between lower federal courts or when a state court interprets a federal law in a new way, the Supreme Court will usually take the case. Of the some 2,000 requests for certiorari each year, more than 1,700 are denied.

Once the Court accepts a case, either on appeal or on certiorari, lawyers for both sides get busy. They must present printed copies of a "brief" in which they argue why they thought the lower court was right or wrong and what they think the Supreme Court should do. On an appointed day, the Justices hear each lawyer's "argument" —sometimes interrupting with fierce and intensive questions. Each lawyer has but one hour. In the following weeks and months, the Justices must each consider this and other cases argued before them. When a decision is reached, one Justice will write the "majority opinion," any who agree with the Court's ruling (but for different reasons) can write "concurring opinions," and those who disagree write "dissenting opinions."

Central to the Court's holding is the written opinion stating the *reasons* for its decision. Conclusions should be made logically. Congress can pass a law without giving any reason at all, but the Supreme Court should not decide a case without giving reasons why it arrived at the result it did.

The importance of "reasoned decision" cannot be overemphasized. Sometimes the Court's decision will be less convincing than it could be, for judicial opinions have a way of masquerading in fancy phrases. But the Court can never stray too far for too long. Without the support of the public and the other branches of government, the Supreme Court's declarations are worthless. The power of the Court is, after all, merely the respect and heed a society pays to its reasons and decisions.

Because people do respect logic and reason, the decisions of the Supreme Court play a crucial role in our day-to-day life. Since the only way to conquer logic is by better logic or by guns, the Court's opinions must be contended with.

The process of interpreting the Constitution is not simple. The nine Justices must draw on a wide variety of materials in deciding on the meaning of the phrase in dispute. Sometimes they look to *The Federalist Papers,* since two of the three men who wrote that collection of essays also helped to write the Constitution. Sometimes they look at Madison's notes of the proceedings at the Convention. Sometimes they read the debates of the first Congress, since many of the men elected to national office had participated in the framing of the Constitution.

The intention of the men who wrote the Constitution can never be fully ascertained, however, and the disputes among themselves show that there was no consensus on the meaning and application of each part of the Constitution. Therefore the Court relies far more often on past decisions—"precedents" which it has made. The meaning of the Constitution is developed on a case-by-case basis. Of the tens of thousands of cases which the Court has decided, more than 4,000 have involved constitutional questions. Hundreds of doctrines have been developed to cope with the innumerable things about which people fight.

But as circumstances change, even these past decisions may not be adequate to the task of determining how the Constitution should be applied in the controversy at hand. Some doctrines which once flourished, like the "original package" doctrine in the field of interstate taxation, have died a graceful death. Some are just beginning to grow, like the doctrine that a person has a "right to privacy." In developing and applying these doctrines, judges must be conscious that a changing society which has grown from horse power to atomic energy, from covered wagons to spaceships, requires an *evolving* law.

Difficult cases can go either way; in the long run they must go the way the people want. "We must never forget it is a Constitution we are expounding," Chief Justice Marshall wrote.[107] He meant simply that when it interprets the Constitution the Court must be conscious of the nation's purpose and not restrict the people in trying to realize their goals.

These purposes and goals are best expressed in the Preamble to the Constitution. Though not part of the law itself, the Preamble has become one of the dimensions of the federal government's powers, indicating the purposes to which such power is to be committed. It reads:

We the People of the United States, in order to form a more perfect Union, establish Justice, insure domestic Tranquility, provide for the common defence, promote the general Welfare, and secure the Blessings of Liberty to ourselves and our Posterity, do ordain and establish this Constitution for the United States of America.

A law that did not meet one of these purposes might have a difficult time in meeting a test of constitutionality. To these principles Congress, the courts, and the President daily refer.

In the days when the Constitution was written, a popular social theory said that the only legitimate government was one in which the people themselves agreed on the form of their government. The Constitution is one of the few examples in history in which a people took charge of their own destiny, consciously shaping their future course, and largely succeeding.

Since 1789 the nation has encountered rapid change, in science, in commerce, in the arts. Not the least significant change is the growing maturity of the American people themselves. There still are intolerant, ruthless, and lawless people in the United States. There still are riots and injustices. But gradually our sense of justice has grown.

We no longer make property a qualification for political rights—for decades at the beginning of United States history, only a small percentage of the citizenry could vote and hold office. We no longer restrict public office to those of a particular religious faith. Well into the 19th century in some states, persons of minority religions were by law barred from serving the public. And we no longer scorn knowledge and education for all; in the early years, many people ridiculed the scientific, inquiring mind. Benjamin Franklin was called an "agent of the devil" for installing lightning rods on buildings and houses.

For a century and three-quarters, the Constitution has

remained a document enabling America to cope with the changes which developments in science, technology, commerce, and culture have brought. Congress, the President, the courts, and the states—all were dealt with in the Constitution, and all exist to this day. But the power relations among these various branches of government have changed tremendously. For the most part, these changes were carried out peacefully, through the established processes of law. In deciding whether a law of Congress or an act of the President is constitutional, the Supreme Court plays its most important role. Through the power of judicial review it determines who is to have what power. For if Congress cannot pass a law, then either some other institution has the power (the President or the states), or else the people are free to act. The relations among the various organs of government and the people are fluid. Later Courts are not forever bound by the decisions of earlier Justices. When corporations became gigantic, far too large for the individual states to exercise effective control over, Congress acted and the Supreme Court approved the Sherman Act and other antitrust laws, through a liberal interpretation of the "commerce clause." These laws reduced the power of the states in this area of commerce and put in it Congress. Thus the interplay of Congress, the Court, and the Constitution has brought about a shift among powers.

Change is effected not alone by judicial interpretation of the Constitution. Congress and the states pass laws, most of which are never contested in the courts. Over a period of time these laws become accepted as part of the culture, as part of the processes and substance of the legal system. Social acceptance is as important as court approval. As society changes its opinions, laws change. Different legislators are elected; different judges are appointed; the Constitution itself is amended.

But the catalogue of changes is long, and this is not the place for its listing. What follows is not a history of the Supreme Court, of the United States, or even of the Constitution. Yet to understand our Constitution it is necessary to explore some of the Supreme Court cases, to see something of United States history, and to look at some of the philosophies which the Constitution is said to contain.

The Constitution was not fixed for all times in 1789. It is a set of fundamental ideas by which orderly change can take place in a stable society. To the degree that violence is avoided while progress is made—to that degree the Constitution is the successful charter of American freedom.

2   Congress

Article I

Section 1

All legislative Powers herein granted shall be vested in a Congress of the United States . . .

Article I of the Constitution creates Congress, the legislative body, giving it the power to pass laws, called statutes. Congress is not the only governmental body which can make federal law, but it is the only body which can *legislate*. That is, Congress on its own initiative can declare what is a crime against the United States and what is not, can create administrative agencies and other governmental bodies, can raise taxes and determine what programs to spend it on, and can make sweeping policies for the future. Congress need not wait for a case to occur to pass law. It can act whenever and however it sees fit, so long as it does not act beyond the power given it by the Constitution. Courts, executive departments, and administrative agencies can also make law, but through different processes—courts decide cases, agencies determine how best to carry out particular laws of Congress. Thus, the Constitution implicitly provides for the separation of powers by vesting legislative power in Congress, executive power in the President (Chapter 3), and judicial power in the courts (Chapter 4).

Only those powers "herein granted"—only those which the Constitution gives to Congress—can be exercised by Congress. It can enact federal law only. This power is huge, in spite of the theoretical limitation. Not only does Congress get powers from specific clauses in the Constitution, it also finds powers by adding up the specific clauses and seeing what results. For instance, from the power of making war and entering into treaties, Congress gets the power to acquire territory, even though acquisition of territories are not mentioned in the Constitution.

Congress also has "inherent powers." For instance, although the Constitution nowhere says it can, Congress conducts investigations. The power to investigate is said, to be a "legislative power." Unless Congress informs itself on a subject—automobile safety, abuses in the drug industry, jamming of the airwaves—it cannot pass intelligent legislation. But Congress cannot go too far. It cannot call witnesses to testify about matters unrelated to the investigation just for the sake of exposing the person to public criticism and ridicule or possible later criminal prosecution.[161]

Congress can even give away some of its power, although it cannot give away too much. Because the Constitution says "ALL legislative powers" are to be vested in Congress, the Court has developed the doctrine of "nondelegability of legislative power." This doctrine says that Congress cannot tell a private association of tax lawyers, "The tax law is too complicated for us so you write the law; whatever you say goes." Except in rare instances, Congress cannot delegate legislative power to private groups.

Nor can Congress give a governmental agency a blank check to make whatever law it wants. During the Depression, the National Recovery Act allowed the President wide authority to make whatever rules he thought were necessary to protect consumers, producers, employees, and others in order to revive commerce and trade. The authority given was so unlimited that when the government sued a poultry dealer in New York to enforce a particular Presidential law dealing with conditions in the industry, the Supreme Court in *Schechter Poultry Corp. v.*

United States (the "sick chicken" case) declared the law unconstitutional because Congress gave away too much power to legislate.[124]

Nonetheless, Congress has created dozens of governmental agencies and given them the power to investigate, to decide cases, and to make rules in a particular field. The National Labor Relations Board can investigate charges of "unfair labor practices" in union or business corporation activities. It can settle disputes which arise out of these "unfair labor practices," such as whether a particular union election should be canceled and a new one conducted. It can also make rules involving union elections: how many months must go by before a second union election can be held if the first one was cricket? (Answer, said the NLRB: twelve months.)

Activities requiring regulation—such as commerce, transportation, labor relations, communications—are so complex that if individual members of Congress had to watch each field daily Congress would need tens of thousands of members and would have no time to consider new legislation. Specialized agencies, therefore, have a legitimate role to play in *administering* Congressional law. If Congress *spells out a clear enough standard* for the agency to use (like defining what an unfair labor practice is), the agency can constitutionally decide cases and make other rules to carry out Congressional policy. Sometimes Congressional standards are very vague: "Regulate in the *public interest*" it may command a particular agency. Nevertheless, as long as the agency operates in accordance with this standard, and as long as Congress *retains power to reverse or revise* agency rules, the delegation of power is constitutional.

Section 1 (continued)

Congress . . . shall consist of a Senate and House of Representatives.

The division of Congress into two separate branches was not novel. Parliament had a House of Commons and a House of Lords. But the particular Congressional scheme resulted from the "great compromise" of the Constitutional Convention. If each state were to have an equal vote in Congress (the New Jersey plan), the big states feared that the small states would exercise a larger power than their size warranted. The small states, on the other hand, disliked the proposal that each state be represented in Congress in proportion to the size of its population (the Virginia plan), for then the large states would drown out the voices of the small states. In the end, a number of other compromises (now embodied in the Constitution) made the "great compromise" (the Connecticut plan) possible. Each state would have two votes in the Senate; each state would be represented in accordance with its population in the House of Representatives.

Section 2 (Clause 1)

The House of Representatives shall be composed of Members chosen every second Year by the People of the several States, and the Electors in each State shall have the Qualifications requisite for Electors of the most numerous Branch of the State Legislature.

Representatives (or Congressmen, as they are informally called) are elected directly by the people of each state every other year. Each Congress is numbered in accordance with this plan. (The 89th Congress, lasting from January, 1965, to October, 1966, was divided into two sessions. The First Session was in 1965 and the 89th Congress, Second Session, covered 1966. The First Session of the 90th Congress began on January 10, 1967.)

Each state may determine its own qualifications for voting in Congressional elections. Georgia and Kentucky allow eighteen-year-olds to vote; voters must be 19 in Alaska, 20 in Hawaii. In all other states citizens must be 21. In all cases, anyone who is entitled to vote for representatives to his state assembly is entitled to vote for his United States Representative.

The Constitution does not talk about Congressional districts. Federal law, however, requires the states to divide themselves into districts. Occasionally a Representative will be chosen as a "member at large" by the voters of the entire state, in states with more than one representative (and as is always the case in those small states which send only one Representative to Congress: Alaska, Delaware, Nevada, Vermont, and Wyoming).

Congressional districts must be more or less equal in population. Before the 1960's, Congressional districts within each state often varied tremendously in population. But in a series of cases decided in 1964, the Supreme Court ruled that when the Constitution gives the "People" the right to choose Representatives, it means each person is entitled to one vote and not more than one. This vote cannot be diluted by allowing, say, 500 people in one district of a state to elect a Representative while giving 5,000 people in a different district in the same state only one Representative. Such an arrangement means that the person's vote in the small district counts for ten times as much as the person's vote in the large district. So Congressional districts must be apportioned according to population.[163] (See p. 218).

Section 2 (Clause 2)

No Person shall be a Representative who shall not have attained to the Age of twenty-five Years, and been seven Years a Citizen of the United States, and who shall not, when elected, be an Inhabitant of that State in which he shall be chosen.

Representatives must be twenty-five years old when they are sworn into office, but they can be younger while campaigning or on election day. Naturalized citizens, like native-born citizens, are eligible to the office of Representative, but no person who has been a citizen for less than seven years can run. (Candidates need not have actually lived *in* the United States; they can live abroad as long as they are citizens.)

The candidates do not have to be citizens of the states from which they run prior to election day; thus a state cannot refuse to let someone run for the House of Representatives because he has not lived in his district for twelve months. In practice, almost all candidates have lived in their states and districts for some time. Only by becoming known to the local community does a politician stand a chance of getting the nomination and winning the election.

Section 2 (Clause 3)

[Representatives and direct Taxes shall be apportioned among the several States which may be included within this Union, according to their respective Numbers, which shall be determined by adding to the whole Number of free Persons, including those bound to Service for a Term of Years, and excluding Indians not taxed, three fifths of all other Persons.]*

This part of Clause 3 has almost no application today. The "all other Persons" refers to slaves. This three-fifths exclusion formula was one of the compromises which made the delegates favorable to the "great compromise" at the Constitutional Convention. The 13th Amendment, in abolishing slavery, did away with these words (as well as "those bound to Service for a Term of Years," which referred to apprentices). The 14th Amendment changed the method for determining how many Representatives should come from each state (see p. 222).

No one is sure what the difference is between "direct" taxes and "indirect" taxes. The necessity for making an apportionment according to population in order for Congress to levy an income tax was ended by the 16th Amendment.

Section 2 (Clause 3, continued)

The actual Enumeration shall be made within three Years after the first Meeting of the Congress of the United States, and within every subsequent Term of ten Years, in such Manner as they shall by Law direct.

Congress is directed to take a "census" of the population every decade to determine how many people live in the states. The 1960 census, however, was undertaken for a purpose far broader. Dozens of questions concerning the social and economic affairs of the family were asked so that Congress would discover the needs and problems of United States citizens.

Section 2 (Clause 3, continued)

The Number of Representatives shall not exceed one for

---

* Note: In this and subsequently quoted text, brackets are used to indicate sections of the Constitution and Amendments that have been repealed or amended.

every thirty Thousand, but Each State shall have at Least one Representative.

Although there has been a census every ten years since 1790, there has not always been a corresponding reapportionment of districts made necessary by growing and shifting populations. It took Congress nine years following the 1920 census to figure out how to reapportion and still keep the number of Congressmen down. The number of Congressmen (not counting Senators) is fixed today at 435 so that the ratio of Congressmen to citizens is one to 410,000, not one to 30,000 as written in the Constitution. If the original ratio had been kept, there would be more than 6,500 Congressmen, and nothing of substance would ever be accomplished. (For the power of Congress to change the ratio, see Section 4, Clause 1, p. 41.)

Section 2 (Clause 3, continued)

[and until such enumeration shall be made, the State of New Hampshire shall be entitled to chuse three, Massachusetts eight, Rhode-Island and Providence Plantations one, Connecticut five, New-York six, New Jersey four, Pennsylvania eight, Delaware one, Maryland six, Virginia ten, North Carolina five, South Carolina five, and Georgia three.]

Since the 1790 census, as populations have changed, these figures have changed correspondingly.

Section 2 (Clause 4)

When vacancies happen in the Representation from any State, the Executive Authority thereof shall issue Writs of Election to fill such Vacancies.

When a Representative dies in office, or resigns, the governor of his state must call for a new election from his district to fill his seat.

Section 2 (Clause 5)

The House of Representatives shall chuse their Speaker and other Officers; and shall have the sole Power of Impeachment.

By this clause, the House is empowered to choose its presiding officer, the "Speaker of the House," and other leaders to conduct business and guide legislation. The House is also given the "sole power of impeachment." In case the President, a federal judge, or some other federal official commits a crime or does something else inconsistent with his duties, Congress can remove him. Removal is a two-step process, and impeachment is the first step. It is really nothing more than a formal accusation, like a charge that a grand jury must make before a person can be brought to trial. (See p. 146.) Once the House impeaches someone—President Andrew Johnson in 1867, for instance—he must be tried before the Senate (Section 3, Clause 6, p. 40). Only then, if judged guilty, can he be removed from office. In 1867, the Senate failed to find President Johnson guilty. The House had impeached him, but when the Senate voted on his removal from office, it lacked one vote for a two-thirds majority. The one vote made all the difference, and Andrew Johnson remained in office for the duration of his term.

Section 3 (Clause 1)

The Senate of the United States shall be composed of two Senators from each State, [chosen by the Legislature thereof,] for six Years; and each Senator shall have one Vote.

Originally, Senators were elected not by the people but by the state legislature. Direct election came in 1913 with the 17th Amendment. Partly as a way of providing a check against the House, each Senator is given a six-year rather than a two-year term. (The Senate was conceived originally as being similar to the House of Lords in the English Parliament. The Lords have life terms; although the Constitutional Convention rejected this feature, it decided that longer terms than those held by Representatives and selection by state legislatures rather by the states' voters would tend to create a body of independent statesmen.)

Section 3 (Clause 2)

[Immediately after they shall be assembled in Consequence of the first Election, they shall be divided as equally as may be into three Classes. The Seats of the Senators of the first Class shall be vacated at the Expiration of the second Year, of the second Class at the Expiration of the fourth Year, and of the third Class at the Expiration of the sixth Year, so that one third may be chosen every second Year; and if Vacancies happen by resignation, or otherwise, during the Recess of the

Legislature of any State, the Executive thereof may make temporary Appointments until the next Meeting of the Legislature, which shall then fill such Vacancies.]

The Senate is no longer divided into separate classes. Regularly elected Senators all serve six-year terms, but only a few more than thirty Senate seats are involved in each election. Unlike the House, which must be entirely elected every two years, only one-third of the Senate is elected at a time, as a result of the original division into three classes. Thus the Senate is said to be a "continuing body." (The last part of this clause, dealing with vacancies in the Senate, was changed by the 17th Amendment.)

Section 3 (Clause 3)
No person shall be a Senator who shall not have attained to the Age of thirty Years, and been nine Years a Citizen of the United States, and who shall not, when elected, be an inhabitant of that State for which he shall be chosen.

Senators must be thirty years old and have been citizens of the United States for nine years. They need not be thirty on election day, or have lived in the United States, or have been a citizen of the state prior to election day. When Robert F. Kennedy ran for the Senate from New York in 1964, some people protested that he was a citizen of Massachusetts (where he had previously voted) and that he therefore could not run. Even though he was ineligible to vote for himself in the election—because he had not lived in New York long enough prior to the election to satisfy the state requirements—he nevertheless was constitutionally entitled to run, since he lived in New York as an inhabitant on election day.

Section 3 (Clause 4)
The Vice President of the United States shall be President of the Senate, but shall have no vote, unless they be equally divided.

Presiding over the Senate is the only constitutional duty a Vice President has, and it is largely ceremonial, except for the rare tie-breaking vote which the Vice President will cast if he happens to be in the Senate that day. Visitors to the Senate galleries will not often see the

Vice President presiding—usually the Senators take turns sitting up front in the Senate President's large chair.

Section 3 (Clause 5)

The Senate shall chuse their other Officers, and also a President pro tempore, in the Absence of the Vice President, or when he shall exercise the Office of President of the United States.

Like the House, the Senate has the power to choose its own officers. The President "pro tempore"—or President pro tem, as he is often called—is simply the temporary presiding officer, who serves when the Vice President has succeeded a President who has died in office. When Vice President Lyndon B. Johnson became President in 1963, Senate President pro tempore Carl Hayden (at eighty-six the eldest Senator) received the Vice Presidential salary though his job was almost completely honorary.

Section 3 (Clause 6)

The Senate shall have the sole Power to try all Impeachments. When sitting for that Purpose, they shall be on Oath or Affirmation. When the President of the United States is tried, the Chief Justice shall preside: And no Person shall be convicted without the Concurrence of two thirds of the Members present.

When any federal official is impeached, the case is referred to the Senate, which acts as a court and holds a trial. Because removal of the President from office is such a drastic step, the Chief Justice presides as the judge, a check on any Senators who might want to act arbitrarily. The members of the Senate are the jury, but a two-thirds vote is necessary. No President has ever been removed from office through the impeachment procedure (supporters of the Andrew Johnson impeachment having failed by one vote to secure the two-thirds majority) and only a very few federal judges have been.

Oaths and affirmations are ceremonies to remind the taker of the seriousness of his endeavor. When sitting as a jury, each Senator must take an oath, swearing before God that he will act according to the rules of law. The Constitutional Fathers were careful of religious belief, and if any Senator has religious scuples against swearing before God, he may *affirm* his willingness to abide by the rules.

Section 3 (Clause 7)

Judgment in Cases of Impeachment shall not extend further than to removal from office, and disqualification to hold and enjoy any Office of Honor, Trust or Profit under the United States: but the Party convicted shall nevertheless be liable and subject to Indictment, Trial, Judgment and Punishment, according to Law.

It was feared that a Congress which was politically motivated to get rid of the President might also want to send him to jail simply because it disagreed with him politically. (Charles I of England had not only been removed from the throne during the political revolution in 1640; his head was chopped off. The Framers of the Constitution wanted to prevent this from happening to a President.) Those who try the President upon his impeachment (the Senate) cannot also sit as a court to try him for his crimes. A regular court of law—the judicial branch—must have charge of the criminal proceeding. The only punishment which the Senate can decree is the loss of office and any right ever to hold another federal office or job.

Section 4 (Clause 1)

The Times, Places and Manner of holding Elections for Senators and Representatives, shall be prescribed in each State by the Legislature thereof; but the Congress may at any time by Law make or alter such Regulations, except as to the Place of chusing Senators.

This clause gives Congress wide powers of regulation, since the word "manner" has been broadly interpreted. Congress first used the power in 1842 when it called for the election of Representatives by district in each state. Congress has made it a criminal offense for anyone to interfere with federal elections—such as the refusal to let qualified people vote, bribery of voters, stuffing ballot boxes. Congress has also changed the ratio of Representatives to the population (from 1:30,000 to 1:410,000) under the power granted by this clause.

Section 4 (Clause 2)

The Congress shall assemble at least once in every Year, and such Meeting shall [be on the first Monday in December,] unless they shall by Law appoint a different Day.

The 20th Amendment changed this. Now Congress begins a new session usually every January 3.

Section 5 (Clause 1)

Each House shall be the Judge of the Elections, Returns and Qualifications of its own Members.

The Senate and House have an absolute power to determine whether a member received a majority of votes in his district. Each house may also judge the "qualifications" of its members, but it is unclear what is included in that word. If the House determined that a newly-elected member was not 25, or had not been a citizen of the United States for seven years, or was not when elected an inhabitant of the state for which he was chosen, then no one would quarrel if the House refused to seat the member.

Honesty, on the other hand, is not a constitutional qualification. Suppose the House refused to seat a member because he was suspected of being dishonest? In 1967, for the third time in the 20th century, the House of Representatives refused to seat a member. Representative Adam Clayton Powell of New York had been sued for libel in New York for a statement he had made outside Congress. He lost the suit but did not pay the judgment. After a series of legal appeals to avoid paying, he was convicted of criminal contempt of court for his delaying tactics, and he could not come into New York without being subject to arrest. A House special investigating committee also charged him with having misappropriated some $40,000 of public funds. The House overruled the special committee (which had recommended less severe penalties) and a majority vote excluded him from his seat.

On previous occasions when the House excluded a duly-elected member—for polygamy, sale of favors, Confederate activity—no court suit was brought to challenge the action. Victor L. Berger of Wisconsin, a socialist, was excluded in 1919 and 1920 for his vigorous opposition to the United States entry into World War I; he had been convicted of sedition. When his conviction was upset by the Supreme Court, however, and the suit against him dropped, he was admitted to the House upon his reelection in 1921, without a dissenting vote.

Representative Powell and his supporters brought court suits seeking to declare the House bar unconstitutional. Meanwhile, his New York district prepared for a new election which he won resoundingly, posing the same problem to the House all over again. Thus, one of the rare moments in American constitutional history when Court is pitted directly against Congress, may come to pass. Because the House might choose to ignore a Court order directing seating, some have speculated that the Supreme Court might refuse to take the case. At the time this book went to press, the whole matter was still unfolding, and the meaning of "qualifications" was still in doubt.

In 1928 the Senate rejected a member-elect because he had received campaign contributions from people subject to a state administrative agency of which he was chairman; his acceptance smacked of corruption and fraud, the Senate found.

Section 5 (Clause 1, continued)

and a Majority of each shall constitute a Quorum to do Business; but a smaller Number may adjourn from day to day, and may be authorized to compel the Attendance of absent Members, in such Manner, and under such Penalties as each House may provide.

In order for a vote of the Senate or House to count, a majority of the members (a "quorum") must be present, even if they do not all vote. Without a quorum, one man in an otherwise empty legislative chamber could pass laws which would affect the entire nation. But members need not be present at all times. There is work to be done in offices as well as on legislative floors.

Section 5 (Clause 2)

Each House may determine the Rules of its Proceedings,

punish its Members for disorderly Behaviour, and, with the Concurrence of two thirds, expel a Member.

Under this power, hundreds of pages of rules have been adopted by each house. Ordinarily, no court may review any rules made by either house for the conduct of its own business. Sometimes these rules will affect private rights secured by other provisions of the Constitution—in that case, the courts have the power to review.[157]

Whether to expel a member is entirely up to the discretion and good sense of each house. Should two-thirds of either house think one of their members is guilty of conduct unbecoming a Senator or Representative—out he goes.

The power to expel is probably more absolute than the power to exclude; had Representative Powell been expelled he would have had a far weaker court case. To be expelled the member must first be admitted to his seat and then be found to have been guilty of "disorderly behavior" while a member.

Section 5 (Clause 3)

Each House shall keep a Journal of its Proceedings, and from time to time publish the same, excepting such Parts as may in their Judgment require Secrecy; and the Yeas and Nays of the Members of either House on any question shall, at the Desire of one fifth of those Present, be entered on the Journal.

Unless the people know what their Representatives have said and how they have voted, it is difficult to judge how well they have performed their duties. For many years, the journal of the Congress has been called the *Congressional Record*. It is published daily and consists of everything that is said on the floor of both the House and the Senate. Speeches are not necessarily recorded exactly as they are spoken—Senators and Representatives reserve the right to rewrite what they said for the *Record* later on in the day when they have cooled down, so the *Record* is not always an accurate report. From time to time committees of Congress publish reports of hearings and investigations, including testimony, statements, and questions. The "yeas and nays" are the votes on particular bills. If at least one-fifth of the members so desire, they can demand that the journal record how *each* member voted.

Section 5 (Clause 4)

Neither House, during the Session of Congress, shall, without the Consent of the other, adjourn for more than three days, nor to any other Place than that in which the two Houses shall be sitting.

Either house may adjourn for the weekend without asking permission of the other. Long weekends (Labor Day, 4th of July or any other time when either house wants to stay away for more than three days) require permission of both houses.

Section 6 (Clause 1)

The Senators and Representatives shall receive a Compensation for their Services, to be ascertained by Law, and paid out of the Treasury of the United States.

It was suggested during the Constitutional Convention that Congress should not be able to change the salary of members while they were in office. But the suggestion was never acted on. An amendment to the Constitution to stop Congress from changing its members' salaries was never ratified. Congressmen and Senators can raise their salaries whenever they feel like it, even though they do not, for political reasons, feel like it very often. (They are, at present, paid $30,000 a year.)

Section 6 (Clause 1, continued)

They shall in all Cases, except Treason, Felony and Breach of the Peace, be privileged from Arrest during their Attendance at the Session of their respective Houses, and in going to and returning from the same;

Little is left of this clause today. "Treason, felony, and breach of the peace" have come to include all criminal offenses, so that a member *can* be arrested for any criminal charge. Only in "civil cases"—for instance, an automobile accident or breach of a contract (cases not involving crimes)—is a member of Congress exempt from arrest. But, except in rare cases such failure of an ex-husband to pay his divorced wife alimony, no one can be "civilly arrested." At the time of the Revolution, civil arrests were far more common than they are today.

Section 6 (Clause 1, continued)

and for any Speech or Debate in either House, they shall not be questioned in any other Place.

No matter how false the statement, or how maliciously it was uttered, a member of Congress cannot be sued for making it. The speech and debate privilege was written to ensure that members of Congress will speak up free of fear that they might be prosecuted. In England in the 1700's, many people were sent to jail or beheaded for "seditious libel" (which often consisted of nothing more than questioning the soundness of laws or the wisdom of official actions) and even Parliamentarians were not free of punishment. The privilege is intended for the public good and not for the legislator's private purposes. Exceptions to the privilege, no matter how minor, might still make a Congressman afraid that someone would try to sue him. The privilege extends also to official investigations, written reports and statements made outside the legislative chamber.

Section 6 (Clause 2)

No Senator or Representative shall, during the Time for which he was elected, be appointed to any civil Office under the Authority of the United States, which shall have been created, or the Emoluments whereof shall have been encreased during such time; and no Person holding any Office under the United States, shall be a Member of either House during his Continuance in Office.

This clause prevents Congress from creating new posts for its members. By denying members of Congress from holding any other public job, it keeps possible conflicts of interest from arising. Congressmen are permitted to serve as directors of public institutions, such as art galleries, however, as long as they are not paid salaries. When President Taft appointed then Senator Knox to be Secretary of State in 1909, Congress reduced the Secretary of State's salary (which had been increased while Knox was Senator) in order that Knox could constitutionally be appointed to the Cabinet.

Section 7 (Clause 1)

All Bills for raising Revenue shall originate in the House of Representatives; but the Senate may propose or concur with Amendments as on other Bills.

Revenue bills are tax bills. It was thought that suggestions for taxing the public ought to be heard first in the house most responsive to the public. The Senate's power to propose amendments to tax bills is broad.

Section 7 (Clause 2)

Every Bill which shall have passed the House of Representatives and the Senate, shall, before it becomes a Law, be presented to the President of the United States; If he approve he shall sign it, but if not he shall return it, with his Objections to that House in which it shall have originated, who shall enter the Objections at large on their Journal, and proceed to reconsider it.

This is the heart of the legislative process. Both houses must agree by majority vote to a bill, *and* the President must sign it (he need not date it or write on it "approved"). If he does sign the bill, it becomes law effective that day (unless the bill states otherwise). If the President dislikes the bill—because he thinks it is unwise, bad policy, unnecessary, poorly written, or unconstitutional —he rejects it, returning it to the house which first proposed it.

Section 7 (Clause 2, continued)

If after such Reconsideration two thirds of that House shall agree to pass the Bill, it shall be sent, together with the Objections, to the other House, by which it shall likewise be reconsidered, and if approved by two thirds of that House, it shall become a Law. But in all such Cases the Votes of both Houses shall be determined by Yeas and Nays, and the Names of the Persons voting for and against the Bill shall be entered on the Journal of each House respectively.

Congress gets another chance if the President vetoes a bill. Should two-thirds of the members present in each house agree, the President's veto will be set aside and the bill will become law without the President's signature. The voting in each house must be done by calling the roll and asking how each member votes; the presiding officer cannot simply say: "All those in favor say aye." The vote must be printed in the *Congressional Record*.

Section 7 (Clause 2, continued)

If any Bill shall not be returned by the President within ten Days (Sundays excepted) after it shall have been presented to him, the Same shall be a Law, in like Manner as if he had signed it, unless the Congress by their Adjournment prevents its Return, in which Case it shall not be a law.

If the President decides that it would not be politically wise to support a bill directly by signing it and unwise to reject it by vetoing it, he can simply do nothing about it at all. The bill becomes law ten days after it was first sent to the White House (Sundays don't count.) If in the meantime Congress has adjourned, however, then the bill dies. This is the so-called pocket veto, since the President can prevent the bill from becoming law by stuffing it in his pocket and forgetting about it. In order to revive the bill, Congress must go through the whole procedure at its next session.

Section 7 (Clause 3)

Every Order, Resolution, or Vote to which the Concurrence of the Senate and House of Representatives may be necessary (except on a question of Adjournment) shall be presented to the President of the United States; and before the Same shall take Effect, shall be approved by him, or being disapproved by him, shall be repassed by two thirds of the Senate and House of Representatives prescribed in the Case of a Bill.

A lot of this is repetitious, thrown in as an afterthought. Taken in its strict sense it would cause the collapse of the whole Congressional system. The trouble is in the word "may." If one house were to take a vote on every matter which *might* eventually come to the other house for a vote, the President would spend his whole working day signing and vetoing votes. If a Congressman submitted a "motion to amend a motion to amend a resolution" and the President had to agree to it before a vote on the amendment itself could be conducted, chaos would result. So from the start this clause was taken to mean simply this: any vote on a *final* bill or resolution must have the President's signature in order to become law.

Preliminary votes do not need a signature. Some final resolutions of Congress do not need the President's signature—for instance a resolution calling on the President to declare the first week in October National Baseball Week. The President could refuse to issue such a proclamation, but in practice he never does.

Section 8 (Clause 1)

The Congress shall have Power To lay and collect Taxes, Duties, Imposts and Excises, to pay the Debts and provide for the Common Defence and general Welfare of the United States; but all Duties, Imposts and Excises shall be uniform throughout the United States.

Where the Articles of Confederation were weak, the Constitution is strong. Congress has the power to create a system of taxation and to enforce the collection of taxes, so that the federal government will have money to finance its operations. Almost every kind of tax is permissible—taxes on income, on property, on sales, on profits, on the manufacture of certain goods.

The taxes cannot be used for all purposes. Taxes can be collected only to pay debts of the United States, to provide for the common defense, and to provide for the general welfare. In practice, these purposes are so broad that any tax which Congress says is for one of these purposes can be justified. (It has sometimes been argued that this clause gives Congress the power to provide for the general welfare in ways other than by raising taxes. For the most part, however, it has been agreed that Congress cannot simply pass a law and justify it by saying that the law is "for the general welfare." Thus, Congress could not pass a law making children ineligible to inherit their parent's property because it is thought desirable to level out large fortunes. But Congress has passed inheritance tax laws, which achieve the same result.)

Duties and imposts are taxes on goods coming into the country. Although in the broad sense, "duties" refers to both import and export taxes, Section 9 of Article I forbids Congress from taxing exports. An "excise" is a tax on the manufacture of a particular object, like tobacco products and liquor. Duties, imposts, and excises must be the same throughout the United States.

Section 8 (Clause 2)

To borrow Money on the credit of the United States;

When Congress passes a law allowing the Treasury Department to sell savings bonds, it is using the power granted by this clause. Once the savings bonds have been sold, Congress can neither pass a later law refusing to pay back the debt nor change the terms under which the debt is to be paid back.

Section 8 (Clause 3)

To regulate Commerce with foreign Nations, and among the several States, and with the Indian Tribes;

One of the major dissatisfactions with the government after the Revolution under the Articles of Confederation was the complete absence of power to regulate commerce among the states. Total economic chaos was imminent. To remedy the prevailing situation, the Constitution made Congress the master regulator.

From this most important "commerce clause," the federal government has developed a vast range of powers over every conceivable aspect of our national economy. An immense body of legislation has been enacted from the very first Congress to the present day, and an impressively large number of cases have come before the federal courts and the Supreme Court in particular.

The commerce clause is one of the few clauses in the Constituion which has expanded in scope almost step by step with the growth of the American economy. That is not at all surprising; the more interdependent the economy becomes, the more justification there is for Congress to regulate in greater areas.

Throughout most of the 19th century, the Supreme Court was not called upon to decide the scope of the power to "regulate." The cases were concerned instead with the meaning of the word "commerce" and the extent to which the power of Congress to regulate interstate commerce means that the states cannot.

In deciding how far the states can go in passing laws that affect commerce, the Court plays one of its chief roles—as umpire determining the powers of others. If Congress decides the Court was wrong and that the states should be allowed to pass certain laws affecting interstate commerce, Congress can simply pass a law overturning the Court's decision and allowing the states to regulate.[107] This, too, is an exercise of the Congress' commerce power: determining when Congressional law should apply and when it is permissible for state law to govern. Congress can even pass a law saying that whatever the states say is all right. In 1890, for instance, Congress passed a law saying that a state could regulate liquor coming from outside the state in the same manner that it regulated liquor made within; Congress would keep hands off. The Court upheld the law.[70]

The first case to come to the Supreme Court involving the commerce clause was in 1824, and Chief Justice Marshall "described the federal commerce power with a breadth never yet exceeded" (as a Justice of the Supreme Court later commented). About ten years earlier the New York legislature had given Livingston and Fulton (the inventor of the steamboat) the exclusive right to navigate New York waters with steamboats. They sold this right to Ogden. Meanwhile, in violation of the New York law, Gibbons ran two steamboats between New York and New Jersey ports. His boats were licensed under a 1793 Act of Congress. Ogden sued Gibbons in state court to have him stopped. The New York court decided for Ogden and ordered Gibbons to cease his boat trips.

Gibbons appealed to the Supreme Court and won his case. In *Gibbons v. Ogden* Chief Justice Marshall wrote that the commerce clause included "that commerce which concerns more states than one . . . The genius and character of the whole government seems to be, that its action is to be applied to all external concerns of the nation, and to those internal concerns which affect the states generally; but not to those which are completely within a particular state, which do not affect other states, and with which it is not necessary to interfere, for the purpose of executing some of the general powers of the government."

The New York law was ruled unconstitutional, since

Congress had already passed legislation, the 1793 Act, under which Gibbons had been given a license to operate his boats. (State laws which conflict with federal laws are invalid, because the Constitution says that federal law is supreme. See p. 124.) *Gibbons v. Ogden* is still relied on today, for as the economy expands, more and more commerce comes to *affect* all the states generally.

Suppose Congress had not passed a law. Would the states then be free to regulate as they see fit? The question came before the Court twenty-seven years later in the case of *Cooley v. Board of Wardens of the Port of Philadelphia.* Pennsylvania had a law which required boats coming from and going to ports outside the state to take on a a pilot from Philadelphia to navigate while in the harbor. Cooley sued, saying that the commerce clause denied the states any power to regulate commerce at all, and that a regulation concerning ships which travel between states is a regulation of interstate commerce.

The Court upheld the Pennsylvania law. Agreeing that a regulation on ships is a regulation of interstate commerce, the Court noted that Congress had not legislated. Until it did, the states were free to act. Said the court (in what has come to be known as the "Cooley doctrine"): "Whatever subjects of [the commerce] power are in their nature national, or admit only of one uniform system, or plan of regulation, may just be said to be of such a nature as to require exclusive legislation by Congress . . . [but the pilotage system] is local and not national . . . it is likely to be the best provided for, not by one system, or plan of regulations, but by as many as the legislative discretion of the several states should deem applicable to the local peculiarities of the ports within their limits."

That is, it is not necessary to have a nationally uniform system of pilots. So the states can do what they want. If Congress were to pass legislation concerning pilots, however, even though national uniformity is not absolutely necessary, then state laws which interfered with Congressional policy would have to cease. The Supreme Court has the responsibility of determining what matters require uniformity and thus absence of state regulation. State taxation of interstate goods and services and state health and safety regulations continue to present difficult and perplexing constitutional problems. In general, the states retain wide powers over the regulation of automobiles, bridges, dams, ferries, and wharves. States also exercise a large authority over corporations and commercial transactions, such as rules governing contracts, checks, and other financial matters. Quarantine laws to control disease and hundreds of other matters are regulated by the states, as long as the state law does not conflict with federal.

Transportation: Land, Water, and Air

In 1887, Congress passed the Interstate Commerce Act, regulating the conduct of railroads. The Act created the Interstate Commerce Commission, and now gives the Commission power to declare which safety devices would have to be installed, to regulate prices charged to passengers, and other powers. Since then, Congress has placed other means of transportation under the Interstate Commerce Commission and has created other agencies, such as the Federal Maritime Commission (for shipping) and the Civil Aeronautics Board and Federal Aviation Agency (for air travel). The functions of many of these boards are being consolidated in the recently created Department of Transportation. Today almost all forms of transportation are regulated in one way or another by Congressional use of the commerce clause power.

Commerce Means More Than Traffic

As Marshall indicated in *Gibbons,* Congress can regulate more than the flow of goods between the states. It can regulate those matters within the states that *concern* or *affect* commerce among the states.

In 1871, in the famous case of *The Daniel Ball,* the owners of a steam vessel, "The Daniel Ball," were fined $500 under a Congressional law requiring all ships operating on navigable waters to be licensed. The owners had not licensed the ship because it operated only between two ports within the state of Michigan, because the ship was so small it could not operate on Lake Michigan, and because the ship did not connect with any other steamers or railway lines running from Michigan to any other state.

But some of the goods which "The Daniel Ball" carried had come from other states and others of the goods were destined to be sold in markets outside Michigan. That was enough. The Supreme Court upheld the law: "She was employed as an instrument of [interstate] commerce; for whenever a commodity *has begun to move* as an article of trade from one State to another, commerce in that commodity between the states has commenced."

Just how far the commerce power extends was demonstrated in 1942 when an Ohio farmer protested a penalty which had been imposed on him by the Secretary of Agriculture for growing more wheat in 1941 than was allowed. A marketing quota had been destablished by the Department of Agriculture under the Agricultural Adjustment Act, passed by Congress in 1938 to help fight the Depression. The Act included wheat that was grown on a farm and used only there; that is, *wheat not sold in any market at all,* inside the state or out.

The Supreme Court ruled in *Wickard v. Filburn* that crops grown on the farm for use on the farm (for feeding livestock) were part of interstate commerce. "That [the specific farmer's] own contribution to the [national] demand for wheat may be trivial by itself is not enough," the Court said, "to remove him from the scope of federal regulation, where, as here, his contribution, *taken together with that of many others similarly situated,* is far from trivial."

The Sherman Antitrust Act of 1890 is another illustration of the extent of the commerce power. The Act forbids companies to take actions which tend to restrain trade and lessen competition. After hesitant starts in upholding the Act,[151] the Court saw the effects that monopoly could have on the national economy.[133] Today, the validity of the antitrust laws is beyond question.

In 1958, Von's Grocery Stores in Los Angeles merged

with a direct competitor, Shopping Bag Food Stores. Although together they accounted for only 7.5 percent of the total retail grocery market in Los Angeles (the total yearly market was $2.5 billion), Von's was the third largest seller in the area and Shopping Bag Food Stores had been the sixth largest. Von's stores had grown from fourteen to twenty-seven and Shopping Bag's from fifteen to thirty-four during the period of 1948-1958, when the merger began. Competitors had been going out of business. From 1950 to 1961, the number of retail grocery stores had dropped from 5,365 to 3,818. Large chain stores were buying up their smaller competitors.

The Justice Department proceeded to prosecute Von's, seeking a court order to break up the merger under the Sherman Act and the Clayton Act (which outlaws mergers that tend to lessen competition). Even though the merger resulted in a grocery unit that controlled only 7.5 percent of the market within the state, the commerce power was held to apply.[158] Ths Supreme Court in 1966 split the stores up again.

Perhaps Mr. Justice Jackson best summed up the extent of the commerce power when he wrote in 1948: "If it is interstate commerce that feels the pinch, it does not matter how local the operation that applies the squeeze." [159]

Production, Industrial Relations, Labor

For many years, the Supreme Court struck down Congressional statutes designed to upgrade standards of production, wages, and hours of workers, and to make working conditions better in a number of industries. The Court was concentrating on the word "commerce." When the Depression struck, the Court eventually shifted its attention to the meaning of the word "regulation."

In 1935, Congress passed the National Labor Relations Act, establishing the National Labor Relations Board and empowering it to hear cases involving companies which engaged in "unfair labor practices," such as discrimination against union members and interference with union organization. The fact that workers could not bargain with their employers—giant companies—because individually they were too weak, led Congress to pass the Act. Congress (and most of the public) felt that one way of helping to wipe out the extreme poverty and joblessness which faced workers throughout the country would be to allow them to combine together in unions. The union would give the workers more nearly equal strength to bargain with companies about such matters as wages, hours, and conditions of employment. Legislation was necessary because most companies at the time were strongly anti-union, and union members often found themselves fired simply for being members. The companies also used numerous other devices to keep unions weak.

The Jones & Laughlin Steel Company tested the constitutionality of the Labor Act by discriminating against union members. The Company discharged certain employees who were active in union organization: Section 8(a)(3) of the N.L.R.A. declared that if the employer fired employees out of anti-union sentiment the company was guilty of an "unfair labor practice." The NLRB found the company guilty of an unfair labor practice and Jones & Laughlin appealed. In *NLRB v. Jones & Laughlin Steel Corp.*, the Supreme Court upheld the law, saying, "The fact remains that the stoppage of those operations by industrial strife would have a most serious effect upon interstate commerce. In view of [the steel company's] far-flung activities, it is idle to say that the effect would be indirect or remote. It is obvious that it would be immediate and might be catastrophic. . . . When industries organize themselves on a national scale, making their relation to interstate commerce the dominant factor in their activities, how can it be maintained that their industrial labor relations constitute a forbidden field into which Congress may not enter when it is necessary to protect interstate commerce from the paralyzing consequences of industrial war?"

This case was followed in 1941 by *United States v. F. W. Darby Lumber Co.* Fred Darby manufactured finished lumber from raw wood in Georgia and then shipped it out of state for sale. Under the Fair Labor Standards Act, he was obliged to pay his workmen the then-current minimum wage, 25 cents per hour, and to keep them at work no longer than forty-four hours per week. He had been paying his workmen between 12½ and 17 cents an hour.

Just before the Act became effective in June, 1938, he called his employees together and said that in order to stay in business he would have to cut their wages down to no more than 9 cents an hour. But, he told them, since he realized this was not enough to live on, he would continue to pay them up to 17½ cents an hour. However, Darby said, he considered the extra part a loan, and he would deduct it from their pay in October, when the Act was in effect. In this way he tried to get around the law and pay his workers less than $572 per *year* required by the Act. His scheme didn't work. The Court said that Congress had the power to control hours and wages involved in production of goods intended for interstate commerce by regulating interstate competition. The lower court was reversed (since it had held that the law was unconstitutional), the case remanded, and after trial Fred Darby was found guilty and fined.

Today all kinds of federal regulations have been upheld, including those on gas, oil, and electricity. The power of Congress to control standards is sweeping.

Communications and Financial Markets

Similarly, Congress has exercised its power to regulate interstate commerce by regulating the radio, television, telephone, and telegraph industries. Communications are under the supervision of the Federal Communications Commission.

Congress also regulates the buying and selling of securities, such as stocks and bonds, and has created a special agency, the Securities and Exchange Commission, to prescribe rules and regulations.

Civil Rights

In very recent years, Congress has used its power to regulate commerce among the states to promote civil rights and to end racial discrimination. The Civil Rights Act of 1964 made discrimination or segregation on the grounds of race, color, religion, or national origin illegal if carried out by hotels, motels, inns, restaurants, cafeterias, and other similar kinds of businesses which serve an interstate public.

In that same year, the proprietors of the Heart of Atlanta Motel in Georgia refused to admit Negroes, solely on the ground of race, even though almost three-quarters of its registered guests were from out of state. The motel owners refused to abide by the Civil Rights Act, contending that it was unconstitutional.

On appeal, the Supreme Court reaffirmed a long line of cases beginning in 1849 [106] which had said that transportation of passengers was a part of interstate commerce. The Court found Congressional testimony overwhelming in its proof that discrimination in accommodations seriously impaired interstate commerce. In *Heart of Atlanta Motel, Inc. v. United States*, the Court upheld the "public accommodations" section of the Act with these words: "That Congress was legislating against moral wrongs in many of these areas rendered its enactments no less valid. In framing [the 'public accommodations' section] of this Act Congress was also dealing with what it considered a moral problem. But that fact does not detract from the overwhelming evidence of the disruptive effect that racial discrimination has had on commercial intercourse. It was this burden which empowered Congress to enact appropriate legislation."

In a similar case decided the same day, the Court upheld the section dealing with restaurants. Ollie McClung, proprietor of Ollie's Barbecue in Birmingham, Alabama, refused to serve Negroes. In *Katzenback v. McClung* he was told to mend his ways, for his refusal was clearly illegal in the face of the Act. If a large group of people cannot eat at public restaurants when away from home, they will tend not to travel, and thus the amount of commerce conducted is reduced. Even if the customers do not all come from out of state, much of the food served does, and this is enough to bring the restaurant within Congress' reach.

Prohibitions against Commerce

Along with the power to regulate goes the power to prohibit altogether. In 1895 Congress passed a law forbidding the carrying of lottery tickets across state lines for the purposes of sale. The Supreme Court, after some soul-searching (the case was argued on three separate occasions before the Court), decided in *The Lottery Case*[16] that the prohibition of interstate gambling was a valid exercise of the commerce power. Since that time, a number of prohibitory statutes have been passed and upheld; among them, the Pure Food and Drug Act (barring commerce in impure food and drugs and giving the Food and Drug Administration and the Federal Trade Commission power to deal with such problems), the White Slave Act (often called the Mann Act, making criminal the transportation of women across state lines for immoral purposes), the Motor Vehicle Theft Act (making interstate dealing in stolen cars a federal crime), and the Webb-Kenyon Act (prohibiting interstate transportation of liquor and prison-made goods where the state laws prohibit such commerce).

Regulation of Foreign Commerce

The power to regulate commerce between the United States and foreign countries is as broad as the interstate commerce power. Under this part of the commerce clause, protective tariffs are permitted, as are laws which prohibit the importation of such goods as impure drugs, opium, inferior teas, sponges taken by divers from the Gulf of Mexico, and prizefight films. The foreign commerce power also extends to antitrust activities abroad. The long arms of Congress can reach across the seas. American businessmen whose activities in foreign countries restrain trade within the United States (such as creating a monopoly to cut off supplies going to the United States) are guilty of violating valid United States laws.

Regulation of Commerce with Indian Tribes

This source of Congressional power was never extensively used; in view of the sorry dealings and tricks which the government played on the Indians during the 19th century, perhaps it would have been misused. The power still exists today, however, and is used mostly to stop the traffic in liquor. Even though Indians are citizens, it is apparently still the law that as long as Indians reside on land given by the United States Government and as long as they remain together as a tribe, governed by Indian agents, Congress can prohibit the sale of liquor to them.[154] But the law has not been tested since 1916.

Section 8 (Clause 4)

To establish an uniform Rule of Naturalization, and uniform Laws on the subject of Bankruptcies throughout the United States;

Congress has an absolute power to decide which people born outside the United States can become citizens and how long and under what conditions aliens may reside in the United States. For many years citizenship was restricted to white persons and those of African descent; Japanese and Chinese, among others, were excluded. Since 1952, Congress has declared that no person is to be kept out because of race.

Once a person is naturalized, his rights are the same as those of people born in the United States. There are no second-class citizens.[75]

Until recently, however, Congress had declared that citizenship could be lost in a number of ways—for example, by voting in a foreign election or serving in the armed forces of another country. Then, in 1963, an American citizen who had lived for the previous ten years in Israel applied to the State Department for a passport renewal. The Department turned him down, declaring that his citizenship had been terminated two years before because he had voted in a local Israeli election. On appeal in 1967 the Supreme Court declared that Congress does not have the power to expatriate a citizen against his wishes. Said the Court: "The people are sovereign and the government cannot sever its relationship to the people." [177]

Under the naturalization power, Congress can allow an alien to enter the country, whether or not he wants to become a citizen. But the alien's rights are not equivalent to the citizen's. True, his life, liberty, and property cannot be taken away without "due process of law" (see p. 178), but many unpleasant things can happen to him.

A foreigner can be deported for belonging to an organization which he was legally entitled to join. Harisiades, Greek by birth, came to the United States at the age of thirteen in 1916. He joined the Communist Party in 1925 and remained a member until 1939. He had married an American citizen and had had two children. He testified that he did not personally believe in the use of force or violence to overthrow the government. In 1930 an order was issued for his deportation, but because he used many aliases, he was not notified of the order until 1946. The Supreme Court said that Congress and the Justice Department acted within their power in evicting Harisiades from the United States, even though membership in the Party was not illegal when Harisiades belonged. [63]

An alien can even be detained indefinitely on a small island—perhaps not punishment, but not unlike being sent to a prison. Ignatz Mezei, a Hungarian cabinetmaker, had lived for twenty-five years in Buffalo, New York. In 1949 he got word from Romania that his mother was ill and he traveled to Europe to see her. Romania refused him entrance and he returned to the United States. Because he was a foreigner (never having taken out citizenship papers) he returned to America by way of Ellis Island in New York (where all aliens then had to report to be cleared by immigration officials). The Department of Justice declared him a security risk and refused him admission. He applied for admission to twenty-five other countries but in each case was refused. By a 5-4 vote, the Supreme Court found no provision in the Constitution that would overcome the power of the Justice Department to keep him locked on an island. [127] Congress, having lawfully delegated power to the Department under the naturalization clause, had doomed Mezei to live on Ellis Island for the rest of his life. After three years, Mezei got a hearing before a board of New York attorneys, who recommended that he be paroled in the United States. This time the Department of Justice agreed and Mezei was released. But the Department did not have to go along with the board's recommendations, and Mezei could have been held for life, without ever knowing why, for the Department never did say what evidence it had against him.

Bankruptcy

Under this section, Congress has the power to pass laws determining what happens when a private individual or a business corporation goes broke and is unable to pay all its debts. This power is an obviously necessary partner to the power to regulate commerce. Bankruptcy legislation can reach *intra*state businesses as well as interstate businesses. Federal bankruptcy laws provide methods of paying off creditors with what remains of a company's funds and allowing the company then to be reorganized and begin operations anew.

Section 8 (Clause 5)

To coin Money, regulate the Value thereof, and of foreign Coin, and fix the Standard of Weights and Measures;

If different units of money were used in different states, business activities would be sorely hampered, to say the least. Congress has the power to fix one value of money throughout the country, to issue paper money, and to make its green-colored dollars a valid way to pay private debts. Because of laws passed under this clause, a person who is owed money cannot refuse to accept paper money and insist on gold instead. Congress can also fix the value of foreign money in relation to United States dollars.

Similarly, to prevent the confusion of having a pound consist of 16 ounces in Florida and thirty-seven ounces in Minnesota, Congress can establish a uniform system of weights and measures. If (as some people would like) the United States were to convert to the metric system (meters and kilometers instead of yards and miles) Congress would have to do the legislating.

Section 8 (Clause 6)

To provide for the Punishment of counterfeiting the Securities and current Coin of the United States;

This clause is unnecessary. The "necessary and proper" clause (see p. 70) allows Congress to punish those who make imitations of money and bonds with the intent of passing them off as the real thing, even if this clause were nonexistent. States can punish counterfeiters as well as Congress, as far as the Constitution is concerned.

Section 8 (Clause 7)

To establish Post Offices and post Roads;

At one time it was thought that the only thing Congress could do under this clause was to designate those places in which post offices and roads could be built. By the last quarter of the 19th century, the clause was broadly interpreted. Today Congress builds not only post offices and highways, but also regulates what may be sent through the mail. Through that power it regulates certain business activities.

Regulations cannot extend too far. Not so long ago the Post Office Department had a regulation requiring the receiver of unsealed political mail from Communist countries to notify the Department if he wanted to receive it. Under this regulation, the Department sent a notice to such persons every time the mail came into the United States. If the Department did not receive an affirmative reply it would not send the mail. A publisher of political pamphlets sued, and the Court agreed the regulation interfered with the freedom of speech and press guaranteed by the 1st Amendment.[80] The law gave the Post Office Department the power to condemn mail as Communist propaganda, a power which might inhibit a person's exercise of his rights. A scholar who reads the mail to see what he can learn about Communist propaganda techniques might be classified as a subversive or security risk by someone with a grudge against him. The mail, said the Court, must go freely.

Section 8 (Clause 8)

To promote the Progress of Science and useful Arts, by securing for limited Times to Authors and Inventors the exclusive Right to their respective Writings and Discoveries;

This is the copyright and patent clause. Congress has passed laws granting exclusive rights to inventors and authors for their inventions and works.

A patent for an invention lasts seventeen years. During that time no one but the patent holder has the right to make or use the invention. Patents can be sold and inventors can license others for money to produce their inventions.

"Writings" has been broadly defined. Copyright can be obtained on books, music, movies, photographs, paintings, sculpture, and other forms of art. The present Copyright Act, enacted in 1909, allows the author a twenty-eight-year copyright, renewable for another twenty-eight years. For many years, pressure has been directed toward Congress to change the Act, which has become outdated in many ways because of new technology, such as coast-to-coast television, communications satellites, and computers. A revision bill now pending before Congress would extend the copyright protection for a period of time equal to the life of the author plus fifty years. Thus, if an author copyrighted a book at the age of twenty-three and died at eighty-three, he and his heirs would have the exclusive rights to the book for 110 years.

The author or inventor must produce his ideas in a tangible form in order to get a copyright or patent. He must build the machine or write the book. No copyright or patent can be given for the idea itself. The theory of relativity, for instance, can be used by anyone in building equipment for physics laboratories. Only the equipment can be patented. Anyone can write about the theory, as long as he does not use the same words that others have used.

Section 8 (Clause 9)
To constitute Tribunals inferior to the supreme Court;

See Article III, p. 100.

Section 8 (Clause 10)
To define and punish Piracies and Felonies committed on the high Seas, and Offences against the Law of Nations;

At the time of the Revolution, a body of law had developed in the courts of many countries concerning relations among nations. Much of this law was common to all nations—crimes on the high seas, crimes during war, rights of nations, rules concerning prisoners of war, duty of countries toward foreigners—and this international law was called the "law of nations." English courts had power to define it themselves, so a particular person might never know whether a law existed for him to violate until the court said Guilty. The Constitution sought to protect United States citizens from this possibility by providing that Congress must define what acts constitute piracy and felonies (serious crimes) committed on the oceans (and even in ports) and what acts are offenses against the law of nations.

Section 8 (Clause 11)

To declare War, grant Letters of Marque and Reprisal, and make Rules concerning Captures on Land and Water;

This clause, and three which follow, make up the "war power" of Congress. Under these clauses, Congress has sweeping powers to deal with military and foreign affairs.

Although Congress alone can *declare* war, the President has a large degree of authority as commander-in-chief (see p. 91). He can move troops, send them into isolated battles, or even plunge them into war. Congress has declared no war since 1941, but United States troops have been called to do battle in many of the years since the end of the Second World War.

In the 18th century, navies were often undersized. To increase fighting power, the government would commission *private* ships to attack enemy ships on the high seas and to seize the ship and its cargo. The "privateer" would be allowed a portion of the plunder. The written commissions were called "letters of marque and reprisal." In the absence of the "letters" deputizing the private vessels, such acts would be piracy. Since private merchant ships are no longer a match for modern warships, letters of marque and reprisal have gone out of fashion.

Enemy property (whether ships on water, or houses, ammunition, and vehicles on land) is disposed of under Congressional regulation when captured, whether or not during time of war.

Section 8 (Clauses 12 and 13)

To raise and support Armies, but no Appropriation of Money

to that Use shall be for a longer Term than two Years;
To provide and maintain a Navy;

The Air Force was created under the power to "raise and support" armies. Congress must pass new laws to appropriate money for the operations of the Army every two years. This is another example of the check Congress exercises over the President. By being required to watch what the "armies" are doing, Congress can control the President's use of the standing Army through its power over the national pocketbook. The power to raise and support the Army and provide and maintain the Navy carries with it the power to draft citizens into the armed forces.

Section 8 (Clause 14)
To make Rules for the Government and Regulation of the land and naval Forces;

The Departments of the Army, Navy, and Air Force, and all military codes and regulations are established under the authority of this clause. Congress has built military procedures and courts for members of the armed services. The court-martial is different from the ordinary trial of civilians accused of crimes. However, the power to enact rules for the military does not extend to wives and dependents. In 1956 the Supreme Court upset as unconstitutional a court-martial of two wives accused of killing their husbands, soldiers in England and Korea. The Bill of Rights, guaranteeing a nonmilitary trial to civilians, follows the flag overseas.[113]

The War Power

By combining clauses 11, 12, 13, and 14, Congress and the President have extensive authority to deal with wartime emergencies. Delegations of power to the President to control rents and regulate prices of hundreds of commodities are allowed—though they might be improper delegations in peacetime.

Sometimes the war power collides with the right of personal liberty. During World War II, the war power won out, and was used to justify locking up, without a trial, citizens who were never proved disloyal.

In Seattle, a University of Washington senior, born in 1918 in the United States to Japanese parents, was arrested for leaving his home after 8 o'clock in the evening. For this violation of a military curfew (imposed on all Japanese in certain areas between 8:00 P.M. and 6:00 A.M.), he was convicted and sent to jail. Because of the fear of possible espionage and sabotage, the Supreme Court agreed that Congress could constitutionally give power to prescribe such regulations to commanding officers.[66]

The entire states of California, Washington, Oregon, Idaho, Montana, Nevada, Utah, and the southern part of Arizona were then declared off-limits to United States citizens of Japanese ancestry. "Civil control stations" and "relocation centers" were established to hold citizens of Japanese ancestry whose homes were in the wrong areas. Commanding General DeWitt said that *all* persons were "subversive" and belonged to "an enemy race."

"I don't want any of them here," he said. "They are a dangerous element. There is no way to determine their loyalty. . . . The West coast contains too many vital installations essential to allow any Japanese on this coast. . . . It makes no difference whether he is an American citizen, he is still a Japanese."

By a 6-3 vote, the Court upheld the lawfulness of the relocation orders, even though they applied only to persons of Japanese descent, and not to those of German or Italian ancestries, countries with which the United States was also at war.[76]

Three Justices sharply dissented from what one called a "legalization of racism." It was charged that agricultural groups put pressure on those in command to get rid of the Japanese because they worked for cheaper wages than their Caucasian counterparts. Said the managing director of the Salinas Vegetable Grower-Shipper Association in California, "And we don't want them back when the war ends, either."

Not one of the 112,000 people sent away without trial had even been accused of sabotage or espionage before being taken to relocation centers. To justify the charge of disloyalty, the "final report" of the Army in February, 1942, two months before the exodus began, said: "The very fact that no sabotage has taken place to date is a disturbing and confirming indication that such action will be taken." Apparently, the less suspicious one was, the more suspicious one became.

There were limits on what could be done, however. In one case, a lucky lady found the government willing to concede that she was loyal to America, even though it insisted on its right to detain her. The Court denied the power. "Loyalty is a matter of the heart and mind, not of race, creed, or color. He who is loyal is by definition not a spy or a saboteur. When the power to detain is derived from the power to protect the war effort against espionage and sabotage, detention which has no relationship to that objective is unauthorized." [38]

The war powers are not limited to actual shooting war. In order to maintain the peace immediately after war and to bring an end to disruptions caused by war, Congress has passed many laws. Perhaps the most outstanding example of peacetime legislation in this field is the Atomic Energy Act, creating the Atomic Energy Commission, giving it authority to do research into nuclear physics, to own almost all laboratories which produce fissionable uranium and plutonium, and to make atomic bombs and other nuclear weapons.

Section 8 (Clause 15)
To provide for calling forth the Militia to execute the Laws of the Union, suppress Insurrections and repel Invasions;

The militia are citizen-soldiers who are not part of the regular Army. Members of the National Guard and National Guard Reserve are militia members. They can be called to active duty in the Army when emergencies arise. The National Guard has been used to help enforce federal court orders concerning school desegregation when state officials have refused to comply. Congress has given the President the authority call up the National Guard to suppress these and other kinds of insurrections.

Section 8 (Clause 16)

To provide for organizing, arming, and disciplining, the Militia, and for governing such Part of them as may be employed in the Service of the United States, reserving to the States respectively, the Appointment of the Officers, and the Authority of training the Militia according to the discipline prescribed by Congress;

Except in two respects, Congress has complete control of the militia. The Congress can tell the states how to organize and what kind of training is necessary. The states have the power to appoint officers (although officers must meet standards prescribed by the President) and to conduct the actual training process. Before 1916 the militia was pretty much a state affair. Since that time the militia has been brought more and more under federal control with the enactment of the National Defense Act. In certain emergencies, the President can draft members of the militia into the regular Army.

Section 8 (Clause 17)

To exercise exclusive Legislation in all Cases whatsoever, over such District (not exceeding ten Miles square) as may, by Cession of particular States, and the Acceptance of Congress, become the Seat of the Government of the United States, and to exercise like Authority over all Places purchased by the Consent of the Legislature of the State in which the Same shall be, for the Erection of Forts, Magazines, Arsenals, dock-Yards, and other needful Buildings;

Maryland and Virginia deeded parts of their states to the United States in order to establish the national capital. In 1800 this land became the District of Columbia, and the next year the city of Washington was established. (In 1846 Virginia was returned its land, so that today Washington, D.C., is smaller in area than it might have been.)

The District of Columbia is not a state and has neither Senators nor Congressmen to represent it in Congress, even though Congress acts as its city council and legislature. It is the only city in American in which the people do not have a voice in their local affairs.

Congress also has the power to govern places purchased from the states, not just for the purpose of building military establishments, such as "forts, magazines, arsenals, and dock-yards," but also such buildings as post offices, hospitals in national parks, and dams. Once the United States comes into possession of the lands sold by the states, Congress alone can punish crimes committed in such places; Congress alone can tax within the places. But until Congress says otherwise, existing state law continues to govern private rights, such as the right to own property and to make contracts.

Section 8 (Clause 18)
—And to make all laws which shall be necessary and proper for carrying into Execution the foregoing Powers, and all other Powers vested by this Constitution in the Government of the United States, or in any Department or Officer thereof.

This is the famous "necessary and proper" or "elastic clause," greatly enlarging the scope of the other powers granted to Congress. "Let the end be legitimate," wrote Chief Justice Marshall in *McCulloch v. Maryland* in 1819, "let it be within the scope of the Constitution, and all means which are appropriate, which are plainly adapted to that end, which are not prohibited, but consist with the letter and spirit of the Constitution, are constitutional." In *McCulloch,* the Court upheld the power of Congress to establish national banks, even though the Constitution nowhere mentions banks and in spite of the fact that a proposal to give Congress the power to charter banks was specifically rejected at the Constitutional Convention. In order to carry out its powers of collecting taxes, borrowing money, regulating commerce, declaring and conducting war, and raising and supporting armies, the establishment of such institutions as federal reserve banks is entirely legitimate.

From Marshall's decision in *McCulloch,* the "necessary and proper clause" has become one of the most important in the Constitution. From it, in fact, has evolved a "fourth branch" of government, nowhere mentioned in the Constitution itself. This fourth branch consists of the executive departments and agencies, such as the Departments of State, Defense, Treasury, and Justice, the Interstate Commerce Commission, the Federal Communications Commission, the Securities and Exchange Commission, the National Labor Relations Board, and more than 50 others.

Executive departments were contemplated by the Framers, for they vested the power of appointment of department heads in the President (see p. 94). President Washington had four cabinet officers, the Secretaries of State, Treasury, War, and the Attorney General, head of the Department of Justice (the prosecutorial arm and legal branch of the federal government). At the outset, these officers were advisers, their departments small. For the most part, the departments did not establish their own laws; they did not hear cases; they did not settle disputes.

After the Civil War, national energy was focused on industrial and corporate development. Railroads became national carriers; products were shipped across the continent. By 1887 the railroads had become so powerful that Congress moved in to control. Acting under the commerce power, with a boost from the necessary and proper clause, Congress created the Interstate Commerce Commission. This agency was empowered to promulgate rules and set standards. It was to be a governmental body that could develop an expertise in the area of railroad transportation, knowledge that Congress could not hope to develop. Because the agency was specialized, it would have the time to investigate, to experience, and to learn about railroad transportation problems. Congress passed the basic laws, but they constituted a bare skeleton. The Commission was to fill in the law around the statutory frame.

From then until the Depression of the 1930's, Congress slowly created more agencies—the Federal Reserve Board and the Railway Labor Adjustment Board, for instance. The Executive Departments and divisions took on a law-making power also: the Treasury Department, the Bureau of Internal Revenue, the Departments of State, Justice, and War all assumed larger roles in the legal process. As commercial life developed, day-to-day tasks arose which legislative bodies and courts were not equipped to handle. Thus the *administration* of the laws was passed on to agencies, departments, and bureaus.

The Depression led to a spate of new agencies. The national economy collapsed; to reactivate it, wide-reaching legislation created boards and commissions to administer many facets of commercial and industrial life. Out of the 1930's came the Federal Power Commission, the Securities and Exchange Commission, the National Labor Relations Board, new powers for the Department of Agriculture. From the procedures and activities of the commissions came a new kind of law—administrative law.

Supplementing the legal process is the administrative process, a vast and far-reaching interplay among courts, Congress, and agencies. Federal labor policy is a case in point. In 1935 Congress enacted the basic National Labor Relations Act (the Wagner Act). This law recognized the right of workers to organize and operate unions; it created the National Labor Relations Board to mediate disputes and controversies in the field of labor relations. It defined certain rights of workers, but only in the broadest of terms. Employers were forbidden from interfering with these rights; such interferences, called "unfair labor practices," could be enjoined by the courts. To develop national labor policy, only the outlines of which were legislated by Congress, the NLRB was given a number of powers. Regional examiners and offices hear complaints and make investigations. They can hear disputes at the trial level, whether brought by business or labor. They can conduct union elections and certify a winning union as "the" union with which the particular employer must negotiate. The union becomes the exclusive bargaining representative for the workers in the unit within the plant or industry, and the employer violates the Wagner Act when he negotiates with individual employees or with other unions. The NLRB can enforce its "cease and desist" orders by going to court and asking for injunctions. The Board hears cases and settles them through hearings and other procedures which closely resemble judicial proceedings. The Board can issue regulations and rules apart from cases (though it usually does not. The Bureau of Internal Revenue, on the other hand, has issued thousands of pages of regulations, under a Congressional delegation of authority in the internal revenue code).

When the losing party before the NLRB dislikes the results, there are ways of appealing the case to the courts. Does a company which enforces a no-solicitation rule on company premises, thus prohibiting union members from discussing union activities during non-working time, interfere with the employees' right to organize? Can the employer hire permanent replacements to take over the jobs left vacant by striking employees, without violating the prohibition against discriminating against the unions? Is the employer under a legal obligation to bargain with the union about sub-contracting of work? (Answers: Yes, No, and Yes.) All these questions have been heard by the Board and reviewed by the Supreme Court. Each decision generates new problems, as employers and unions seek somewhat different ways to do things they are forbidden from doing. (Thus, an employer cannot refuse to take back a striking worker if the employer has not already hired a replacement when the striker returns.)

Most cases heard by the Labor Board, and most rules announced, are not appealed to the courts. The delays and costs are usually prohibitive, or simply not worth the bother. Furthermore, the role of the courts on appeal is strictly limited. Because the NLRB is assumed to possess an expertise in labor matters, the Supreme Court limits its consideration to whether the Board has exceeded its authority as given by Congressional Act. Most of the procedures, presumptions, and factual conclusions of the Board are not reviewable.

Together the Board and the federal courts have developed a national labor policy. From time to time, aspects of the policy have drifted from what a certain Congress, given the economic and political considerations which it faces, thinks desirable. Thus the Wagner Act was aimed at increasing union strength, so almost anything which unions did was permissible. It was impossible for a union to commit an unfair labor practice, because the Wagner Act defined such practices in terms of employer actions only. By 1947 unions had grown mightily in size, the mood of the country and Congress had shifted. The Taft-Hartley Act was enacted to amend the National Labor Relations Act in important respects. Certain activities unions had engaged in were made unfair labor practices; the President was given power to go to federal courts to enjoin strikes for a 80-day period. (The Norris-LaGuardia Act of 1932 had prohibited federal courts from issuing injunctions against unions, because the courts at that time were hostile to union purposes.)

So agencies, Congress, and the courts interact in a variety of ways to create and administer federal law. The agencies and the administrative process are fundamentally a creation of Congress under its power to enact legislation necessary and proper to the carrying on of its own powers and *of the powers which the Constitution vests in other branches of the government.* Congress has mixed the executive and judicial powers with its own legislative powers and created the hybrid, independent agency—part legislature, part executive, part court. Without the fourth branch of government it would be difficult to manage and control a large industrial, technological society; without the necessary and proper clause, it would have been far more difficult to create the fourth branch.

The necessary and proper clause has also been used in a much different way: to create a body of admiralty and maritime legislation—the law of the sea. The Constitution gives the federal courts jurisdiction to hear cases involving admiralty and maritime law (see p. 109), but it does not say what that law is, who is to make it or change it. The Supreme Court held in the early 1800's that it had the power to apply as federal law the maritime law that had existed in the states at the time the Constitution was written. But it was not long before Congress desired to change and modify the law that had been created by the courts of the various seafaring states and nations during the course of several centuries. The Supreme Court held in a number of cases that the Congress possessed the power to change the law of the sea, under the necessary and proper clause. In the 19th century, Congress extended the jurisdiction to navigable rivers and lakes. In 1948 it extended the jurisdiction to land structures such as docks and bridges; it has also brought airplanes into the admiralty, a law that was developed to regulate the affairs of ships. Through a subtle blending of the commerce power and the necessary and proper clause, Congress has transformed a clause in Article III of the Constitution, giving jurisdiction to courts, into a grant of great legislative power.

Section 9 (Clause 1)

[The Migration or Importation of such Persons as any of the States now existing shall think proper to admit, shall not be prohibited by the Congress prior to the Year one thousand eight hundred and eight, but a Tax or duty may be imposed on such Importation, not exceeding ten dollars for each person.]

This was a compromise between those who favored slavery and those who wanted to abolish it. Congress could not end the slave trade between 1789 and 1808. This clause died at midnight, December 31, 1807.

Section 9 (Clause 2)

The Privilege of the Writ of Habeas Corpus shall not be suspended, unless when in Cases of Rebellion or Invasion the public safety may require it.

Habeas corpus (Latin for "you have the body") is one of the greatest guarantees of personal liberty in our entire constitutional system. The writ of habeas corpus is an order by a court to state or federal officials to release a person in custody unless they can show a legal justification for his detention. Because of habeas corpus it is almost impossible for a person to be arrested by police and simply sent to jail without trial, since upon application by the person in jail the court will grant the writ of habeas corpus and order the government to try the suspect or let him go.

The right of habeas corpus applies only against the federal government, insofar as the Constitution is concerned. In 1867 Congress passed a law giving federal courts the power "to grant writs of habeas corpus in all cases where any person may be restrained of his or her liberty in violation of the Constitution, or of any treaty or law of the United States." One year later the 14th Amendment was ratified, making it unlawful for any state to deprive any person of "life, liberty, or property without due process of law." Since the right not to be deprived of liberty without due process is a constitutional one, federal courts have had the power since 1868 to issue writs of habeas corpus to free persons from illegal state proceedings as well as federal ones.

During wartime—just when habeas corpus may most be needed (since the fear of invasion may cause officials to lock up anyone interfering with their conduct of the war)—the writ may be suspended by Congress if "the public safety may require it." Lincoln authorized the United States commanding general to suspend the writ during the Civil War and the Supreme Court upheld the action, but only because Congress later gave its approval.

After the Japanese attack on Pearl Harbor in 1941, the governor of Hawaii turned the territory over to an Army general. Even after the immediate danger was over, regular trial procedures were short-circuited for crimes unrelated to the war (like embezzlement). When prisoners began applying for habeas corpus, the general resisted, until a local judge ordered him to justify the proceedings. The general continued to resist, the judge held him in contempt of court and fined him, and when the dust of battle settled, habeas corpus defeated the general. He produced the prisoners and they were eventually released when the Supreme Court ruled that the proceedings had been illegal.

Said the Court: "From time immemorial despots have used real or imagined threats to the public welfare as an excuse for needlessly abrogating human rights. The . . . Constitutional rights of an accused individual are too fundamental to be sacrificed merely through a reasonable fear of military assault. There must be some overpowering factor that makes a recognition of these rights incompatible with the public safety before we should consent to their temporary suspension." [31] The Supreme Court, not the general, has the right to determine what that "overpowering factor" is.

Section 9 (Clause 3)
No Bill of Attainder or ex post facto Law shall be passed.

Bills of Attainder

The old English Parliament used to pass laws declaring a named person guilty of a certain crime and ordering him punished without trial. This was a "bill of attainder"—an exercise of judicial power by the legislative branch. In a system of separation of powers, this kind of law could not be permitted. Both Congress and the states are forbidden from using it.

During the 1940's Congress prohibited the Treasury Department from paying three government employees their salary because, it was said, they had engaged in subversive activities. Without trial, Congress declared that they could never receive federal salaries (except for service on juries or in the Army) unless the President were to appoint them to public office and the Senate consented. This was a bill of attainder, said the Court, and tossed out the law.[153]

Ex Post Facto Laws

Parliamentary practice gave rise to this prohibition also. Laws were passed which made illegal an act entirely lawful at the time when it was done. By this device, anyone could be arrested and imprisoned. The prohibition against ex post facto ("after the fact") laws applies as well to the states as to the federal government, but only with respect to *criminal* laws. "Retroactive" legislation (laws reaching back into the past) is valid if it concerns property and other private rights. For instance, a law passed in June, raising the income tax rates effective the preceding January, is a retroactive law, but it is not ex post facto because it does not relate to criminal matters. If the law also said that people who had not paid the higher rate during the previous February were guilty of a crime, that would be ex post facto and unconstitutional.

The distinction between criminal and "civil" laws is not an easy one to draw. Harisiades, the Greek alien who was deported because he was a member of the Communist Party when it wasn't illegal to belong, was not "punished" by an ex post facto law, though he was no doubt the victim of one. Deportation proceedings are said to be civil, rather than criminal, and so such retroactive legislation is valid.

Section 9 (Clause 4)

No Capitation, or other direct, Tax shall be laid, unless in Proportion to the Census or Enumeration herein before directed to be taken.

A capitation tax is a poll tax, a tax on the right to vote. Poll taxes are now unconstitutional (see the 24th Amendment). The only other important "direct" tax is the income tax, and because of the 16th Amendment, no apportionment need be made. This clause has little use today, partly because the meaning of "direct" is so unclear that most important taxes have been declared "indirect." (This clause applies only to the federal government.)

Section 9 (Clause 5)

No Tax or Duty shall be laid on Articles exported from any State.

Whenever goods are shipped overseas for sale in a foreign country, neither the United States nor the state governments may tax them. However, a tax on a whole class of goods, only some of which are exported, is constitutional. For example, a tax on the manufacture of automobiles is constitutional, even though some are sold abroad.

Section 9 (Clause 6)

No Preference shall be given by any Regulation of Commerce or Revenue to the Ports of one State over those of another: nor shall Vessels bound to, or from, one State, be obliged to enter, clear, or pay Duties in another.

The "no preference" clause has a limited meaning. Congress cannot discriminate between ports just because they are in different states. Discrimination resulting from some other cause is permissible.

Congress is free, however, to improve harbors and build lighthouses and other structures in select ports, even though other ports may be disadvantaged.

Section 9 (Clause 7)

No Money shall be drawn from the Treasury, but in Consequence of Appropriations made by Law; and a regular Statement and Account of the Receipts and Expenditures of all public Money shall be published from time to time.

Congress is not restricted in what it can spend. This clause talks only to the executive branch. Under no circumstance can the Secretary of the Treasury authorize payments to be made from the public monies of the United States unless Congress has first passed a law allowing him to. Even if a court has ruled that the federal government owes someone money, Congress must first approve the payment. (Every year Congress appropriates a certain sum of money to the "general fund" to pay for court judgments against the United States, in order to spare itself the bother of having to consider each case as it is decided by the courts.) The books of account of federal funds are prepared by the Division of Internal Audits of the Bureau of Accounts of the Treasury Department.

Section 9 (Clause 8)

No Title of Nobility shall be granted by the United States: And no Person holding any Office of Profit or Trust under them, shall, without the Consent of the Congress, accept of any present, Emolument, Office, or Title, of any kind whatever, from any King, Prince, or foreign State.

Thus the hereditary, self-perpetuating, aristocratic class was done away with. But nothing prevents a private citizen from being honored by a foreign government.

Even a photograph of a foreign head of state, sent as a remembrance to a United States official, might be an illegal gift. The public officer should ask Congress for permission to receive it. In practice, no one much worries about the little things.

Section 10 (Clause 1)

No State shall enter into any Treaty, Alliance, or Confederation; grant Letters of Marque and Reprisal; coin Money; emit Bills of Credit; make any Thing but gold and silver Coin a Tender in Payment of Debts; pass any Bill of Attainder, ex post facto Law, or Law impairing the Obligation of Contracts, or grant any Title of Nobility.

The prohibition against granting letters of marque and reprisal is another way of saying that only Congress has the right to grant them. The prohibitions against bills of attainder, ex post facto laws, and titles of nobility apply in the same way as the prohibitions placed on the federal government.

Treaties, Alliances, and Confederations

Because the states are forbidden from entering into alliances, the attempted secession of the southern states during the Confederacy was declared unconstitutional, and the Confederacy has never been considered to have had a legal existence. Today the clause prohibits the states from dealing directly with foreign governments.

Money, Credit, and Legal Tender

A national economy requires a uniform monetary system. Therefore, the states were forbidden from making their own money. Money regulated by Congress is good in all states.

Bills of credit are paper notes intended for general circulation as a substitute for money. These too are taboo, although there is nothing to prevent a state from borrowing money and signing a contract promising to pay back the debt. Similarly, until the past few decades, the states could not insist that anything other than gold or silver coins be accepted in payment of state debts. But now, because of federal law, ownership of gold except in special circumstances is unlawful. States can lawfully pay debts in federal reserve notes (the regular green paper money of the United States).

Impairing the Obligation of Contracts

Once upon a time, the "contract clause" was one of the most important parts of the Constitution; in eight years after the Civil War, twenty attempts by the states to hinder the carrying out of public contracts were thwarted by the Supreme Court. Today the contract clause has almost dried up as a source of protection.

The first case in which the Supreme Court overturned a state law as unconstitutional involved the attempt by Georgia to take back land it had sold. Four land companies had bought millions of acres of land in Yazoo River Valley (almost the entire land areas of Alabama and Mississippi) dirt cheap; part of the land was sold to Peck who then sold some of the land to Fletcher.

It was then that the "Yazoo land scandal" broke: members of the state legislature had been bribed into passing the law authorizing the sale of public land. Georgia voters promptly kicked them out of office, and the next legislature tried to repair the damage by repealing the law which had deeded the property to the real estate companies.

Fletcher then refused to pay Peck for the land, because he thought that the second Georgia law would get the land back for Georgia. In *Fletcher v. Peck* the Supreme Court said that the contract with Peck was good, that Peck's title to the land was good, and that Georgia's attempt to retake the land was unconstitutional. The deed of land by the first Georgia legislature was a contract, and it makes no difference as to third parties that it was corruptly made. To take it back would be to impair unlawfully the continuing obligation of the contract to the third party, Peck. The contract clause commands the states to respect their own contracts, as well as those between private individuals. (Had the *original* buyer—those who had fraudulently bought from the Georgia legislature—not yet sold the land, Georgia could have nullified the contract because of the fraud. The chain of buyers makes the difference.)

This principle is still good law, but the next case provided a way by which the states could get around the clause. In 1769 King George III established Dartmouth College in the state of New Hampshire, putting its affairs in the hands of private "trustees" or caretakers. The royal charter passed on to the state after the Revolution. In

1816 New Hampshire tried to change Dartmouth into a public college. Dartmouth hired Daniel Webster to defend it. (Webster reportedly remarked during argument before the Supreme Court that "it is a small college but there are those who love it," a statement said to have brought tears to the eyes of many in the courtroom.)

Webster won his argument. In the *Dartmouth College* case the Supreme Court recognized the charter as a valid contract. The state must promise to recognize the chartered institution in return for the private organization's agreement to conduct the business for which it was chartered.

From then on, when states granted charters to corporations (and later on when corporation laws allowed companies to be incorporated simply by filing the proper papers), the state expressly reserved the right to alter or amend the contract of incorporation. Since the companies and other organizations must agree to this condition before the contract goes into effect, states now exercise much larger power over private corporations. But Dartmouth College remains private.

The final end to the importance of the contract clause came more than half a century after the *Dartmouth College* case. In 1877 the Supreme Court decided in *Munn v. Illinois* (a case involving state regulation of private grain-storage facilities, see p. 204) that some businesses are "affected with a public interest" and that they become "quasi-public." With an increasingly broad power to regulate private companies upon a finding that they affect the public interest (what activity today does not affect the public interest?), the states can get around the contract clause. This does not mean that the states can do whatever they want. Private rights are now protected by the "due process" clauses of the 5th and 14th Amendments.

Section 10 (Clause 2)

No State shall, without the Consent of the Congress, lay any Imposts or Duties on Imports or Exports, except what may be absolutely necessary for executing its inspection Laws: and the net Produce of all Duties and Imposts, laid by any State on Imports or Exports, shall be for the Use of the

Treasury of the United States; and all such Laws shall be subject to the Revision and Controul of the Congress.

The states have a legitimate interest in determining whether a product entering or leaving its borders is disease-ridden (spoiled food, for instance) or illegal (narcotics). So it may inspect imported goods and charge a fee when "absolutely necessary." (The fact that the Constitution used the word "absolutely" here helped Chief Justice Marshall when interpreting the "necessary and proper clause," which does not use the word "absolutely." Laws need not be "absolutely necessary" in order for Congress to have the authority to pass them to aid its other powers; they need be only an appropriate way of achieving a legitimate goal.)

If money is left over from the inspection fees it goes into the United States Treasury. Congress retains power to change state inspection laws, including the power to lower fees, as part of its power to regulate interstate and foreign commerce.

Section 10 (Clause 3)

No State shall, without the Consent of Congress, lay any Duty of Tonnage, keep Troops, or Ships of War in time of Peace, enter into any Agreement or Compact with another State, or with a foreign Power, or engage in War, unless actually invaded, or in such imminent Danger as will not admit of delay.

Tonnage duties are taxes imposed purely for the privilege of entering ports. "Troops" here does not mean "militia"; it means that the states cannot maintain standing armies.

Interstate Compacts

Originally, the "compact clause" was used primarily for boundary disputes. Negotiations between states over mutual boundary lines had to be ratified by Congress in order to fix the property of each. Today the compact clause is of importance in such undertakings as flood control, pollution, conservation, and control of water supply. The Port of New York was created by the Port Authority, a compact between New York and New Jersey, approved by Congress.

Congress can give its consent in advance. Thus the Crime Compact of 1934 was created after Congress agreed to let the states set up methods of controlling interstate crime. The Council of State Governments, another interstate organization, is a permanent association which explores common state problems, including highway and traffic safety, crime, and business activities.

The Constitution gives Congress immense powers —some are expressly delegated, as for instance, the commerce power and the others of Section 8. Some powers are inherent in any legislative body—the power to conduct investigations. Some result from the implications of express provisions—the power to acquire territories and to create administrative agencies. For all its power, however, there are some extremely important things which Congress cannot do. It cannot enforce its own laws; it cannot prosecute criminals; it cannot resolve disputes between two parties who claim rights under existing laws. These powers are given to other organs of government to which the Constitution now turns. Nor can Congress enact certain kinds of laws—laws restricting various freedoms of the people themselves are prohibited by the Amendments to the Constitution. The powers of Congress can never be considered without remembering the significant restraints which the Constitution imposes throughout.

3   The President

Article 2

Section 1 (Clause 1)
The executive Power shall be vested in a President of the United States of America.

The vast "executive power" is given to one man, the President of the United States. Article 2 of the Constitution outlines the basic duties and functions of the President, but there is little detail. How the Presidents have used their executive power, augmented by increasing delegations of power by Congress to carry out specific legislative plans, accounts for a good deal of American history itself.

If the power of the President is great, the incredible size of the executive department of the United States is perhaps more than any one man can cope with. It has been estimated that without the electronic equipment (computers, etc.) employed by the federal government, it would take every person in the United States—more than 200,000,000 people—just to do the paperwork every year. It is not surprising that President Harry S Truman once remarked, "I sit here all day trying to persuade people to do the things they ought to have sense enough to do without my persuading them. . . . That's all the powers of the President amount to."

That may be the way it looks to the man in the White House, but to the outsider the executive powers are enormous (but not unlimited). Although members of the first Congress proposed that the President be addressed as "His Excellency" and "Elective Majesty," the ideas were rejected, and the executive powers have not come to be a substitution for the British monarch's former powers.

In the spring of 1952, President Truman found this out. The previous December it was evident that talks between United States Steelworkers of America and the major steel producing companies to resolve differences in wage policies were headed for an impasse. From then until April, President Truman tried almost every means at his disposal (but not Taft-Hartley) to head off a strike, including a personal plea to the workers to continue even after the contract had run out and a referral of the case to the Wage Stabilization Board. It was thought at the time that if a strike caused a halt in steel production, the United States efforts in the Korean War would be seriously endangered.

Compromises failed. Two hours before the strike, the

President "seized" the mills, ordered the Secretary of Commerce to operate them as government property, and asked the workers to resume production as government employees. The workers returned, but Youngstown Sheet & Tube Company and other companies sued and quickly won their case in a federal district court. Since the property once again belonged to the companies, the workers went out on strike.

The federal Court of Appeals ruled that the strike must stop, pending an appeal in the Supreme Court. With the workers once again returning, the Supreme Court put aside other business and on June 2 ruled that the President had no power to seize the mills without Congressional authorization. The President returned the property immediately and the strike began again. (It was settled seven weeks later.)

The President had justified his seizure on the grounds that the Constitution vested in him the "executive power" and that inherent in this power was the right to do what he did when the national security required it. Presidents had seized property on a number of occasions during wartime and the Court had approved. Conceding that Congress could have seized the mills, the Supreme Court answered that "the Constitution does not subject this lawmaking power of Congress to Presidential or military supervision or control." [172]

Nevertheless, in some areas the President's power is supreme. In negotiating treaties, in conducting the foreign policy of the United States, in his role as chief tactician of the military, neither the Supreme Court nor Congress can tell him how to act. Moreover, in those areas where the Congress and President share responsibility—war and peace, relationships with foreign governments—Congress can delegate its power to the President without constitutional objection. In these fields the "separate" branches share powers; their powers are not limited, but spring from the very nature and function of government.[149]

Section 1 (Clause 1, continued)

He shall hold his Office during the Term of four Years, and, together with the Vice President, chosen for the same Term, be elected, as follows:

The President's term of office begins at 12:00 noon January 20 of every fourth year. (Until 1937 the President began his term on March 4, but the 20th Amendment changed the date.)

Section 1 (Clause 2)

Each State shall appoint, in such Manner as the Legislature thereof may direct, a Number of Electors, equal to the whole Number of Senators and Representatives to which the State may be entitled in the Congress; but no Senator or Representative, or Person holding an Office of Trust or Profit under the United States, shall be appointed an Elector.

The President is not elected directly by the people, as are Senators and Representatives. Rather, the people vote for "electors" who later choose a President. Each state is entitled to as many electors as the sum of its Representatives and Senators. Today there are 538 electors, so a majority of at least 270 votes is necessary for election. (Total electors: 435 Congressmen, 100 Senators, 3 from the District of Columbia.) Senators and Representatives themselves cannot be electors, nor can anyone employed by the federal government.

In practice, electors are pledged to vote for the person whom the majority of the people in the state vote for; indeed, in most states only the names of the Presidential candidates appear on the ballots. The electors, unknown to the people, must vote for the candidate who receives the majority of votes. In 1960 an Oklahoma elector broke his pledge to vote for Vice President Nixon and voted for Senator Harry F. Byrd instead. This was only the eighth time such a defection has occurred in the some 14,000 votes since 1789.

Section 1 (Clause 3)

[The Electors shall meet in their respective States, and vote by Ballot for two Persons, of whom one at least shall not be an Inhabitant of the same State with themselves. And they shall make a List of all the Persons voted for, and of the Number of Votes for each; which List they shall sign and certify, and transmit sealed to the Seat of the Government of the United States, directed to the President of the Senate. The President of the Senate shall, in the Presence of the Senate and House of Representatives, open all the Certificates, and the Votes shall then be counted. The Person having the greatest Number of Votes shall be the President, if such Number be a Majority of the whole Number of Electors appointed; and if there be more than one who have such Majority, and have an equal Number of Votes, then the House of Representatives shall immediately chuse by Ballot one of them for President; and if no Person have a Majority, then from the five highest on the List the said House shall in like Manner chuse the President. But in chusing the President, the Votes shall be taken by States, the Representation from each State having one Vote; A quorum for this Purpose shall consist of a Member or Members from two thirds of the States, and a Majority of all the States shall be necessary to a Choice. In very Case, after the Choice of the President, the Person having the greatest Number of Votes of the Electors shall be the Vice President. But if there should remain two or more who have equal Votes, the Senate shall chuse from them by Ballot the Vice-President.]

The original method by which the electors were to vote was changed by the 12th Amendment. (See p. 196.)

Section 1 (Clause 4)
The Congress may determine the Time of chusing the Electors, and the Day on which they shall give their Votes; which Day shall be the same throughout the United States.

Electors are chosen on Election Day, which is the first Tuesday after the first Monday in November, two and one-half months before the President is to take office. The Electors themselves meet in their respective state capitals in December and send the results to the President of the Senate (the Vice President of the United States) who counts the votes before a joint session of Congress when it convenes in January.

Section 1 (Clause 5)
No Person except a natural born Citizen, [or a Citizen of the United States, at the time of the Adoption of this Constitution], shall be eligible to the Office of President; neither shall any Person be eligible to that Office who shall not have attained to the Age of thirty-five Years, and been fourteen Years a Resident within the United States.

The President must be at least thirty five years old,

must have lived in the United States for fourteen years prior to his election; and he must have been born within the United States. It has never been decided whether a person born to American parents outside the territory of the United States is a "natural born" citizen. Certainly a person born in a territory, as distinct from a state, is not disqualified. Senator Barry Goldwater, Republican Presidential candidate in 1964, was born in Arizona in 1912, before it became a state.

To be sure that those born before the Constitution was ratified would be eligible for the Presidency, the Constitution qualified anyone who was a citizen in 1789. Eight Presidents fell into this category (Washington, Adams, Jefferson, Madison, Monroe, John Quincy Adams, Jackson, and William Henry Harrison). Since the time Vice President Tyler became President upon Harrison's death in 1841, this provision has become unnecessary.

Section 1 (Clause 6)

In Case of the Removal of the President from office, or of his Death, Resignation, or Inability to discharge the Powers and Duties of the said Office, the Same shall devolve on the Vice President . . .

The Constitution does not make it clear whether the Vice President is to become President or merely Acting President when the Chief Executive dies in office. The first Vice President faced with the dilemma, John Tyler in 1841, took the oath of office and assumed the full powers of the Presidency. He struck a precedent which has been constitutionally accepted ever since.

No President has ever resigned, but a few have been temporarily disabled. President Wilson was very ill for the last year and more of his term in 1919-1920. Exactly what the powers of the Vice President are in such a situation are very unclear. President Eisenhower and succeeding Presidents have made private agreements with their Vice Presidents. (And see the 25th Amendment, p. 239.)

Section 1 (Clause 6, continued)

and the Congress may by Law provide for the Case of [Removal,] Death, Resignation [or Inability, both] of the President [and Vice President,] declaring what Officer shall then act as President, and such Officer shall act accordingly, until [the Disability be removed, or] a President shall be elected.

In 1947, Congress passed the present succession law. Should a President leave office for any reason, and there is no Vice President, the following people will succeed to the office of President: the Speaker of the House of Representatives, and if he leaves office, the President pro tem of the Senate, then the Cabinet officers (the Secretary of State, Secretary of the Treasury, Secretary of Defense, the Attorney General, the Postmaster General, the Secretary of the Interior, the Secretary of Agriculture, the Secretary of Commerce, the Secretary of Labor, the Secretary of Health, Education and Welfare, the Secretary of Housing and Urban Affairs, and finally, the Secretary of Transportation). But before assuming the Presidency, he must first resign his position as member of Congress or Cabinet. The likelihood that there will no Vice President has been greatly diminished by the 25th Amendment.

Section 1 (Clause 7)

The President shall, at stated Times, receive for his Services, a Compensation, which shall neither be encreased nor diminished during the Period for which he shall have been elected, and he shall not receive within that Period any other Emolument from the United States, or any of them.

The President receives a salary of $100,000 per year, an official expense account of $50,000, and a nontaxable expense account of $40,000 for purposes of official travel and entertainment expenses. (Ex-Presidents receive $25,000, free mailing expenses, and $50,000 per year for office help; widows of Presidents receive $10,000 yearly.) The operation of the White House, its staffs, and the Presidency itself cost far more than that, and additional appropriations are provided in various ways. But the President is forbidden from receiving specific personal pay or financial rewards from the United States Treasury or from state treasuries.

Section 1 (Clause 8)

Before he enter on the Execution of his Office, he shall take the following Oath or Affirmation: — "I do solemnly swear (or affirm) that I will faithfully execute the Office of President of the United States, and will to the best of my Ability, preserve, protect and defend the Constitution of the United States."

President John F. Kennedy began his Inaugural in 1960 with these words: "We observe today not a victory of party, but a celebration of freedom—symbolizing an end, as well as a beginning—signifying renewal, as well as change. For I have sworn before you and Almighty God the same solemn oath our forebears prescribed nearly a century and three quarters ago."

The oath is ceremonial though serious; a President can take the oath after assuming office. President-elect Kennedy became President Kennedy at noon on January 20, 1960, even though he did not take the oath until fifty-one minutes later. When President Kennedy was assassinated, Vice President Johnson became Chief Executive immediately, and was sworn in later.

Section 2 (Clause 1)

The President shall be Commander in Chief of the Army and Navy of the United States, and of the Militia of the several States, when called into the actual Service of the United States;

The President is the supreme commander of all United States military forces. His orders supersede those of any general or admiral. Yet the President is a civilian officer; an unbroken tradition in the United States requires the government to control the military. In the habeas corpus case in which the general was told to obey the orders of a judge (see p. 76), the Supreme Court said: "The supremacy of the civil over the military is one of our great heritages." [31]

The Commander-in-Chief is not restricted to the authority to command troops and devise strategies during war. In 1861, on July 4th, President Lincoln proclaimed that he had authority to make war, and he sent ships to blockade Southern ports following an attack on Fort Sumter, even though Congress had not declared war. In the *Prize Cases,* the Supreme Court affirmed the constitutionality of his actions. During the Second World War,

President Roosevelt used his powers as Commander-in-Chief to establish a host of executive agencies to deal with war emergencies, such as the Office of Emergency Management, the War Labor Board, the War Production Board, and the Office of Economic Stabilization. Congress gave him the authority to create dozens of others, such as the Office of Price Administration.

Section 2 (Clause 1, continued)

he may require the Opinion in writing, of the principal Officer in each of the executive Departments, upon any Subject relating to the Duties of their respective Offices,

Some of the delegates to the Constitutional Convention wanted to require the President to consult an official council. But no compromise could be reached on what that council could be, and its opponents were able to kill the proposal. The President may, if he wishes, consult his Cabinet officers, though he does not have to. The size of the government and complexity of its operations in fact insure that the President speak to the Secretaries of State, Defense, and Treasury, the Attorney General, and others many times every week. Formal Cabinet meetings have become a tradition, but the President may go without them if he wishes.

Section 2 (Clause 1, continued)

and he shall have Power to grant Reprieves and Pardons for Offenses against the United States, except in Cases of Impeachment.

The Presidential pardon restores all rights to the person convicted of crimes, such as the right to practice his profession.[39] The President can suspend a convict's federal jail sentence. A Presidential pardon does not give the convicted person the right to be reimbursed for the fine he paid, however, or to be compensated for the time he spent in prison. He must appeal to Congress to pass an "amnesty law," and there is no assurance that he will get it. Congress cannot revoke a Presidential pardon.

Section 2 (Clause 2)

He shall have Power, by and with the Advice and Consent of the Senate, to make Treaties, provided two thirds of the Senators present concur;

The President's treaty-making power is one of his most important. Although the Senate must approve a final treaty by a two-thirds vote in order for it to become binding law, the President has the sole power to negotiate the terms of treaties with foreign countries.

Treaties are entered into for a variety of purposes. To provide a means by which the countries of the world can solve common problems, the United Nations was formed through a complex series of treaties. To bring a halt to the explosion of radioactive bombs in the atmosphere, many nations have signed the Nuclear Test-Ban Treaty proposed by President Kennedy in 1963. Perhaps the most common kind is the treaty of "Friendship, Commerce, and Navigation," which two nations will sign, granting rights to each other's citizens, establishing means of settling disputes between the countries, providing agreements concerning trade and commerce, and allowing embassies and ambassadors. The United States has signed such treaties with scores of countries.

Some treaties are "self-executing." If a treaty grants a right to a foreigner, such as the right to own property in the United States, he can sue in the courts to enforce his right if it is infringed, since the treaty becomes federal law. Other kinds of treaties depend on the independent support of Congress even after ratification by the Senate. If the treaty calls for expenditure of United States funds, for instance, for the construction of defense establishments, the Congress must first appropriate the funds and authorize the expenditure, and its refusal to do so can thwart the entire treaty. Thus, the House of Representatives exercises an indirect check over Presidential treaty-making power, even though the Constitution does not spell it out.

Usually the President negotiates and signs a treaty, and then presents it to the Senate. Politically, the Senate is forced to go along, since the United States would have a hard time justifying to world opinion why it refused to honor a treaty already signed. Sometimes the President will withhold his signature pending Senate approval. But the Senate does not always consent: the treaty bringing the United States into the League of Nations in 1920 was rejected by the Senate.

Treaties are not the only methods of international agreement. Very frequently today, the President enters into "executive agreements"—agreements authorized by Congress under its power to regulate commerce, the mail, and copyright and patents. Executive agreements do not require a two-thirds vote of the Senate and for this reason are coming into wide use. The treaty power often overlaps with the power to make executive agreements.

Section 2 (Clause 2, continued)

and he shall nominate, and by and with the Advice and Consent of the Senate, shall appoint Ambassadors, other public Ministers and Consuls, Judges of the supreme Court, and all other Officers of the United States, whose Appointments are not herein otherwise provided for, and which shall be established by Law: but the Congress may by Law vest the Appointment of such inferior Officers, as they think proper, in the President alone, in the Courts of Law, or in the Heads of Departments.

A government of laws must be run by men. To the President is committed the responsibility of naming all the high officers of the federal government—Cabinet officers, heads of administrative agencies and members of their boards, all federal judges, ambassadors to foreign countries and others in the diplomatic service. Through this power the President can place his stamp on the policies of the nation, by choosing men who share his views. The Senate must approve his nominations by a majority vote.

Once the officer is commissioned, the Senate cannot revoke its vote. The Senate does not have the power to remove officers of the United States, unless an officer is first impeached by the House. But in many cases, the President acting alone may fire an executive official if he chooses, including Cabinet officers and other political agents.

The President cannot, however, remove all federal officers. The so-called independent agencies, such as the Federal Trade Commission, were created by Act of Congress to enforce Congressional policy. The FTC and many other agencies have legislative and judicial functions which are supposed to be independent of day-to-day politics. If the President could remove members of these agencies, he could curtail their independence. In a case arising out of President Roosevelt's attempts to fire a member of the FTC, the Supreme Court denied the power of the President to remove independent officials (even though he appoints them): "It is quite evident that one who holds his office only during the pleasure of another, cannot be depended upon to maintain an attitude of independence against the latter's will." [67]

Congress cannot tell the President whom to pick, but it can fix the qualifications for all federal jobs except those specifically spelled out in the Constitution itself. In fact, Congress has gone to such great lengths in prescribing the standards for persons in many public offices (party affiliation, age, citizenship, residence, professional experience) that the President must sometimes choose from a small number of men.

Perhaps the most sweeping setting of standards by Congress is the Hatch Act of 1940. This law prohibits all persons in the executive branch, including employees of agencies and departments, from taking an "active part in political management or political campaigns." Only the President, Vice President, and certain "policy determining officers," such as Cabinet members, are exempted.

George P. Poole, a "roller" in the United States mint at Philadelphia, had been a ward executive committeeman in that city. He worked actively for his party on election day at the polls. Rejecting his position that the Hatch Act (which would force him out of his job) violated his 1st Amendment rights of speech and association, the Supreme Court in 1947 upheld the law. [145]

The purpose of the Act was to make public employees more efficient by removing them from pressures which would come from engaging in politics. It would be difficult for a civil service employee who disagreed with the party in power to refuse to go along with his boss's request that he campaign for his boss's party. The Act allows employees to say, "Sorry, sir, it's not that I dislike you or your party, but only that federal law forbids me." Said the Court: "It is only partisan political activity that is [forbidden]. . . . Expressions, public or private, on public affairs, personalities, and matters of public interest, not an objective of party action, are unrestricted by law so long as the government employee does not direct his activities toward party success."

Section 2 (Clause 3)

The President shall have Power to fill up all Vacancies that may happen during the recess of the Senate, by granting Commissions which shall expire at the End of their next Session.

If a vacancy in a public office exists, whether or not it arose before the Senate adjourned, the President can name whomever he pleases to the job. But the appointment only lasts until the end of the next session, usually not much more than a year from the time when the President fills the vacancy.

Section 3 (Clause 1)

He shall from time to time give to the Congress Information of the State of the Union,

Section 3 not only gives the President power to act, it prescribes certain duties, acts which he must undertake. Not that Presidents have been loathe to carry out these duties; indeed, this section is the kernel of the Presidential power.

Usually the President gives the State of the Union address every year in January. But the timing is up to the President and there have been years in which more than one such speech was given. The "information" on conditions in the United States is today as much (or more) for the benefit of the citizens as it is for individual Congressmen, with whom the President communicates privately all the time. The fact that he must give a formal address forces the President to give some consideration to how he can explain the condition of the country to the voters and what he plans to do for the year to come.

Section 3 (Clause 2)

and recommend to their Consideration such Measures as he shall judge necessary and expedient;

One of the most important functions of the President is to recommend legislation to Congress. Although bills are independently proposed by Congressmen and Senators, the most important legislation is prepared by the executive department. The federal budget, including appropriations for the military, for domestic programs, and foreign aid, is worked out in advance and submitted to Congress by Senators and Congressmen of the President's party. Similarly, such legislative programs as reorganization of the federal government, creation of new agencies and departments, traffic safety, conservation, labor relations, taxation, and numerous others originate in the appropriate government department and are sent along to Congress for consideration. The laws which eventually emerge from Congress are the result of extensive compromise between President and Congress, between the two parties, and among conflicting interests throughout the nation.

Section 3 (Clause 3)

he may, on extraordinary Occasions, convene both Houses, or either of them, and in Case of Disagreement between them, with Respect to the Time of Adjournment, he may adjourn them to such Time as he shall think proper;

On a number of occasions, Presidents have called the houses of Congress together for consideration of legislation; sometimes, the Senate alone has been convened in order to approve nominations and treaties. But no President has ever adjourned Congress.

Section 3 (Clause 4)

he shall receive Ambassadors and other public Ministers;

These few words, along with those which give the President power to make treaties, to appoint ambassadors, and to act as Commander-in-Chief, give him enormous powers in the field of foreign relations. From the power to receive ambassadors and other public ministers of foreign countries, the President has derived the power to refuse to admit all foreign diplomats of whatever country he chooses. Thus the President has the sole power to "recognize" foreign nations when new ones are formed. He can also refuse to recognize foreign countries, when a government is overthrown. The United States did not recognize the Soviet Union from 1917 until 1933, when President Roosevelt negotiated a complex set of treaties. The United States does not recognize Communist China, and the few dealings which the United States has with that country are done indirectly through the embassies of countries which do recognize China.

When the President exercises his foreign relations powers, his decisions cannot be challenged in the courts. Disputes arising from Presidential policy in this area raise questions which the courts will not look into.

Section 3 (Clause 5)
he shall take Care that the Laws be faithfully executed,

When Congress passes a law or a federal court hands down a decision, the matter is only at a beginning. Laws exist to control and regulate the behavior of people; the mere statement that a law exists is not likely to produce much compliance unless some power backs up the law, either to call an offender to account by bringing him before the courts for trial or to administer the law by making the countless daily decisions which Congress and courts cannot do. The power to "take care that the laws be faithfully executed" is the power to prosecute criminals, to staff the administrative and executive agencies, and to carry on the daily interpreting of Congressional regulatory statutes such as the antitrust laws, the food and drug laws, and the labor laws. Here is the central instance of the executive's domestic power.

Section 3 (Clause 6)
and shall Commission all the Officers of the United States.

The nomination, approval, and commissioning of United States officers is a three-step process. First the President nominates the person for office (Section 2, Clause 2, see pp. 94–5) and then by a majority vote the Senate must approve the nomination. At this point the President may sign the commission—that is, formally install his nominee in office—or he may not. The approval of Congress does not make the person an officer and the President can change his mind.

Section 4

The President, Vice President and all civil Officers of the United States, shall be removed from Office on Impeachment for, and Conviction of, Treason, Bribery, or other High Crimes and Misdemeanors.

Members of Congress, military officers, and private citizens cannot be impeached. But all executive officials can be, including those in independent administrative agencies. It has never been clearly settled whether "other high crimes and misdemeanors" means something broader than violations of criminal law for which the person could also be tried in court. At President Andrew Johnson's impeachment trial in 1867 the radical Republicans urged that an abuse of discretion or an improperly motivated act (meaning a political act with which Congress disagreed), while not criminal, was nevertheless an offense for which a President could be impeached and removed from office. Though the impeachment succeeded, the conviction did not and the narrower view seems to have won out.

4   The Federal Courts

Article 3

Section 1 (Clause 1)

The judicial Power of the United States, shall be vested in one supreme Court, and in such inferior Courts as the Congress may from time to time ordain and establish.

Like legislative and executive power, the judicial power is nowhere defined in the Constitution. It was assumed that the Supreme Court and any other federal courts which Congress might establish would exercise the same general powers which courts in England and in the colonies had long exercised.

The judicial power has come to mean the power of a

court, following regular procedures, to hear the arguments of both sides of a real dispute, and to make a final and binding judgment as to which party to the dispute is entitled to the relief he seeks. Once the judgment is made, neither Congress nor the President can legally upset the decision in the particular case. This principle, that judgments of courts are final, is another element in the separation of powers. (The attentive reader will recall that in one kind of case Congress can reverse the Court in the decision of the particular case: when the Court rules that a state cannot enforce a regulation of commerce because it conflicts with the need for uniformity, Congress can pass a law permitting the state to continue as before.[107] This rarely happens.) Of course, Congress can often change the rules handed down by courts. Whenever the Court interprets a federal statute and Congress disapproves, the law can be changed. The Court's decisions can also be changed by later cases in the Court itself and also by constitutional amendment. But these changes affect only *future* cases, not the parties to the case the Court has already decided. (However, see the discussion of retroactivity in connection with the 6th Amendment, see p. 189.)

A number of particular powers make up the general judicial power. Courts can determine their own guidelines for interpreting statutes and the Constitution (called "rules of construction"). They can make their own rules of procedure when authorized by Congress. They can hold a person in "contempt of court" when he interferes with the orderly processes of the court (he can be put in jail until he promises to obey). Courts can fashion remedies called for by the case before them, unless Congress specifically prohibits them from using a particular remedy. Thus in accident suits the courts can order one person to pay another money (called "money damages" or simply "damages"). The courts can issue writs of habeas corpus and orders (called "injunctions") prohibiting a person from doing something or compelling him to act. (These are by no means all the remedies.) Courts can issue a "subpoena," an order to a person to appear in court as a witness. Courts can appoint special assistants temporarily to aid in a given case and can admit or "disbar" attorneys from practicing before them.

The Constitution deals only with the judicial power of the United States; the states are free to experiment with their judicial power as they see fit (within the limits imposed by the Bill of Rights and the 14th Amendment; see, for instance, p. 171), and Congress cannot regulate the procedures and powers of state courts.

Although the Supreme Court is the only court required by the Constitution, Congress has created a number of "inferior" or "lower" federal courts, under the power granted to it by this section and by Section 8, Clause 9, of Article 1. Generally, the federal court system is divided into three parts.

First is the system of "federal district courts," which handle all federal trials and a great bulk of other judicial work. The United States is now divided into ninety-two districts in each of which sits a district court with from one to twenty-four judges. Each state has at least one district court.

The next higher set of federal courts is the "court of appeals." The nation is divided into eleven "circuits," in which a court of appeals sits. These courts do not have trials; they take appeals from the judgment of the district courts. Each circuit has from three to twelve judges. Almost always, three judges sit on each case, never less. On some occasions all the judges sit "en banc."

At the top of the federal courts stands the Supreme Court. In certain kinds of cases, appeals from the various circuits can be taken to the Supreme Court. But it can also hear cases on appeal from the state supreme courts. Since almost every case which comes to it will have been heard in at least one appellate court, the Supreme Court does not serve as merely another court to take an appeal to—from the more than 2,700 cases which are appealed to it, the Court generally chooses those whose settlement would most contribute to a development of the law and a resolution of great public controversies.

There are also a number of other federal courts which do not fit into the three-tier system. These are the specialized courts which hear specific kinds of cases; they include the Tax Court, the Court of Claims, and the Court of Customs and Patent Appeals. Appeals from their decisions may be taken to the circuit courts and then to the Supreme Court.

Some governmental bodies—such as the National Labor Relations Board, the Federal Trade Commission, and the Securities and Exchange Commission—have been given power by Congress to decide certain kinds of cases at the trial level. Yet they are not courts within the meaning of Article 3. Although the courts of appeals and the Supreme Court have the power to review cases which the agencies have decided, in practice very few of the total number of administrative cases are decided by the federal courts.

Section 1 (Clause 2)

The Judges, both of the supreme and inferior Courts, shall hold their Offices during good Behaviour, and shall, at stated Times, receive for their Services, a Compensation, which shall not be diminished during their Continuance in Office.

Congress has the power to determine how many Supreme Court and other federal judges there should be. For a century, the Supreme Court has consisted of nine Justices, but this was not always true. At the beginning, the Chief Justice of the United States and five Associate Justices served on the Court. Congress added Justices over the years until the number reached ten in 1863. Three years later Congress provided that as vacancies occurred, the number should be reduced to seven. But the number never dropped below eight and in 1869 Congress set the number at nine where it has since remained.

Federal judges hold their office for life and cannot be removed from office except by impeachment for lack of "good behavior." What constitutes lack of good behavior is not clear, but it has usually meant conduct of a criminal or morally reprehensible nature, like taking bribes.

The salary of the federal judge cannot be reduced while he is in office (though it can be increased). At one time it was said that the passage of federal income tax laws could not apply to judges since the income tax is a reduction in the salary. In 1939 the Supreme Court reversed its earlier opinion and allowed itself to be taxed. Permitting judges to be taxed on the same basis as everyone else "is merely to recognize that judges are also citizens, and that their particular function in government does not generate an immunity from sharing with their fellow citizens the material burden of the government whose Constitution and laws they are charged with administering." [104]

Section 2 (Clause 1)

The judicial Power shall extend to all Cases, in Law and Equity arising under this Constitution, the Laws of the United States, and Treaties made, or which shall be made, under their Authority;

Jurisdiction

Just because the courts have judicial power does not mean that they can exercise it whenever they want. The court must first have "jurisdiction" over the case before it can be brought for trial and appeal. The Constitution says that federal courts have jurisdiction over certain classes of cases only. If one of these cases comes up, then the courts can exercise their full judicial power over it. But if the court does not have jurisdiction, it must dismiss the case at the outset. Jurisdiction deals with what cases the courts can hear; judicial power with what they can do with those cases over which they have jurisdiction.

Definition of "Case" and "Controversy"

Furthermore, the courts can exercise their judicial power only when a "case" or "controversy" has arisen. The courts cannot give out advice. When in 1793 President Washington asked the Supreme Court for its opinion concerning the meaning of certain treaties, Chief Justice John Jay replied for the Court that it was powerless to do so.

What constitutes a "case" or "controversy" is not always easy to ascertain. Various doctrines have been developed to clarify when a case is a case and when not.

For instance, the Court will not decide an abstract question just for the sake of decision. In 1906 Congress passed a law allowing David Muskrat and other Cherokee Indians to bring suit in the federal courts to determine whether prior acts of Congress regulating the Cherokee's title to their lands were constitutional. In *Muskrat v. United States,* the Court dismissed the suit on the grounds that it had no jurisdiction to consider the claim. There was no concrete dispute between the United States and Muskrat; he was merely suing because Congress said he could. The Act was unconstitutional, since Congress authorized a suit not allowed by the Constitution, namely, one in which there was no case or controversy.

Not only must there be a *real* dispute, but the person who is suing must have a *substantial interest* in the controversy. You cannot sue on behalf of your neighbor who was hurt in an accident. You do not have "standing."

Even if you do have an interest it cannot be a minor one. Mrs. Frothingham found that out when she sued the government to stop the payment of federal funds to programs designed to protect the health of newborn children. She claimed that the MaternityAct of 1921 was unconstitutional because Congress had no power to spend federal tax money in such a manner. Her injury, she claimed, was in having to pay more taxes than would otherwise be necessary. Said the Court: "[Her] interest in the moneys of the Treasury—partly realized from taxation and partly from other sources—is shared with millions of others; is comparatively minute and indeterminable; and the effect upon future taxation of any payment out of the funds so remote, fluctuating, and uncertain that no basis is afforded for an appeal to the preventive powers of a court." [46] Thus the "taxpayer suit" cannot be brought in federal courts.

The *Frothingham* case has made it difficult to contest federal laws which establish aid to education programs. Opponents of aid to religious schools object that such programs violate the 1st Amendment's ban on making "laws respecting an establishment of religion." In 1968 the Supreme Court decided to rethink the *Frothingham* doctrine, at least insofar as it affects 1st Amendment suits. The 1968 case was brought by seven taxpayers who object to federal funds being spent on parochial schools and argued on their behalf by Senator Sam J. Ervin of North Carolina. At press time, the Court had not rendered its decision.

A "case" or "controversy" does not have to be one in which the injury or damage has already happened. The Court has upheld the Declaratory Judgment Act of 1934, allowing federal courts to declare the rights of parties where an actual dispute exists and an injury has not yet happened but is likely to, if the parties act as they say they will. For instance, before a person breaks a contract, he will want to find out if he has the legal right to. If the Court says he does not, he may reconsider his decision.

Cases "Arising Under" the Constitution and Federal Laws

1. Law and Equity. Among the cases which the Court has jurisdiction to hear are those "in law and equity" arising under the Constitution, federal law, and treaties. In this context, the word "law" refers to a special kind of law—that which was decided by "common law courts" in England. Centuries ago, English courts developed a very rigid set of procedures and remedies. For instance, the most common remedy was the "money judgment," and it could be obtained only by pleading the case according to intricate rules. And what good was a money judgment when your neighbor was about to do irreparable injury to you, for which money would be no compensation?

More and more dissatisfied people appealed to the King and his ministers for a justice that the courts could not give. One of the King's closest ministers, the Chancellor, was put in charge of these appeals and during the 16th and 17th centuries, the courts of "chancery" developed much looser and more flexible remedies than those available in the older, "common law" courts. Because the remedies were fairer or more "equitable," this new type of court came in time to be called a court of "equity" and its remedies were known as "equitable remedies." The usual common law remedy was the "money judgment." Equity devised such remedies as the injunction.

At the time the Constitution was written, the two separate court systems existed side by side in America, and they each applied their different law to the cases over which they had jurisdiction. The Constitution recognized the distinction, but gave federal courts the power to hear both kinds of cases—those which common law courts could hear and those which equity courts could hear. (By the middle of the 19th century, it became evident that much unnecessary confusion and even injustice resulted from the division between the two kinds of law. So a reform movement on both the state and federal level began to merge "common law" and "equity" into a single court. Except for a very few states today, the states and the federal system each have one set of courts which can apply both the common law and equity and which can give common law and equitable remedies.)

2. *The Meaning of "Arising under the Constitution."* The federal courts cannot take just any case which involves common law or equity disputes. It can take only those disputes which "arise under" the Constitution, federal law, and treaties. Cases so arise whenever a court must interpret the meaning of the Constitution, federal statutes, or treaties in order to decide the case. As Chief Justice Marshall said in 1821: "A case in law or equity consists of the right of one party, as well as of the other, and may truly be said to arise under the Constitution or laws of the United States, whenever its *correct decision* depends on the construction of either." [20] By giving federal courts the power to interpret the Constitution, federal law, and treaties, this clause gives the federal courts, and the Supreme Court in particular, the most important aspect of "judicial review": the power to declare unconstitutional those laws which conflict with the Constitution, whether they be federal or state.

Although the Constitution does not specifically say that the courts should have this power, Article 6 (see p. 124) makes the Constitution, the laws of the United States and treaties, the "supreme law of the land." This being so, the power of the Supreme Court to decide questions of constitutionality is inescapable. Most people at the Constitutional Convention probably assumed the power. State courts had upset laws of their legislatures when the laws conflicted with the state constitutions. The power of judicial review—the power to interpret constitutions, statutes, and other laws—was long held to be a part of the "judicial power."

Some people disagreed. Why shouldn't Congress be able to interpret the Constitution equally as well as the Court? The supremacy of the Court over Congress in matters of constitutional meaning was settled in 1803 in *Marbury v. Madison,* probably the most famous of all Supreme Court cases.

Marbury had been named by President John Adams to a justice of the peace court in Washington, D.C., just before President Adams' term of office expired. Marbury's commission had been signed but not delivered when Thomas Jefferson took the oath of office. President Jefferson told his Secretary of State, James Madison, not to deliver any commissions which remained in the White House. Jefferson, the Democrat, was anxious not to have in United States courts any more judges appointed by Adams, the Federalist, than were legally necessary.

So Marbury went to the Supreme Court and sued for a "writ of mandamus" against Secretary Madison. The writ of mandamus is a court order directing a government official to carry out a task which he is under a legal obligation to do.

The Court was faced with a dilemma. Jefferson intensely disliked the Federalist philosophy; Chief Justice Marshall was highly suspicious of the Democratic philosophy. Marshall was, in fact, the same man who had earlier signed Marbury's commission, while Secretary of State in Adams' Administration. If Jefferson defied the Court, its power as the third element in the system of checks and balances might be seriously weakened, even destroyed.

Marshall was equal to the task. He noted that Marbury had brought his suit to the Supreme Court, instead of to a lower federal court, because of the Judiciary Act of 1789. This Congressional law gave to the Supreme Court the power to issue a writ of mandamus. This law, Marshall said, was unconstitutional, since the Constitution gave the Court jurisdiction to hear such a case *only on appeal.* That is, Marbury was asking the Court to act as a trial court, and the Constitution allowed it to act as an appellate court only (except in two rare types of cases). Since the Congressional law went further than the Constitution allowed, and since the Constitution is the supreme law of the land, the mandamus section of the Judiciary Act of 1789 was void. When the Court must choose between Constitution or federal law, it is bound to pick the Constitution.

Before striking down the law, Chief Justice Marshall declared that Marbury was legally entitled to the office of justice of the peace, since the commission had already been signed by President Adams. Marshall thus began a tradition of constitutional interpretation which is still more or less followed today: usually the Court will not interpret the Constitution unless there is no other way to settle the given case. If Marbury had not been entitled to the judgeship, for instance, the Court would not have had to inquire into the meaning of the Constitution.

In most instances when it is forced to interpret the Constitution because of a law which is said to conflict, the Court will presume that the statute is constitutional and find a way (if it can) of construing the statute so that it does not conflict with the Constitution. The Court has a number of other self-imposed rules which limit its power to interpret the Constitution.

By far, the bulk of the Court's work consists of cases dealing with federal law and not with the Constitution. Of the thousands of laws passed by the states and Congress since 1789, no more than 90 federal laws and 800 state laws have been declared unconstitutional. It is significant that far more state than federal laws have been invalidated. The power of judicial review is most importantly a power to create uniformity of federal law. State laws, by their very nature, tend to conflict with the uniformity of a national Constitution. Said Mr. Justice Holmes, "I do not think the United States would come to an end if we lost our power to declare an act of Congress void. I do think the Union would be imperiled if we could not make that declaration as to the laws of the several states."

Section 2 (Clause 1, continued)
—to all Cases affecting Ambassadors, other public Ministers and Consuls;

When representatives of foreign governments get into legal trouble in America, their cases can be heard by the Supreme Court. By itself, this clause does not prevent state courts from deciding divorce and similar cases involving foreign ambassadors and diplomats. But Congress has made the jursidiction of such cases exclusive in the Supreme Court because relations with foreign governments and their representatives are delicate. Rather than having possibly fifty different rules, the Court can decide cases with uniformity. (However, cases brought *by* ambassadors and ministers and cases involving consuls can be brought in state courts as well.)

Section 2 (Clause 1, continued)
—to all Cases of admiralty and maritime Jurisdiction;

A third system of courts sprang up in England some 800 years ago. These were the courts of the admirals, and they dealt with cases involving the high seas. The special admiralty courts were necessary because the merchants who engaged in commercial transactions among many countries had to depend upon courts which understood their particular problems. All sea-traveling countries had admiralty courts. Thus, in addition to cases of common law and equity, federal courts are empowered to hear cases of "admiralty and maritime jurisdiction."

Today this is a broad jurisdiction. It includes the following kinds of cases, among others: accidents and injuries which happen at sea or on navigable inland waters and lakes, whether on ship or on a crashing airplane; injuries which ships or other water vessels cause to people or buildings on land; maritime contracts, such as those that concern employment of seamen, the supplying of ships with goods, and insurance policies on vessels; and injuries to stevedores and others who unload and do work on ships while docked.

Because Congress under the "necessary and proper clause" can pass laws which help the courts carry out their powers and because maritime matters are almost always matters of interstate commerce, Congress has steadily enlarged the scope of the admiralty and maritime jurisdiction.

Section 2 (Clause 1, continued)
—to Controversies to which the United States shall be a Party;

The United States government has an obvious interest in being able to bring lawsuits in its own courts. Congress has made this jurisdiction exclusive, so whenever the United States is a party to a lawsuit, state courts cannot hear the case.

This clause does not give private individuals the right to sue the federal government, however. In England, it was long held that the King, who made the laws, was above the law and could not be sued. The doctrine of "sovereign immunity" is a holdover from that belief—the government cannot be sued without its consent. There are a number of statutes passed by Congress which allow individuals to sue the government in many, though not all, kinds of cases.

Section 2 (Clause 1, continued)
—to Controversies between two or more States;

When states get into disputes over boundary lines, or the pollution or diversion of each others' water systems, an independent referee is necessary. The Constitution and Congress have made the Supreme Court the exclusive umpire.

Section 2 (Clause 1, continued)
[—between a State and Citizens of another State—]

This clause was repealed by the 11th Amendment (see p. 195).

Section 2 (Clause 1, continued)
between Citizens of different States;

The Diversity Jurisdiction

When residents of different states get into a legal hassle

(because, for instance, they disagree over the interpretation of a contract they signed, or one of them injured another in an auto accident), they may turn to the federal courts to resolve the dispute, even though the plaintiff could also sue in a state court. Because the states were independent sovereignties after the Revolution, it was feared that a citizen of one state might not be fairly treated in another state. So the "diversity jurisdiction" was created to give people of diverse state citizenships an independent forum. (The District of Columbia is not a state for purposes of this clause; and a United States citizen who lives abroad cannot sue in federal courts under this clause because he is not a citizen of a state.)

If citizens of different states have a dispute involving federal law, they do not need to point to this clause in order to get their case into federal court, since under this same clause, as we have seen, federal courts have jurisdiction over cases involving federal law. Except in rare cases, therefore, the "diversity jurisdiction" deals with cases involving *state* law.

But what is state law?

One of the most important powers of courts is the power to make up the law themselves, when no act of the legislature covers the situation. For hundreds of years in England, the courts developed a body of law known as the "common law." It dealt with physical injuries caused by assault, with unintentional accidents resulting in damage to person or property, with rules relating to contracts, and with dozens of other everyday occurrences.

Because the courts took one case at a time, they could decide each case on narrow grounds. Thus if the next case in the general area was somewhat different, the courts were free to decide it as justice required. Gradually, the precedents and principles which emerged became guiding policies of the common law. The unwritten rules (actually written down in the judges' opinions) were equal in importance to acts of Parliament.

Of course, Parliament could change the common law whenever it wanted. But unless Parliament acted, the courts had a free hand.

So in each state, the courts exercise this same power to

declare the common law. State legislatures can modify or abolish the rules, but the courts have the power in turn to interpret the legislation. State law, then, is twofold: it is the combination of the legislature's statutes and the common law of the courts.

When the federal courts have jurisdiction to hear cases, because the parties come from different states, their disputes concern the meaning of state law. The Judiciary Act of 1789 told the federal courts that when a state *statute* is involved, they must apply the state law.

But the Judiciary Act was silent on what to do when the common law only was involved. Must the federal courts turn to the state common law or could they make up their own, a *federal* common law?

For nearly a century, from 1842 until 1938, the Supreme Court said that federal courts could *ignore* state court decisions, and make up their own law. In 1938 in *Erie Railroad v. Tompkins* the Supreme Court reversed a century of precedents and said that from then on the federal courts must apply state court decisions.

In the *Erie* case, Tompkins was injured by a railroad car while he was walking along the track. He was a Pennsylvania citizen and the railroad had its business offices in New York, so he sued in federal district court in New York. The legislature had left the law of negligence (carelessness resulting in injury) in the hands of the courts, as have most states. The state common law said that the railroad was not responsible for the accident given the particular circumstances; the federal rule said that it was. The district court decided in favor of Tompkins, applying the federal rule. The Court of Appeals for the Second Circuit (which covers New York, Connecticut and Vermont) affirmed.

The Supreme Court reversed, saying that there was no such thing as federal common law. Federal courts can interpret federal statutes, treaties, and the Constitution, but unlike the state legislatures, they cannot make up their own rules. The common law deals mostly with injury and contract cases, which always come up in the state courts (unless, as here, the parties are residents of different states and want to go to federal court). When the parties are in federal court only because of the diversity jurisdiction, it makes no sense to have one rule in the state court and an opposite one in the federal court across the street, since the plaintiff could "shop around" and pick the forum whose rules gave him the best deal. So in 1938, the federal common law came crashing down.

Almost. There are still a very few types of situations in which Congress has passed no statutes and in which state legislatures have no power to act. Take the case of a contract between the United States and a private citizen, for instance. The state legislatures cannot pass laws regulating the federal government's contracts, and state courts cannot hear cases to which the United States is a party. Congress, furthermore, has not enacted a code of contract law. So the federal courts are free to fashion rules when such cases come to them. Similarly, when two states dicker over boundary lines or water rights, subjects on which Congress has not acted, the federal courts can develop a federal common law.

Section 2 (Clause 1, continued)
—between Citizens of the same State claiming Lands under Grants of different States.

In the early years of the country, states granted land to citizens while the boundary of the state was in dispute. Two different states could claim the same land and sell it to different persons. This situation does not happen any longer and the clause has fallen into disuse.

Section 2 (Clause 1, continued)
and between a State, or the Citizens thereof, and foreign States, Citizens or Subjects.

The 11th Amendment repealed part of this clause by forbidding federal courts from hearing suits against the states by anyone except other states or the United States Government. Similarly, under the doctrine of "sovereign immunity," foreign countries without their consent cannot be sued in federal courts. The practical importance of the clause is in allowing foreign countries or citizens to sue residents of the states in federal courts and permitting United States citizens to sue foreigners who happen to be in the United States in federal court.

Section 2 (Clause 2)

In all Cases affecting Ambassadors, other public Ministers and Consuls, and those in which a State shall be Party, the Supreme Court shall have original Jurisdiction.

In two of the classes of cases dealt with in the previous section, the Supreme Court alone has the power to hear them. Lower federal courts cannot. This is called "original jurisdiction" because the case must originate in the Supreme Court. The Court does not conduct regular trials, however. It refers the factual issues to special "masters" chosen for the purpose of uncovering the facts.

Section 2 (Clause 2, continued)

In all the other Cases before mentioned, the Supreme Court shall have appellate Jurisdiction, both as to Law and Fact, with such Exceptions, and under such Regulations as the Congress shall make.

Coupled with its power to create and regulate lower federal courts, Congress can also control the jurisdiction of the Supreme Court. This section is another in the federal system of checks and balances. All cases, except those involving ambassadors and those in which a state is a party, must be begun in the federal district courts. The Supreme Court can only review the decisions. (Thus Marbury's writ of mandamus case was dismissed in *Marbury v. Madison.*)

The review power extends both to "law" and "fact." The "facts" are those aspects of the case on which a jury would be called to decide were there a jury sitting; for instance, did the defendant act reasonably? how much damage was suffered? Under this clause, the Supreme Court can review both legal and factual aspects of a case, insofar as Congress authorizes. The 6th and 7th Amendments limit the Court's power to review the facts, however. Usually the jury's decision as to the facts is final and beyond the power of review.

The Supreme Court does not automatically get the jurisdiction. Congress must first grant it, and it does not have to grant the full jurisdiction allowed by the Constitution. In the early years, in fact, the lower federal courts were established mainly to hear maritime and admiralty claims (as well as suits involving citizens of different states where the amount in controversy was more than $500, and some kinds of suits involving federal laws, mostly trade and navigation). All other cases involving federal law had to be tried in *state* courts.

Today the jurisdiction of federal courts is much expanded, but it is still not as great as Congress could make it. For instance, suits involving federal law cannot be heard in federal courts today unless the amount in controversy is more than $10,000. When the state courts hear federal cases, they must use federal law, just as when federal courts hear cases involving state law, they must use state law.

Although Congress cannot expand the jurisdiction beyond the limits laid out in the Constitution, it can withdraw jurisdiction whenever it wants, even for the limited purpose of stopping the Supreme Court from deciding a case already argued. In 1869, for instance, military authorities in Mississippi placed a newspaper editor under custody. He sued for a writ of habeas corpus and when he remained in custody, he appealed to the Supreme Court. Congress was afraid that in considering the appeal, which rested in part on the Reconstruction laws passed after the Civil War, the Court might find some of them unconstitutional. So a statute was enacted withdrawing the Supreme Court's appellate jurisdiction in cases involving habeas corpus. Even though lawyers had already argued the case before the Court, the case was dismissed for lack of jurisdiction.[41] (Jurisdiction in habeas corpus has been restored.)

The power of Congress over the courts is thus very broad; an unwise use of Congressional power to curtail jurisdiction of the courts could seriously hamper law and order. If cases cannot be settled by courts, they may be settled by violence. So for the most part, Congress has resisted proposals to limit the courts' power to hear cases. When the Supreme Court ruled in 1964 that equal numbers of people must be allowed to vote for each state assemblyman and senator (see p. 187), some members of Congress wanted to withdraw jurisdiction from the federal courts in this kind of case. But the proposal was killed: even some who disliked the Court's decisions concerning state reapportionment were against curtailing its power to hear the cases.

Section 2 (Clause 3)

The Trial of all Crimes, except in Cases of Impeachment, shall be by Jury; and such Trial shall be held in the State where the said Crimes shall have been committed; but when not committed within any State, the Trial shall be at such Place or Places as the Congress may by Law have directed.

This clause has been refined by the 6th Amendment (see p. 180).

Section 3 (Clause 1)

Treason against the United States, shall consist only in levying War against them, or in adhering to their Enemies, giving them Aid and Comfort. No Person shall be convicted of Treason unless on the Testimony of two Witnesses to the same overt Act, or on Confession in open Court.

Treason is the only crime defined in the Constitution. Congress has no power to change the definition.

The language in this clause dates back to the English Statute of Treasons of 1350. People were being convicted of treason for acts which only by a stretch of wild imagination, were related to what we today think of as treason. Under the Constitution, two witnesses must both actually have seen the treasonous acts; circumstantial evidence will not do. When a citizen joins the army of an enemy nation, his treason is clear enough. But it is almost impossible to define what is meant by giving aid and comfort to the enemy; and cases of such treason have been rare. Nevertheless, the fact that an act does not constitute treason or cannot be proved as such, does not mean that Congress cannot make the act illegal. Thus Congress outlaws espionage and sabotage, and the two-witness rule does not apply.

Section 3 (Clause 2)

The Congress shall have Power to declare the Punishment of Treason, but no Attainder of Treason shall work Corruption of Blood, or Forfeiture except during the Life of the Person attainted.

Treason in early England was punished severely and often unfairly. The relatives of the traitor—who was often convicted on flimsy evidence—lost their property ("forfeiture"), simply for the crime of being related. Children were barred from inheriting the traitor's property after he was executed; the traitor's estate would go to the King, instead. This was known as "corruption of blood." The taking from those not convicted of treason was outlawed in the United States.

5   Federal-State Relations

Articles 4-7

ARTICLE 4: Section 1

Full Faith and Credit shall be given in each State to the public Acts, Records, and judicial Proceedings of every other State. And the Congress may by general Laws prescribe the Manner in which such Acts, Records and Proceedings shall be proved, and the Effect thereof.

Without the "full faith and credit" clause, people would continually be uncertain of their rights. If a person wins a judgment against someone who broke a contract or caused an automobile accident, the decision of the court would not be much good if the loser could simply leave the state in order to avoid paying. If a marriage in one was invalid in another, people might never travel or move. To insure the stability of the legal system, each state is required to give binding effect to the laws of the sister states.

The most important aspect of full faith and credit is the enforcement of court judgments. A final judgment is not open to question in other state courts, except in rare circumstances. If the loser leaves the state, all that the winning party has to do is contact a lawyer in the state where the losing party has gone. The lawyer will take a copy of the court's judgment (prepared according to the rules laid down by Congress under its power to regulate in this area) and present it to the court of his state. That court will then issue a judgment declaring the original judgment valid and ordering the losing party to pay. If he still refuses, his property can be "attached" (taken) by the court and sold at a public auction; the proceeds of the sale will then go to the winning party in the other state.

If applied strictly and literally, full faith and credit could be harsh. Oftentimes this is true in divorce cases, where the wife leaves her home to go to another state (often Nevada because of its liberal divorce laws). Suppose the wife gets her divorce and an award of alimony, but the husband had no chance to contest the case. Should the alimony decree be recognized in the ex-husband's state? If it is, the former husband will have been deprived of his right to a hearing in court. So the full faith and credit clause has its exceptions.

Acts of the legislature are not always enforced by sister states, either. The criminal laws of one state are never enforced by another. But a judgment in one state that a person owes taxes can be enforced in another state.

The situations which arise under the full faith and credit clause can be exceedingly complicated, and Congress has done little to untangle the confusions.

Section 2 (Clause 1)

The Citizens of each State shall be entitled to all Privileges and Immunities of Citizens in the several States.

No state may discriminate against citizens of other states in order to benefit its own citizens. States cannot prevent nonresidents from freely traveling through them, from owning property in the state, or from settling down. A law which made nonresidents pay higher taxes than residents on property within the state would be invalid. Nor can a state refuse to permit nonresidents from suing in its courts on substantially the same terms as those which its citizens enjoy.

Section 2 (Clause 2)

A Person charged in any State with Treason, Felony, or other Crime, who shall flee from Justice, and be found in another

State, shall on Demand of the executive Authority of the State from which he fled, be delivered up, to be removed to the State having Jurisdiction of the Crime.

If a person is in another state when he is charged with crime, the governor can request the governor of the state in which he is found to return him for trial. This is called "extradition." Having been returned, the defendant can be tried for the crime with which he was first charged or any other crime which it was later discovered he committed. A person who is kidnapped and illegally returned to the state where he committed a crime cannot protest his trial. But a state does not always have to return a fugitive from justice; if the state to which he has fled wants to try him for a crime first, it can.

Section 2 (Clause 3)

[No Person held to Service or Labour in one State, under the Laws thereof, escaping into another, shall, in Consequence of any Law or Regulation therein, be discharged from such Service or Labour, but shall be delivered up on Claim of the Party to whom such Service or Labour may be due.]

Even in the Middle Ages, serfs who escaped from farms and lived in the cities for a year and a day became free men. But this clause was made obsolete by the 13th Amendment.

Section 3 (Clause 1)

New States may be admitted by the Congress into this Union; but no new State shall be formed or erected within the Jurisdiction of any other State; nor any State be formed by the Junction of two or more States, or Parts of States, without the Consent of the Legislatures of the States concerned as well as of the Congress.

Once admitted, each new state is equal to all the other states in powers and rights of the people. Congress has sole power to admit new states into the union. Whether or not to admit a state is a political question beyond the reach of the courts. When West Virginia split apart from Virginia during the Civil War and was admitted by Congress as a separate state in 1863, the original Virginia did not give its consent, as required by the Constitution. But the status of West Virginia as an equal state has never been challenged.

Section 3 (Clause 2)

The Congress shall have Power to dispose of and make all needful Rules and Regulations respecting the Territory or other Property belonging to the United States; and nothing in this Constitution shall be so construed as to Prejudice any Claims of the United States, or of any particular State.

How to dispose of public property is a question for Congress alone; it can lease as well as sell or give away. The states are forbidden from taxing the public lands of the United States. Congress also has the power to act as a state legislature over the territorial lands of the United States, such as Guam and American Samoa.

The power to govern the territories is somewhat different from the power the federal government exercises in the states. Grand juries and 12-man juries are not constitutionally required in territories, for instance, though they are constitutionally required in all federal criminal cases in the states (see p. 174). Furthermore, Congress can pass laws with respect to territories which would violate Article I, Section 8, Clause 1 (see p. 49) requiring uniformity of duties throughout the United States. Territories are not considered part of the United States for this purpose.

Section 4

The United States shall guarantee to every State in this Union a Republican Form of Government, and shall protect each of them against Invasion; and on Application of the Legislature, or of the Executive (when the Legislature cannot be convened) against domestic Violence.

What a "republican form of government" means has never been made clear. It does not mean that states cannot experiment with their governmental institutions, such as having a one-house legislation (Nebraska) or utilizing the procedures of petition, referendum, and recall. A governor who tried to abolish the legislature and the courts and act as a dictator might find no cause to complain if the United States Government moved in to protect the state, however. The phrase was intended to mean, as

Madison wrote in *The Federalist Papers* (No. 43), that "aristocratic or monarchical innovations" in the states are unwelcome. The guarantee is needed, said Madison, because "who can say what experiments may be produced by the caprice of particular states; by the ambition of enterprising leaders, or by the intrigues and influence of foreign powers?"

The Supreme Court has had few occasions to consider the phrase. In the famous case of *Luther v. Borden,* the Supreme Court declared that it could not judge between two factions in a state, each claiming to be the only legitimate government. The case arose out of Dorr's rebellion in Rhode Island in 1841. Dorr and his followers wrote a new state constitution, liberalizing the right to vote, and proclaimed it in effect. The state government appealed to the President for help, but federal troops were not sent. When the state militia invaded Luther's house (he was a supporter of the rebellion), he sued. The court dismissed the case, refusing to decide which side was the lawful government. The decision to protect the states against invasion is up to the President and Congress. (Dorr and his followers lost, and the original government regained control; but the constitution of Rhode Island was soon changed anyway.)

The Supreme Court has consistently refused to decide disputes in which was questioned the power of the states to organize governmental functions in certain ways and to establish certain political procedures. Exceptions to the Court's general reluctance to consider political questions are its recent holdings in cases involving the apportionment of state legislatures (see p. 218).

Congress has authorized the President to call out the National Guard when riots or rebellion occur in the states. Presidents have had occasion to use this power when local riots became too violent for the city and state police to put down.

ARTICLE 5

The Congress, whenever two thirds of both Houses shall deem it necessary, shall propose Amendments to this Constitution, or, on the Application of the Legislatures of two thirds of the several States, shall call a Convention for proposing Amendments, which, in either Case, shall be valid to all Intents and Purposes, as part of this Constitution, when ratified by the Legislatures of three fourths of the several States, or by Conventions in three fourths thereof, as the one or the other Mode of Ratification may be proposed by Congress; Provided [that no Amendment which may be made prior to the Year One thousand eight hundred and eight shall in any Manner affect the first and fourth Clauses in the Ninth Section of the first Article; and] that no State, without its Consent, shall be deprived of its equal suffrage in the Senate.

Although the Constitution was written to endure, it needed an escape valve in order to prevent it from blowing up should any of its parts fall into widespread disfavor. A Constitution which is easy to amend, on the other hand, is not much of a Constitution, as the experience of many foreign countries shows, because the whim of the majority can change fundamental rights at any time. So the amendment procedure was made difficult, but not impossible. Only twenty-five amendments have been passed since 1787; and when it is considered that ten of these, the Bill of Rights, were passed by the first Congress and ratified by the states within two years, the rate of change has been small.

All amendments to date have been proposed to the states by a two-thirds vote of each house of Congress. (The President is not required to sign them.) The amendments have then been sent to each of the states; when a majority vote in the legislatures of three-quarters of the states (thirty-eight) has ratified the amendment, it goes into effect as a full part of the Constitution, in no way inferior to any other clause, and superior to those which it changes.

Only one amendment was ratified by the alternative procedure spelled out in this Article. The 21st Amendment, which repealed the 18th Amendment (prohibiting liquor in the United States), was ratified by special conventions in each of the states rather than the state legislatures. It was thought that conventions elected by the people of each state, meeting for the sole purpose of debating the amendment, would be more likely to ratify it. The legislatures were dominated by representatives from rural areas, and it was feared that they might still support the 18th Amendment.

Amendments can also be brought about by the action of the states, rather than Congress. If two-thirds of the states petition Congress, it must call a national convention to consider amendments. This has never happened, although at press time a serious effort to call a Convention was being made. Thirty-two of the necessary 34 state legislatures had passed resolutions calling for a Constitutional Convention to propose an amendment to overturn the Supreme Court's "one man, one vote" decision (see p. 218). The resolutions were all passed quietly, and a public counter-reaction did not set in until *The New York Times* noted that a movement was afoot. Critics of the Convention pointed to the danger that, once called, it might propose all sorts of amendments, as reactions against recent Supreme Court rulings concerning school prayer (see p. 143) and criminal procedures, (see p. 169). Even if 34 states applied to Congress, it is unclear whether Congress would be compelled to call a Convention or what kind it would have to call. If the resolutions adopted by the states were worded differently could it be said that two-thirds had not "applied"? Would Congress be able to tell the convention what amendments to consider? Would it be able to make rules for the Convention? Would it be able to change the amendments proposed? These are unanswered questions. (If a Convention were to write an amendment, three-fourths of the state legislatures would still have to ratify.)

Some proposed amendments have not been ratified by three-quarters of the states. There are still two amendments lingering from 1789, one from 1810, and one from 1861. The Supreme Court has hinted that these amendments are so far out of date that they cannot now be ratified. But what about an amendment which has waited for only thirty years?

In 1938 the Kansas legislature ratified the proposed "child labor" amendment which the Kansas senate had previously rejected. The Kansas Supreme Court had denied a writ of mandamus to compel the secretary of state of Kansas to cancel the ratification. On appeal the Supreme Court upheld the state Supreme Court, in effect allowing the ratification by Kansas to stand. The Court ruled that it would not question whether an amendment has been lawfully ratified. That is a question solely for the states, and when the Secretary of State declares an amendment to have been ratified by a sufficient number of states, it becomes part of the Constitution. Amending the Constitution is a political process with which the Court will not interfere.[21]

Because of the uncertainty resulting from this case, as to how long a time can go by before an amendment grows out of date, some recent amendments have specified that they shall not become operative unless ratified within seven years of their proposal by Congress.

Only one part of the Constitution cannot be amended: the provision giving each state two Senators. Unless the state agrees (which presumably no state ever will) two Senators are required. This provision in Article 5 was part of the "great compromise" which led to the establishment of two houses of Congress.

(The provision in brackets concerned the slave trade; it is now obsolete.)

ARTICLE 6: Clause 1

All Debts contracted and Engagements entered into, before the Adoption of this Constitution, shall be as valid against the United States under this Constitution, as under the Confederation.

This clause was put in the Constitution to insure that debts would be paid and the continuity of government recognized. A new nation was not formed with the adoption of the Constitution, only a new form of government.

Clause 2

This Constitution, and the Laws of the United States which shall be made in Pursuance thereof; and all Treaties made, or which shall be made, under the Authority of the United States, shall be the supreme Law of the Land; and the Judges in every State shall be bound thereby, any Thing in the Constitution or Laws of any State to the Contrary notwithstanding.

This is the "supremacy clause" and it remains to this day one of the most important provisions in the Constitution. It was partly on the basis of this clause that Chief

Justice Marshall was able to rule that the Supreme Court had the power to invalidate laws of Congress which conflicted with the Constitution. Similarly, the Supreme Court has the power to rule on the constitutionality of state laws. Whenever a state law conflicts with the Constitution, *or* a statute of Congress, *or* a treaty, the state law must fall.

Because federal law is superior to state law, the states cannot tax the property or transactions of the federal government. In *McCulloch v. Maryland,* the state tried to tax the United States Bank chartered by Congress. "The power to tax involves the power to destroy," Chief Justice Marshall wrote, and denied the power.

The supremacy of federal law is far-reaching. In 1916, England and the United States signed a treaty for the protection of migratory birds. Congress then passed a law, regulating the killing, capturing, and selling of many species of birds. The state of Missouri protested. Congress could not regulate birds which the state owned within its borders, it said. Missouri pointed to the fact that Congress had earlier tried to pass the same kind of law when there was no treaty, and the law was declared unconstitutional. The Supreme Court recognized that the law unsupported by treaty might be bad, but the treaty made the constitutional difference.

The United States had the power to enter into the treaty—once it did, the supremacy clause demands that state law must go, especially since Congress can pass legislation to help enforce lawful treaties. "Here a national interest of very nearly the first magnitude is involved. It can be protected only by a national action in concert with that of another power. The [birds have] no permanent habitat [in the state]. But for the treaty and the statute, there soon might be no birds for any powers to deal with. We see nothing in the Constitution that compels the government to sit by while a food supply is cut off and the protectors of our forests and of our crops are destroyed." So spoke Justice Holmes for the Court.[92]

The supremacy clause also shows that though the United States is a federalism, the state governments and federal government are not wholly separate and distinct things. The supreme court of Rhode Island once dismissed a case in which the defendant was sued for a violation of federal law. The state court said that the United States and the state of Rhode Island were separate sovereignties and that neither had to enforce the penal law of the other. Rhode Island pointed to the fact that under the full faith and credit clause, states were allowed to deny enforcement of the criminal laws of sister states. But the Supreme Court reversed. The penal law of the United States, it said, by virtue of the supremacy clause is the policy of the states also.[137] (Most federal crimes are not taken to state courts because Congress has declared that only federal courts can try the cases.)

State court judges are bound to follow the Constitution and federal laws, even if the law of their own state tells them not to. State judges are thus responsible first to the United States Constitution.

Although the Constitution is superior both to federal laws and to treaties, federal statutes and treaties are on the same level with respect to each other. Even though in the eyes of the world the revocation may be illegal, a later Congressional law can nullify a previous treaty, at least with respect to domestic applications; the courts cannot then uphold the treaty. Likewise, a later treaty nullifies a prior conflicting law of Congress.

Clause 3

The Senators and Representatives before mentioned, and the Members of the several State Legislatures, and all executive and judicial Officers, both of the United States and of the several States, shall be bound by Oath or Affirmation, to support this Constitution;

Upon entering office, Senators, Representatives, state legislators, federal and state judges, and all members of the executive departments of federal and state governments must take an oath to support the Constitution.

When Abe Fortas took the oath of office on becoming Associate Justice of the Supreme Court in October, 1965, he took the following oath to fulfill his constitutional obligation: "I, Abe Fortas, do solemnly swear that I will support and defend the Constitution of the United States against all enemies, foreign and domestic; that I will bear true faith and allegiance to the same; that I will take this obligation freely, without any mental reservation or purpose of evasion; and that I will well and faithfully discharge the duties of the office on which I am about to enter. So help me God."

Clause 3 (continued)

but no religious Test shall ever be required as a Qualification to any office or public Trust under the United States.

It is unconstitutional to deny someone public office because of his religion. Strictly speaking, this clause applies only to federal office. But the freedom of religion sections of the 1st Amendment make it equally applicable to the state governments (see p. 117). In 1961, for instance, the Supreme Court struck down a Maryland statute which required all persons to declare a belief in God before they could become notary publics in the state. The states have no right to ask a person about his beliefs concerning God or religion, even whether he has any beliefs at all.[140]

ARTICLE 7

The Ratification of the Conventions of nine States shall be sufficient for the Establishment of this Constitution between the States so ratifying the same.

DONE in Convention by the Unanimous Consent of the States present the Seventeenth Day of September in the Year of our Lord one thousand seven hundred and Eighty seven and of the Independence of the United States of America the Twelfth. In Witness whereof We have hereunto subscribed our Names.

[Here follow thirty-nine names; see pp. 308ff.]

The men at the Constitutional Convention were not completely unanimous in their support of the Constitution as it had been drafted. As a show of unity, the Pennsylvania delegate who actually wrote the final version of the Constitution, Gouverneur Morris, suggested that the Constitution say that it had been signed by the unanimous consent of the *states present*. This was done; although many members of the Convention refused to sign, at least one member of every state placed his signature on the document (except for Rhode Island, which had no delegates).

The Framers chose conventions, rather than state legislatures, as the means of ratifying the Constitution. Even the formality of presenting the document to the Congress was dispensed with. The delegates wanted no delays or obstacles to ratification. They thought that the already established national Congress and state legislatures might stand in the way. State conventions, elected by the people, constituted solely for the purpose of passing on the new constitution, would expedite the ratification, the Constitutional Convention hoped. The delegates to the state conventions would not feel as bound to uphold the status quo as might the state legislators. By July, 1788, the conventions had acted.

The Constitution officially took effect March 4, 1789, even though General Washington was not inaugurated until April 30. Laws which conflicted with the Constitution before this date were not invalid until March 4.

PART TWO

THE RIGHTS OF THE PEOPLE

The Job Is Never Done

Even before the Constitution was ratified in the summer of 1788, people were asking for changes. They were not meek about it. Many state legislators declared they would vote against ratification because basic rights were not guaranteed to the people. Others said they would vote for the Constitution—provided it was amended immediately by the first Congress. Still others wanted it rewritten by another convention. In the end, of course, the Constitution was ratified by more than the necessary nine states, but to their yes votes a number of state legislatures had attached a recommendation that a Bill of Rights be added.

The men who had written the Constitution were not indifferent or sloppy or simply forgetful. They had completed a war not so many years before against many of the tyrannies which were to be prohibited by the Bill of Rights. But they thought that a Bill of Rights, spelling out what individual liberties the people were to have, would be unnecessary. Why? Because the Constitution which we have just explored contains no grant of power to Congress to legislate against any of the freedoms which a Bill of Rights would contain.

In urging New York to ratify, Hamilton argued: "I go further and affirm that Bills of Rights are not only unnecessary in the proposed Constitution but would even be dangerous. They would contain various exceptions to powers not granted, and on this very account would afford a colorable pretext to claim more than were granted. For why declare that things shall not be done, which there is no power to do?" Furthermore, eight states (New Hampshire, Massachusetts, Pennsylvania, Delaware, Maryland, Virginia, North Carolina, and South Carolina) had all adopted bills of rights, and three other states (New York, New Jersey and Georgia) had specific guarantees written in their own constitutions. This would be enough protection, thought the men in Philadelphia.

The delegates to the Convention miscalculated. From all quarters of the country, the demand was insistent: a Bill of Rights was necessary. The people remembered the war they had just fought. It was not the benevolence of a friendly government which led them to proclaim in the Declaration of Independence: "We hold these Truths to be self-evident, that all Men are created equal, that they are endowed by their Creator with certain unalienable Rights, that among these are Life, Liberty, and the Pursuit of Happiness." Against a background of centuries, it was all too clear how a government, any government, could deny the "unalienable rights" of free men. The denial of rights could even be justified, for as we have seen, the necessary and proper clause gives Congress great scope in legislative enactment.

When government has power, even when it springs from the people, it has a tendency to become a thing unto itself, a separate body operating under its own momentum. Elections were supposed to prevent the federal government from becoming a dictatorship. But what of the years between elections, when the politicians are not faced by immediate pressure to justify their actions? The elected bodies of government can act. Then the Congress and the Executive may forget their responsibilities. They may grow apart from the people. They may forget what it's like to be poor, or not know what it's like to be rich, may choose not to remember that "all men are created equal." They may decide that people who are different do not deserve to remain different or should not be allowed to become the same. And a zealous majority of common people, blinded by passion, may become a mob of the moment, intent on forcing obedience to a social code or religious belief. The majority may be bent on stopping people with different views from expressing them, and may condemn a minority without trial to prison for beliefs, thoughts, and conduct that harm only the moral indignation of the jailer. Against such actualities, the colonists had rebelled.

Oppression is mankind's oldest story. A few examples from English history will explain the fear of the revolutionaries that without a Bill of Rights an old kind of tyranny would replace their new kind of government.

The first English trials were not by juries—they were by ordeal. An accused person would be dropped into a lake; if he sank he was innocent, and if he rose to the top he was guilty. If he was found guilty, he would be executed; if he was innocent (and not drowned) he would be banished from the kingdom because he was still a suspected felon. This barbarism was brought to an end only with difficulty.

When jury trials were first substituted, they were juries composed of witnesses, not neutral persons. The accused had to consent to be tried by jury, and often his consent was forced by placing heavy weights upon him until he agreed or died.

A few hundred years later, even though the jury system had matured, an elaborate censorship system was in full swing. In the 1600's nothing could be printed without a license granted by the King and his ministers. Severe penalties were dealt to those who wrote and those who printed unlicensed works. In practice, anything could be forbidden.

Strangely enough, the crime of "seditious libel" (including attacks on any officials, inciting religious or political changes through unlawful means, or promoting ill feeling between classes) was graver if the statements were *true!* For if passions would be aroused to violence by false reports of why England ailed, imagine how much more upset the people would be if they knew the facts were true. Reports of real injustice would inflame the people far more than exaggerated tales. So the press was at the mercy of King or censor. Those who disagreed had the "choice" of being executed.

King Henry VIII in 1534 split from the Catholic Church, disavowed the Pope, and in the Act of Supremacy, declared himself the head of the Church of England. Henry sent one of his attendants to John Fischer, Bishop of Rochester, to determine what the Bishop thought about Henry's new law. The messenger told Fischer that he could speak his mind, that no harm would come to him whatever his opinion. Fischer then humbly said that he could not approve of the Act of Supremacy, for under the law of God, King could not be set above Pope. For this opinion, the King broke his word, imprisoned Fischer, and tried him for treason; after a rubber-stamp jury found him guilty, the Lord Chancellor sentenced him as follows: "You shall be led to the place from whence you came, and from thence shall be drawn through the city to the place of execution at Tyborne, where your body shall be hanged by the neck, half alive you shall be cut down and throwne to the ground, your bowels to be taken out of your body before you, being alive, your head to be smitten off, and your body to be divided into quarters, and after your head and quarters to be set up, where the King shall appoint; and God have mercy upon your soule." The King reduced the sentence to simple death, and Fischer was beheaded.

In 1619, William of Essex wrote a book in which he predicted King James I would die in two years unless he renounced his evil ways. The prediction was based on an analysis of various biblical warnings concerning tyrants. Only one copy of the book was made and it was placed in a box and secretly transmitted to the King. For this effrontery, William was sentenced to death, guilty of high treason.

The examples are endless—confessions beaten from people, the accused denied defense lawyers for certain crimes, religious minorities persecuted. And the revolutionaries realized that this sort of thing might continue to happen, unless a Bill of Rights was established.

With the hindsight of a century and three-quarters, it was fortunate the first Congress felt compelled to carry out the recommendations of the people. For even with the Bill of Rights, American history is still full of examples of attempts by state and federal governments to restrict freedom. Even before the federal Bill of Rights was written, three men were convicted in Massachusetts of "political libel" in the face of a specific prohibition in the state constitution against such convictions. Seven years after the federal Bill of Rights was adopted, the Sedition Act was passed by Congress, outlawing speech and writing which was offensive to President John Adams and the Federalist party then in power. Quite a performance for a Congress which, according to Hamilton and Madison, had been given no power by the Constitution to do this in the first place, and had then specifically been denied the power in the Bill of Rights. (The Act lapsed three years later and the Congress did not repass it, the Federalists having lost control. The Court never passed on its constitutionality.)

The fears of those who advocated a Bill of Rights were justified, and the first Congress in 1789 settled down to the task of drafting such a bill. In the House of Representatives, Madison, who had originally opposed a Bill of Rights on the grounds that it was unnecessary, now sat down to work out a politically acceptable solution. He combed all the state proposals and came up with less than twenty amendments. After a special committee shaped them, the House passed seventeen. The Senate knocked out three of the proposed amendments, and the joint Senate-House conference committee deleted two more, bringing the number to twelve. These were approved and sent to the state legislatures, and by December, 1791, all but two survived. The first two amendments—relating to the number of Representatives in Congress and to the pay of Congressmen—failed to gain support. The remaining ten were ratified and these constitute the Bill of Rights. (Massachusetts, curiously enough, failed to ratify the ten amendments. This state, which had pressed so vigorously for a Bill of Rights, finally got around to ratifying in 1941—on the 150th anniversary of the Bill of Rights.)

Since 1791, only fifteen other amendments have been added. Most of the later amendments related to structural changes in the government. Some, however, dealt with basic, "unalienable rights": the abolition of slavery, the right of women to vote. And one amendment above all

—the 14th—radically altered the meaning and application of the Bill of Rights and the power of the federal government.

Originally, the Bill of Rights prohibited only the federal government from interfering with basic rights of citizens. Thus, although the Congress could not pass laws abridging the freedom of speech or religion or take away the right to jury trials, the states could, and did. An amendment to restrict the state legislatures in this regard —said by Madison to be the most valuable amendment —had been defeated in the Senate during debate on the Bill of Rights, partly because many states already guaranteed these rights in their own constitutions. Nevertheless, it was often argued that the Bill of Rights applied to the states also.

In 1833, the Supreme Court settled the point. Barron owned a wharf in Baltimore. The city had diverted the waters in which the wharf sat in order to build a system of smooth, straight, paved roads. As a result, Barron's wharf dried up and his commercial business was ruined. Baltimore did not offer to reimburse him for his losses, and he sued the city in 1822. The case finally reached the Supreme Court eleven years later. Barron argued that when the 5th Amendment said "no person shall be deprived of life, liberty, or property without due process of law," it meant the state could not ruin his business without paying. The Court disagreed. If the federal government had done the same thing, it would have had to pay. But the 5th Amendment, and the rest of the Bill of Rights, was "intended solely as a limitation of power by the government of the United States and is not applicable" to states or cities. Since the only ground of jurisdiction was a case "arising under the Constitution," the Court had to dismiss the suit when it ruled that the Constitution did not apply. *Barron v. Baltimore* thus gave the states the green light to deny to their citizens rights which the federal government could not deny. There matters stood for more than thirty years.

After the Civil War, however, in an effort to guarantee freedom and full opportunity to ex-slaves, Congress proposed, and the states in 1868 ratified, the 14th Amendment, which reads in part: "nor shall any State deprive any person of life, liberty or property without due process of law." Within the last half-century, that clause has been used to make the Bill of Rights apply against the states also.

"Due process of law" originally meant fair and just procedures. Because justice to one man may be tyranny to another, the "due process clause" is perhaps the vaguest in the Constitution. Nevertheless, since the 1920's, the word "liberty" has come to take on a broad meaning. The freedoms of speech, religion, and press are now firmly established liberties, secure against state interference as well as federal. Many of the guarantees of fair procedure in Amendments 4 through 8 have also come within the protection of due process (though not all).

"The history of liberty has largely been the history of observance of procedural safeguards." So said Mr. Justice Frankfurter in a case involving the issue of how many hours at one sitting the police could question a suspect. (The answer: Not too many.[89])

Some have found it strange that the Supreme Court has increasingly become a kind of arbitrator of police and court regulations concerning crimes and criminals. Unless fair procedures are employed, however, all other rights are hollow. Crime menaces freedom, but unjust imprisonments and high-handed police tactics infringe on freedom also.

Article 1 defined some procedures that were so unfair that they were never to be used by state or federal governments—the ex post facto laws and bills of attainder were among them. These prohibitions were believed to be insufficient, so other specific procedural requirements were written into the Bill of Rights. These include prohibitions against unreasonable searches and seizures, coerced confessions, and cruel and unusual punishments.

At various times since the passage of the 14th Amendment, it has been asserted that: none of the Bill of Rights applies to the states; the entire Bill of Rights applies to the states; and some, but only some, of the procedural requirements of the Bill of Rights are applicable equally to the states. This last view has won out. The Bill of Rights has not been "absorbed" into the due process clause of the 14th Amendment in one large chunk. Instead, it is being "selectively incorporated" case by case, clause by clause, into the 14th Amendment. As more and more provisions have been incorporated in recent years, it appears more and more likely that someday perhaps almost the entire Bill of Rights will find a home in the 14th Amendment.

But whether "absorption" or "incorporation" (call it whatever you want), by what justification has the Bill of Rights come to be increasingly swallowed up by a clause in the 14th Amendment which reads as follows: "nor shall any State deprive any person of life, liberty, or property without due process of law"? The 5th Amendment has a "due process" clause also. If other parts of the Bill of Rights (such as the right against unreasonable searches) are *not* part of the due process clause of the 5th Amendment (otherwise why would these other rights have been put in?), how is it that they are part of the substance of the *identically worded* due process clause in the 14th Amendment? This redundancy once worried the guardians of the Constitution; today the repetition is favored. For against the oppressions of two governments, two clauses must stand ready to protect the individual.

Focus on the words of the due process clause: "No person shall be deprived of life, liberty, or property without due process of law." The Constitution does not say that life, liberty or property can *never* be taken away; but it does say that these can be taken away only if due process of the law—the fair procedures—are followed. All criminal penalties prescribe the deprivation of at least one of these: life (the death penalty), liberty (jail sentences, loss of the right to vote), property (monetary fines). Before any of these can be taken away, then, all organs of government—legislative, executive, and judicial—must observe certain procedures.

The essence of due process requirements has been described in a number of ways. Fair procedures have been said to be those "implicit in the concept of ordered liberty." They are "principles of justice so rooted in the traditions and conscience of our people as to be ranked as fundamental." They are principles such that a "fair and enlightened system of justice would be impossible without them." "Neither liberty nor justice would exist if they were sacrificed." They are the "fundamental principles of liberty and justice which lie at the base of all our civil and political institutions." [105] The absence of these procedures would "offend those canons of decency and fairness which express the notions of justice of English-speaking peoples even toward those charged with the most heinous offenses." [8] If the government violates the required procedures, it engages in "conduct that shocks the conscience." [118]

If unfair procedures do any of these things, they offend "due process of law." Such descriptions are necessarily vague. They suggest the spirit of the principle, not the principle itself. They indicate that what shocks the conscience of one set of judges at one time (and hence what is within the meaning of the due process clause) may not shock the conscience of another Court at another time. So the most fundamental fact to be observed about the due process clauses is that they never stop growing; they are constantly developing. What those who wrote the amendments thought they were trying to do in the 4th or 5th or 8th Amendment is of small concern. The real question is, what are *today's* standards? Four centuries ago, the cutting off of ears was not considered "cruel and unusual punishment." It was a commonplace. Today it would be automatically prohibited by the 8th Amendment. As the sense of American justice develops, so also does the Constitution.

An increasing number of cases coming to the Supreme Court in the 1960's have concerned the incorporation of parts of the Bill of Rights into the 14th Amendment. At an almost furious pace, the Court has absorbed more and more provisions, and greatly enlarged their scope. The evolution of the 14th Amendment has become almost a judicial revolution. Taken together, the Bill of Rights and the 14th Amendment represent an enormously expanding system by which freedom continues to be guaranteed to the people in the face of rapidly growing federal and state governments.

7   The Basic Freedoms

The 1st Amendment

Amendment 1

Congress shall make no law respecting an establishment of religion, or prohibiting the free exercise thereof; or abridging the freedom of speech, or of the press; or the right of the people peaceably to assemble, and to petition the Government for a redress of grievances.

"When men have realized that time has upset many fighting faiths, they may come to believe even more than they believe the very foundations of their own conduct that the ultimate good desired is better reached by a free trade in ideas—that the best test of truth is the power of the thought to get itself accepted in the competition of the market, and that truth is the only ground upon which their wishes safely can be carried out. That at any rate is the theory of our Constitution. It is an experiment, as all life is an experiment." Thus Mr. Justice Holmes dissented, protesting the jailing of those who had published political propaganda in 1919.[2]

On the face of it, the freedoms protected in the 1st Amendment seem to be absolutely protected against any laws. "Congress shall make NO law," says the 1st Amendment. But this would mean that anyone would be free to ruin a man's reputation by telling lies about him, or that a person could justify a murder on the grounds that his religion demanded it. (Some primitive religions, of course, have long believed in ritual killing.)

The 1st Amendment freedoms cannot be so absolute. They are "majestic generalities" which must be translated into "concrete restraints on officials." [163] But Congress and state legislatures must be able to pass laws to protect society and individuals against grave harms. The Supreme

Court faces its most delicate task when it must draw that judicial line between laws which so directly interfere with the precious freedoms that they are unconstitutional and those laws which are constitutional because they are aimed at other evils, even though they may indirectly curtail our basic freedoms.

Religion

Throughout much of the world's history, most countries have had "national religions," particular state-supported faiths. Many countries have forbidden practice of any other religion at all. Other countries do not forbid free worship but give the national religion certain benefits, such as limiting public office-holding to those of the national faith.

Many of the American colonies, also, had their own religions. Although minority groups had fled England and other countries to escape religious persecution, upon arriving in America they promptly persecuted those who disagreed with them. The Puritans in Massachusetts exiled people preaching doctrines which were unorthodox to them; they even went so far as to condemn Quakers, Anabaptists, and others to death. Most states had established official state religions; some had not. Even Rhode Island, which had no state church, and was generally tolerant, guaranteed religious freedom for Christian faiths only. It was to ensure that the federal government would not set up its own religion that the first part of the amendment was written.

In 1802 President Jefferson wrote that the 1st Amendment established a "wall of separation between Church and State." To a large degree, these words have become the guiding principles in deciding religion cases.

1. The Establishment Clause

A. SCHOOL ATTENDANCE. A New Jersey law allows local school boards to make contracts in connection with transportation of students. One township in 1947 decided to repay bus money to parents whose children went to

Catholic parochial schools. The Supreme Court held in *Everson v. Board of Education* that such a payment was not unconstitutional, that it did not tend to establish a religion because it was used for a purely nonsectarian purpose. In that landmark case, the Court went far in defining what the constitutional rule is: "The 'establishment of religion' clause of the First Amendment means at least this: Neither a state nor the Federal Government can set up a church. Neither can pass laws which aid one religion, aid all religions, or prefer one religion over another. Neither can force nor influence a person to go to or to remain away from church against his will or force him to profess a belief or disbelief in any religion. No person can be punished for entertaining or professing religious beliefs or disbeliefs, for church attendance or nonattendance. No tax in any amount, large or small, can be levied to support any religious activities or institutions, whatever they may be called, or whatever form they may adopt to teach or practice religion. Neither a state nor the Federal Government can, openly or secretly, participate in the affairs of any religious organizations or groups and *vice versa.*"

These words were put to the test one year later. The school board of Champaign, Illinois, allowed public schools to be used for religious instruction during school hours. If a parent signed a "request card," the student would leave his regular schoolroom and receive religious instruction. Other students would continue to study their regular subjects. This so-called released time arrangement was struck down. Said the Court: "Here not only are the State's tax-supported public school buildings used for the dissemination of religious doctrines. The State also affords sectarian groups an invaluable aid in that it helps to provide pupils for the religious classes through use of the State's compulsory public school machinery. This is not separation of Church and State." [69]

New York has a different version of "released time." In New York, students who want to receive religious training are excused from school during a certain hour to go to a church or other religious institution. The public schools make no announcements of who attends or does not attend the outside schools; the public schools do not ask their pupils to engage in religious training; they do not pass around cards; they do not approve the religious teachers, as did the Illinois schools. Because of these substantially different facts, the Court distinguished the Illinois case from the New York case, saying, "The government must be neutral when it comes to competition between sects," not that the government cannot "cooperate with religious authorities by adjusting the schedule of public events to sectarian needs." When it does cooperate, the government "follows the best of our traditions." [173] The New York program was upheld.

B. BIBLE READING AND PRAYER IN SCHOOL. A number of recent decisions have held that Bible reading and the saying of prayers in public schools are a violation of the establishment clause. In a typical situation, a particular passage from the Bible would be read to a class during a homeroom period by student or teacher, and those who wished could leave.

How does this constitute an establishment of religion? At the trial in *School District of Abington v. Schempp*, Edward Schempp, a Unitarian and member of the Unitarian Church in Germantown, Pennsylvania, testified that the doctrines in the Bible which were read to the class were contrary to his family's religious beliefs.

Why not have his children leave the room? The trial judge summarized the argument as follows: "Edward Schempp, the children's father, testified that after careful consideration he had decided that he should not have Roger or Donna excused from attendance at these morning ceremonies. Among his reasons were the following. He said that he thought his children would be 'labeled as "odd balls" ' before their teachers and classmates every school day; that children, like Roger's and Donna's classmates, were liable 'to lump all particular religious difference[s] or religious objections [together] as "atheism" ' and that today the word 'atheism' is often connected with 'atheistic communism,' and has 'very bad connotations, such as 'un-American' or '[pro]-Red,' overtones of possible immorality. Mr. Schempp pointed out that due to the events of the morning exercises following in rapid succession, the Bible reading, the Lord's Prayer, the Flag Salute, and the announcements, excusing his children from the Bible reading would mean that probably they would miss hearing the announcements so important to children. He testified also that if Roger and Donna were excused from Bible reading they would have to stand in the hall outside their 'homeroom' and that this carried with it the imputation of punishment for bad conduct."

Anyone who has ever attended school can probably testify that often pressure to conform will cause one to think somewhat less of the person who is different. By making this difference hinge on religion, by establishing an atmosphere in which the school seemed to be saying that a certain religion was a good thing, the school went beyond its constitutional power. Furthermore, in putting an indirect coercion on the minority, the school abridges the individual's free exercise of religion.

None of this is to say that today schools cannot study the Bible as the brilliant literature that it is; none of this is to say that the cultural and historical study of religion is forbidden in public schools. Far from it. The Court specifically said in *Schempp* that such studies would be entirely permissible under the Constitution. What is forbidden is the conducting of a religious exercise.

The public did not receive the school prayer decision quietly. Many who perhaps did not fully understand what was said pressed for an amendment to the Constitution, which would allow prayers in public schools. Part of the impetus for such an amendment came from those who thought the Supreme Court outlawed prayers; of course it did not. In fact, the Court stressed just the opposite: other avenues of prayer are open and should be used. Prayers in church and prayers every day with the family at home for those who want them are obviously acceptable. Only when the machinery of the state comes into play to foster prayer and Bible reading is the worship objectionable. These arguments convinced Congress, and efforts to overrule these decisions by amendment have failed.

2. The Free Exercise Clause

An establishment of religion does not necessarily coerce the individual. When the state *forces* the individual to act contrary to his religious beliefs, then it violates the second part of the 1st Amendment's guarantee of religious freedom.

A 1925 Oregon law which required every student to attend public schools was attacked by the Society of Sisters, a Catholic orphanage whose existence was threatened by the law. The Supreme Court struck down the law; religious schools cannot be outlawed in such a manner and a person cannot be forced to attend a nonreligious school.[108]

Across the country in West Virginia, a law required all students to salute the flag. Some objected that the required "stiff-arm salute" was too much like Hitler's (this was in 1942). Although the manner of salute was modified somewhat, the law was enforced against Jehovah's Witnesses. The Witnesses objected to saying the pledge of allegiance on the grounds that it conflicted with their literal reading of the Bible, which says, "Thou shalt not make unto thee any graven image" (Exodus, 20:4). The children were expelled from school and both children and parents were threatened with prosecution unless they agreed to salute. They offered to give another pledge publicly, including the following statement: "I respect the flag of the United States and acknowledge it as a symbol of freedom and justice for all." West Virginia defended on the ground that "national unity is the basis of national security" and that the states have "the right to select appropriate means for its attainment." West Virginia was quoting the language of a Supreme Court decision three years before in which the power to compel the salute was upheld.

Now the Supreme Court reversed itself. In *West Virginia State Board of Education v. Barnette,* the Court said: "Ultimate futility of such attempts to compel coherence is the lesson of every such effort from the Roman drive to stamp out Christianity as a disturber of its pagan unity, the Inquisition as a means to religious and dynastic unity, the Siberian exiles as a means to Russian unity, down to the fast failing efforts of our present totalitarian enemies. Those who begin coercive elimination of dissent soon find themselves exterminating dissenters. Compulsory unification of opinion achieves only the unanimity of the graveyard.

"It seems trite but necessary to say that the First Amendment to our Constitution was designed to avoid these ends by avoiding these beginnings. There is no mysticism in the American concept of the State or of the nature or origin of its authority. We set up government by consent of the governed, and the Bill of Rights denies those in power any legal opportunity to coerce that consent. Authority here is to be controlled by public opinion not public opinion by authority."

In striking down the flag salute law, Justice Jackson went on to say, "If there is any fixed star in our constitutional constellation, it is that no official, high or petty, can prescribe what shall be orthodox in politics, nationalism, religion, or other matters of opinion or force citizens to confess by word or act their faith therein."

More recently, a woman was fired from her job in South Carolina because she was a Seventh Day Adventist, and could not work on Saturday. When she was unable to find work anywhere else, because no employer wanted her unless she could work on Saturday, she applied for state unemployment compensation benefits. These were denied. The Supreme Court reversed the South Carolina Supreme Court, which had held that she was not entitled to the payments. The refusal to pay her conflicted with her free exercise of religion, by penalizing her for belief that Saturday, instead of Sunday, should be observed as the Sabbath.[129]

3. Laws Restraining Religious Practices

The wisdom of forbidding the government to pass laws "respecting an establishment of religion or prohibiting the free exercise thereof" will probably not be denied in a country such as the United States, where there are at least eighty-three separate religious groups of 50,000 members or more, as well as hundreds of smaller groups. Nevertheless, some activities, though they can be justified in the name of religion, would disrupt our society too much and have been outlawed. The freedom to believe is wider than the freedom to act.

Polygamy, the practice of having more than one wife or husband, has been banned throughout the nation. The prohibition has been upheld as constitutional, even though polygamy is advocated by the Mormons.[115]

Sunday closing laws are another set of constitutional statutes which affect religion. Many states have legislation requiring stores to remain closed on Sunday. Proprietors who for religious reasons close their stores on Saturdays have protested that they lose business by being forced to close their stores on Sunday as well. This argument has so far proved unavailing. Although Sunday closing laws had religious origins, today they merely provide a day of rest for the great majority of people, who, according to the Court, should not have to be bothered by the noise and crowds of shoppers and traffic. It would be difficult, furthermore, to work out an administrative system to make sure that those stores which stayed open on Sunday were closed on Saturday. On the other hand, some people have urged that there is an obvious distinction between a large discount department store, as in the case of *Two Guys from Harrison v. McGinley,* and the small Orthodox Jewish food stores, as in *Gallagher v. Crown Kosher Supermarket,* in which the consumers complained also. Since their religion demanded that they buy only from a kosher market, they could shop neither on Saturday nor on Sunday. But the Supreme Court has not made the distinction.

A number of cases have arisen concerning government financial aid to religion. States often furnish textbooks to students in public and parochial schools alike; in the *Everson* case, the state reimbursed parents of parochial school children for bus transportation. Usually these arrangements have been upheld by the Court, on the ground that the government is aiding not the religious aspect of the parochial schools but rather the secular, nonreligious functions.

Freedom of Speech and Press

It is not surprising that in a society which cherishes the individual, one of the most precious freedoms is the right of anyone to speak and publish. These are the only ways we know to communicate our ideas; from this communication has come religion, science, literature, commerce, art, and politics.

Ideas are powerful, and all new ideas have been resisted by some group at some time. When truly radical ideas appear, they can be stamped out by killing those who advocate them. During the Middle Ages, scientists who thought the earth revolved around the sun were actually burned to death. Thomas Paine's neighbors vilified him because he did not believe in the literal truth of biblical stories. In England, people advocating "improvements" in political and social life were condemned to death. People everywhere have been intolerant of anything new, and the fear of punishment—whether it be death, exile from country, prison, or the fact that the heretic is excommunicated—stifles not only the ideas that have been condemned, but also any other idea which a person thinks *might* be condemned.

"Those who won our independence had confidence in the power of free and fearless reasoning and communication of ideas to discover and spread political and economic truth. Noxious doctrines in those fields may be refused and their evil averted by the courageous exercise of the right of free discussion. Abridgement of freedom of speech and of the press, however, impairs those opportunities for public education that are essential to effective exercise of the power of correcting error through the processes of popular government." [139]

But because ideas incite, some to right injustices and others to riot for wrongs, a line has always been drawn between speech which advances society and that which is destructive. In America, a narrow view has been taken of what is destructive. Merely because an idea—such as birth control, allowing women to vote, or saying that God is dead—may lead to widespread social changes if it is accepted, perhaps to a disappearance of an old way of life, is not to say that it is destructive.

This thought, that freedom of speech and press and related rights should not lightly be interfered with, has given birth to a doctrine of constitutional law known as the "preferred position" of 1st Amendment rights. Usually, when Congress or a state legislature passes a law, and a case involving the law is being litigated, the Supreme Court will presume it to be valid, and will require those who would have the law declared unconstitutional prove that in the *particular circumstances* it does in fact conflict with the Constitution. When a case arises involving the 1st Amendment or a related right (such as liberty to travel abroad, protected by the due process clause), the presumption is just the reverse. The law is presumed invalid, unless the maker of the law, who is claiming it does not collide with the Constitution, can show that in *no circumstance* will it conflict with a 1st Amendment right or related right.[4] The Court will examine the law "on its face"; it will not narrowly interpret a law which allegedly infringes the 1st Amendment in order to avoid a constitutional question.[139] Some have protested that no constitutional right should be higher than any other, but the "preferred position" doctrine seems likely to remain. This should not be shocking, since the 1st Amendment says "no law" can abridge the freedom, whereas other amendments indicate that a weighing of interests must be made.

Yet a weighing even of 1st Amendment rights must be made. Some speech can be destructive. Slander and libel hurt. A speaker who urges a restless crowd to take arms against imagined tyrannies can cause riots, physical injuries, and property damage. A pornographic book can harm the very young. Someone who conspires with others to commit a crime can also be dangerous. So because there are reasons why society needs to curb certain communications, some methods of controlling speech and press are permissible.

1. Prior Restraint: Licensing

The most obvious way to control is to require everyone who wants to talk or to publish to submit what he wants to say to an official censor first. Only if his work is approved can he then speak his mind. This is also the most effective way to shut everyone up. Prior licensing is usually not valid; where it is allowed it must be surrounded by the utmost procedural precaution.

A Maryland statute required all movie exhibitors to submit their films first to the Maryland Motion Picture Censor Board. In 1965 a theater refused. The "prior restraint" inherent in the system—so obnoxious even four hundred years ago—was unconstitutional, the owners said. The Supreme Court agreed. Under the Maryland law, the exhibitor had to prove the film should be given a license by proving that it was not obscene. The Court laid down the opposite rule: the censor board must prove that the film is not worthy of a license. Furthermore, the censor board could deny or delay the license on its own. The Supreme Court ruled that the censor must either give the license within a short period of time or go to court to stop the film from being shown, with the assurance that a court will decide the question promptly.[45]

The 1st Amendment protects public meetings as well as movies. New York City passed an ordinance making religious meetings on the streets illegal, unless a permit from the police commissioner was first secured. The ordinance did not specify any standards for the commissioner to apply, before granting or denying a permit; applicants were at his mercy. The ordinance suggested that in addition to controlling meetings to prevent congestion in the streets, the commissioner could refuse a permit if the speaker was likely to "ridicule" any religious belief or to preach atheism or agnosticism. Carl Jacob Kunz, a Baptist minister, had received a permit in 1946. At meetings in Columbus Circle he violently attacked Catholics and Jews, calling Catholicism a "religion of the devil," and Jews, "Christ-killers." The police commissioner revoked his permit after receiving a "flood of complaints" and refused him one when he reapplied in 1947 and 1948.

Finally, Kunz held his meetings anyway, continuing his derogatory language and was arrested and fined $10. Coming to his rescue, the American Civil Liberties Union financed his ultimate appeal to the Supreme Court. which reversed his convictions. The power of the commissioner to refuse a permit was an unconstitutional prior restraint on speech The commissioner did not have to justify his refusal, and in fact did not. even though Kunz admitted he would continue to agitate. The reason for the Court decision is clear enough: to stop Kunz means the police could stop anyone with whom they disagreed.[78]

In fact. this once happened in Jersey City, New Jersey, where Mayor Hague was empowered to refuse permits for speaking in public if there was a likelihood of public disturbances or riots. The mayor seemed intent not to preserve the peace but to use his power as an "instrument of arbitrary suppression of free expression of views on national affairs." Every time the Congress of Industrial Organizations (CIO), a group seeking to organize the industrial workers in the town into unions, sought a permit to discuss national issues in public, Mayor Hague (a violent opponent of unionization) denied the request. It was clear that he was abridging the freedom of political opponents to speak. The CIO sued the mayor, and the Supreme Court eventually ruled that his power to grant permits was unconstitutional.[61]

Not all licensing is unconstitutional, however. When the permit system is used not to discriminate against speech but to protect a public need, the system may be constitutional even if it does cut down the right to express opinions. For instance, Trenton, N.J., had a city ordinance forbidding *all* "sound trucks" from going on the public streets and emitting "loud and raucous noises." Trenton wanted to end the public nuisance of having phonograph, radio, or loudspeaker noise play out on the streets. Since alternative methods of disseminating information were available, the regulation designed to preserve public tranquility was upheld.[77] On the other hand, where *some* sound trucks are allowed and the police chief can use his discretion as to which ones, the statute is invalid.[122] It's either all or nothing.

The protection against prior restraint is a wide one. A specific license system does not need to be in force in order for a governmental action to be declared unconstitutional. For instance, a Minnesota law declared that a "malicious, scandalous, and defamatory newspaper, magazine, or other periodical" could be prevented from being published ("abated") as a "public" nuisance." A Minneapolis periodical called *The Saturday Press* was enjoined from further publication because it had attacked the police chief and other city officials, declaring in inflammatory language that they were grossly negligent in their duty, associated with gangsters, and took bribes. The paper was not stopped because it had not secured a license; no newspapers are licensed. Rather it was told not to publish any more, on the theory that it might continue to criticize public officials. But this is just as surely prior restraint, said the Court: "The fact that the liberty of the press may be abused by miscreant purveyors of scandal does not make any the less necessary the immunity of the press from previous restraint in dealing with official misconduct. Subsequent punishment for such abuses as may exist is the appropriate remedy, consistent with constitutional privilege." In *Near v. Minnesota,* the Court ordered the state to keep hands off.

2. Subsequent Punishment

The alternative to prior restraint through licensing is to make certain kinds of speech punishable *after* the speech is made. This kind of restraint is not quite as drastic as a licensing system, since no one has the power to refuse to let the speech be given. But the power to put in jail is nevertheless a serious one, and the mere existence of laws on the statute books will tend to keep people silent for fear they might be prosecuted.

A. CLEAR AND PRESENT DANGER. Perhaps the most important justification for curtailing speech is the doctrine of "clear and present danger," first stated by Justice Holmes in 1919: "The most stringent protection of free speech would not protect a man in falsely shouting fire in a theater, and causing a panic. . . . The question in every case is whether the words used are used in such circumstances and are of such a nature as to create a clear and present danger that they will bring about the substantive evils that Congress has a right to prevent." [125]

Justification springs from the very nature of the test: if the best test of truth is the power of thought to get it accepted in the competition of the market, when there is no market—that is, when there is *not enough time for debate* —an inflammatory speech which will cause rioting or revolution must be within the power of the police to prevent. As Justice Brandeis said in *Whitney v. California,* "Those who won our independence by revolution were not cowards. They did not fear political change. They did not exalt order at the cost of liberty. To courageous, self-reliant men, with confidence in the power of free and fearless reasoning applied through the processes of popular government, no danger flowing from speech can be deemed clear and present, unless the incidence of the evil apprehended is so imminent that it may befall before there is opportunity for full discussion. If there be time to expose through discussion the falsehood and fallacies, to avert the evil by the process of education, the *remedy to be applied is more speech, not enforced silence.* Only an emergency can justify repression. Such must be the rule if authority is to be reconciled with freedom."

The "clear and present danger" test has given the Supreme Court much difficulty. Like all doctrines which come complete with a name, "clear and present danger" is a deceptively simple test. How clear and how present the danger must be has never been settled.

In a 1919 case, five people were sent to jail for twenty years for publishing two leaflets denouncing President Wilson for sending troops to Russia and demanding that workers who emigrated from Russia and were working in munitions factories strike.[2] In a 1925 case, Benjamin Gitlow published a pamphlet called the "Left-Wing Manifesto," calling for the overthrow of the American form of government by mass industrial strikes; although there was no evidence that any of the 16,000 copies he distributed had any effects, he was convicted under a 1902 New York criminal anarchy statute.[52] Then in 1927, Anita Whitney was convicted of violating a "criminal syndicalism" statute by being a leader of the Communist Labor Party and attending meetings, despite the fact that the Party voted down a proposal for widespread political action and that without contradiction, Miss Whitney herself testified that she did not intend to violate any law.[165]

The Supreme Court upheld the convictions in all these cases, in the face of dissents in the first two by Justices Holmes and Brandeis and of their disagreement with the reasoning in the last. In none of these cases did the danger seem to be imminent, even if it was clear. The majority in *Gitlow v. New York* said, in fact, that "it cannot be said that the state is acting arbitrarily or unreasonably when, in the exercise of its judgment as to the measures necessary to protect the public peace and safety, it seeks to extinguish the spark without waiting until it has enkindled the flame or blazed into the conflagration." In other words, the clear and present danger can be fuzzy and distant.

An even more troublesome question had arisen throughout. How "substantive" (serious) must the danger be in order for Congress or the states to have the constitutional power to forbid the speech which is supposedly about to prove the danger? At various times the clear and present danger test has been used to outlaw obscenity, labor union picketing, speeches before hostile crowds, and criticism of courts. Often in these latter cases, the Supreme Court has reversed the lower courts, permitting the speech. But it has never been clear whether the "clear and present danger" test is the proper one for these kinds of cases.

Finally, in 1951, the clear and present danger test was turned upside down. Although it was originally framed to insure that convictions would be sustained only if a serious danger was both clear and present, the Supreme Court in *Dennis v. United States* upheld the conviction of people charged with having conspired to teach the necessity for the use of force in overthrowing the government. They were NOT accused of having agreed to overthrow the government someday. They were NOT accused of having taken action designed someday to overthrow the government. Nor were they accused of actually having taught anyone how to go about using force and violence. They were charged merely with getting together and agreeing that the teaching of violent revolution would be a good thing.

The Supreme Court applied a new test: "whether the gravity of the 'evil,' discounted by its improbability, justifies such invasion of free speech as is necessary to avoid the danger." In other words, if the danger is very serious, it need not be clear and present at all; only if the danger is small, must it be clear and present. A sliding scale was introduced. This is precisely what the original test was designed to avoid.

The case arose in the early 1950's under the Smith Act of 1940, designed to curb Communist activity. In itself, curtailing Russian Communists is not bad, if they really do intend to try to overthrow the government by force and violence. But the case provided fuel for the fire of fear.

It now became all too easy to abridge the freedom of speech and press. It is not difficult to label as a Communist anyone with whom the police or prosecutors or employers disagree. Regardless of whether he really is—for who can tell what it means to be a "real" Communist as opposed to somebody who merely has "strange" or "different" ideas?—he who advocates something less than "100 percent Americanism" runs the risk of being called a Communist and arrested, prosecuted, and convicted.

In the early 1950's thousands of people were affected because they spoke out. Some were fired from public employment, not because they were convicted of crime but only because they were "suspected" of being disloyal or un-American. Others lost their jobs with private employers when they espoused beliefs with which their employers disagreed. Sometimes a person could be alienated from his community simply because he questioned the sanity of a society which allowed such head-hunting to go on.

The temper of the times was strikingly close to the hysteria in Salem, Massachusetts, in 1692, when some young girls came across a book which discussed how witches were supposed to behave. Mostly as a joke, they accused a young half-Indian, half-Negro girl—a family slave—of being a witch. In order to save her life, the girl confessed not only that she was a witch but that others in the community were also. If her master had not beaten her quite so hard, he might not have got so many confessions from her. These people accused others, and from the stories told, skies must have been dark with witches riding brooms. Some people said the whole thing was downright nonsense, and they were promptly accused of being in league with the devil. More than twenty "witches" were killed; nineteen of them hanged. The whole thing only came to a halt when witch-hunters started accusing proper Bostonians, such as the clergy and merchants. At that point the special witch courts were dissolved and some 150 prisoners were released from jail.

So, too, when Senator Joseph McCarthy attacked proper Americans, such as officers in the United States Army, the Communist scare subsided. And with the passing of the scare went the Supreme Court's willingness to water down the clear and present danger test. In cases which arose during the later 1950's and early 1960's, *Dennis v. United States* was limited. Today before a person can be convicted he must be an active member of an illegal organization, he must know about and support the illegal organization. [32, 102, 123, 170] Mere advocacy without more is permissible.

The danger of infringing the right to speak is not limited to the fact that speech in general is curtailed. The danger is also that the outlawed speech is driven underground where underground reasoning flourishes, where fanatic Communists and others who want to overthrow the government by force and violence are not subjected to the potency of logic which would destroy their reasoning. When the public does not hear the Communists' arguments, or the arguments of ultra right-wing groups, it cannot counter their arguments. Channels for peaceful change are closed.

The history of the past forty years should be sufficient to demonstrate that there never has been a clear and present danger of a violent revolution. "Clear and present danger" at the outermost must mean within a matter of days. In riot cases, when a person by speaking to a crowd has caused the mob to become violent so that injury is soon to occur, the time period is usually taken to be minutes. But there has been no serious violent attempt on the government since possibly 1919, when these cases first arose. Perhaps it is as President Woodrow Wilson once said: "The best thing to do [with a fool] is to encourage him to advertise the fact by speaking. It cannot be so easily discovered if you allow him to remain silent and look wise, but if you let him speak, the secret is out and the world knows that he is a fool."

B. LIBEL AND SLANDER. The 1st Amendment, it is generally agreed, was never intended to give people the freedom to tell lies about others. A doctor's livelihood can be ruined if someone falsely says he knows nothing about medicine. A woman wrongly said to be "immoral" may quickly lose old friends and develop a collection of new and unwanted ones. People who have been falsely accused are allowed to sue their accusers and collect money damages for the wrongs. It doesn't matter whether time will prove the accuser wrong; the damage will already have been done. Even a criminal penalty imposed on someone for libeling an entire group of people, such as racial or religious minorities, is not unconstitutional.[9]

When in the heat of politics, however, a public official or a candidate is falsely accused of having done something wrong, the accuser *is* protected by the 1st Amendment.

In one recent case, *The New York Times* was sued for $500,000 for printing an ad paid for by a "Committee to defend Martin Luther King and the Struggle for Freedom in the South." Among other things it stated that police "ringed" the Alabama State College Campus, armed with shotguns and teargas. Police Commissioner Sullivan brought suit; he charged that the police did not "ring" the campus, although they were there; that the students did not sing the song which the advertisement had said they did, and so on. He also said that though the ad did not mention his name his reputation was injured because many people read the word "police" to mean him. He introduced no evidence to show whether his reputation suffered a $500,000 loss. The staff of *The New York*

Times did not check the statements in the advertisement for accuracy, not finding any reason to believe anything so stated was false. The Supreme Court reversed the state judgment. Criticism of *public officials,* the Court said, is protected by the 1st Amendment.[98]

The danger, of course, was that libel suits could be used to stop dissent in newspapers. The fact that the statements were false does not matter. If people knew that they could be sued for political libel, they would be wary of talking at all. Occasional misstatements of fact, or even frequent misstatements, do not lessen the need for constitutional protection. The Court noted that any number of lawsuits could be instituted against newspapers; the sheer cost of defending the suits would force the paper out of business. "Whether or not a newspaper can survive a succession of such judgments, the pall of fear and timidity imposed upon those who give voice to public criticism is an atmosphere in which the First Amendment freedoms cannot survive."

C. CENSORSHIP OF MORALS. The justification for outlawing publication of "obscene" books and pictures is not that otherwise a clear and present danger of a serious evil will be presented. The justification is, rather, that a serious evil will have already been done. Pornography cannot be counteracted by large dosages of wholesome reading, such as the works of Benjamin Franklin. Pornography disturbs the mind once it is read, and the mind stays harmed.

The trouble is that the line between what is worthy literature and what is trash is exceedingly difficult to draw. Literary works of both Mark Twain and Benjamin Franklin have been banned in some communities within recent decades on the grounds that they were obscene. From time to time such classics as Boccaccio's *Decameron,* Flaubert's *Madame Bovary,* Zola's *Nana* have been declared obscene, as have modern novels such as Joyce's *Ulysses* and Michener's *Tales of the South Pacific.* There have been hundreds of others. More than fiction has been outlawed: sex education books by reputable doctors have been removed from bookshelves by force of law. Even some eminent dictionaries have toppled.

Today, as far as the Constitution is concerned, these

books can freely be read. Laws which attempt to take them from bookstores or libraries are unconstitutional.

In 1957, the Supreme Court held that obscenity is not protected by the 1st Amendment. At the same time, the Court devised a test which makes the definition of obscenity narrow: "Whether to the average persons, applying contemporary community standards, the dominant theme of the material taken as a whole appeals to prurient interest." [121] In subsequent cases this test was taken to mean that three things must be shown: (1) the "dominant theme of the material taken as a whole appeals to a prurient interest in sex"; (2) "the material is patently offensive because it affronts contemporary community standards relating to the description or representation of sexual matters"; and (3) "the material is *utterly* without redeeming social value." [90]

This test has not made it any easier to decide what is obscene. A movie ("Lady Chatterly's Lover") advocating adultery "as a desirable, acceptable and proper pattern of behavior" was held *not* obscene. [74] "That adultery under certain circumstances may be proper behavior" is the advocacy of an idea. "The First Amendment's basic guarantee is of freedom to advocate ideas," said the Court.

Another time the Court struck down a law which forbade the showing of "The Miracle." The movie was the story of a young Italian goat tender who thought her baby had come from St. Joseph, as a miracle. A New York censor board said the movie ridiculed the story of Christ and was therefore "sacrilegious." The state court of appeals (New York's highest court) had said "no religion, as that word is understood by the ordinary, reasonable person, shall be treated with contempt, mockery, scorn, and ridicule." Answered the Supreme Court, reversing: "This is far from the kind of narrow exception to freedom of expression which a state may carve out to satisfy the adverse demands of other interests of society. . . . The censor is set adrift upon a boundless sea amid a myriad of conflicting currents of religious views, with no charts but those provided by the most vocal and powerful orthodoxies." [72]

Even a minimum amount of "social value" makes a book or movie acceptable. Some books which might otherwise be taken as obscene have final chapters which show that lust does not pay—a moral ending of redeeming social value. In one recent case, the publisher of *Eros Magazine* was convicted and sent to jail under a federal statute making it criminal to send obscene books and magazines through the mail. He advertised his magazine as "the result of recent court decisions that have realistically interpreted America's obscenity laws and that have given to this country a new breadth of freedom of expression . . . *Eros* takes full advantage of this new freedom of expression. It is *the* magazine of sexual candor." [51] The Court had difficulty determining whether the magazine was obscene, but because it was advertised as going *as far as* the law would allow, the Supreme Court ruled that since it "pandered" to prurient interest it was obscene and went *further* than the law allowed. In other words, in a close case, evidence that a publisher *advertises* a book in certain ways may be enough to stamp the book itself as unfit.

The 1st Amendment has not been fully clarified in this area. When a Justice of the Supreme Court can say, "Perhaps I could never succeed in intelligibly [defining 'hard-core pornography']. But I know it when I see it," it is clear that the Court is still struggling for a standard, trying to walk the fine line between having to decide each year whether or not hundreds of books are obscene (leaving no time for anything else) and having to let the really pornographic works go unpunished by default. It has been suggested by some who think that books, magazines and movies cannot be constitutionally censored that a law forbidding sale of pornography to minors would nevertheless be constitutional because it aims at protecting the young.

Freedom of Association, Assembly, and Petition

America is a nation of joiners. From the very beginning of the nation's history, groups of citizens have formed associations and organizations as diverse in nature as the purposes and values of man. Although the words "freedom of association" do not appear in the Constitution, the freedom has developed from the overlap between the guarantees of freedom of speech and freedom of assembly. Freedom of speech and assembly would not amount to much if people could not form associations to discuss their ideas, to plan political or economic or social action, to debate proposals, to pass resolutions, or to decide how to influence the organs of government.

1. Public Meetings and Demonstrations

The right to come together for meetings is fairly well defined. Mayor Hague could not deny union members the right to assemble on the streets, assuming their behavior was orderly, to discuss federally protected rights, assuming other groups were given the right to assemble also. Unlike the case of the sound trucks, which can be banned outright, an ordinance forbidding *all* groups from meeting in public parks and other public places in order to get at one disliked group would not be constitutional.

The right of association and assembly applies equally to peaceful meetings indoors as well as outdoors, regardless of the nature of the meeting's sponsor. In one case, Thomas, president of a national union, arrived in Houston, Texas, to address a mass meeting called by the Oil Workers Industrial Union for the purpose of forming a local union. Wide publicity had been given to the meeting, which was scheduled two days after Thomas' arrival. On the afternoon of the speech, Thomas was ordered by a Texas district court, on proceedings initiated by the Texas attorney general, to refrain from talking, on the grounds that he had not complied with a state law requiring all persons soliciting labor union membership to have a state license. Thomas went ahead with the speech, in which he discussed the court order and said that he had not intended to break any law, but convinced of the illegality of the court's order, he would test it by "earnestly ask[ing] those of you who are not now members of the Oil Workers International Union to join now. I solicit you to become a member of the union of your fellow workers and thereby join hands with labor throughout the country in all industries." He was arrested and convicted. The Supreme Court reversed.

The state argued it had an interest in protecting workers from imposters who pretended to be union organizers. Not objecting to this goal, the Supreme Court held that the state regulation went far beyond this purpose. "The assembly was entirely peaceable, and had no other than a wholly lawful purpose. The statements forbidden were not in themselves unlawful, had no tendency to incite to unlawful action, involved no element of clear and present, grave and immediate danger to the public welfare . . . The restraint is not small when it is considered what was restrained. The right is a national right, federally guaranteed. There is some modicum of freedom of thought, speech and assembly which all citizens of the Republic may exercise throughout its length and breadth, which no State, nor all together, nor the Nation itself, can prohibit, restrain or impede. If the restraint were smaller than it is, it is from petty tyrannies that large ones take root and grow. This fact can be no more plain than when they are imposed on the most basic rights of all. Seedlings planted in that soil grow great and growing, break down the foundations of liberty." Furthermore, "If one who solicits support for the cause of labor may be required to register as a condition to the exercise of his right to make a public speech, so may he who seeks to rally support for any social, business, religious, or political cause." [138]

Similarly, a person who helps conduct an entirely peaceful meeting, called under the auspices of the Communist Party, cannot be jailed under a law which forbids "criminal syndicalism" ("the doctrine which advocates crime, physical violence, sabotage or any unlawful acts or methods as a mean of accomplishing or effecting industrial or political change or revolution"). If the speakers at the meeting do not advocate unlawful conduct, the persons in attendance have a constitutionally protected right to be there. [28]

Meetings of a disorderly nature present more of a problem. People who agitate in public to incite immediate riot or violence do not have a constitutional right to be allowed to speak. [42] But meetings which are otherwise lawful, which become disorderly because of outside violence, may be entitled to constitutional protection.

Jesse Cantwell, a Jehovah's Witness, played phonograph records on the streets of New Haven, Connecticut, after asking permission of two passersby. The records attacked all organized religions and specifically the church of the two men, who happened to be Catholics. Cantwell was arrested on the grounds that he had incited others to breach of the peace. The two had threatened Cantwell with physical harm unless he took his records and departed, which he did. The Supreme Court reversed. Connecticut had not convicted Cantwell on the grounds that he was being noisy or making traffic conditions difficult. "We find only an effort to persuade a willing listener to buy a book or to contribute money in the interest of what Cantwell, however misguided others may think him, conceived to be true religion . . . To persuade others to his own point of view, the pleader, as we know, at times resorts to exaggeration, to vilification of men who have been or are, prominent in church or state, and even to false statement. But the people of this nation have ordained in the light of history that, in spite of the probability of excesses and abuses, these liberties are, in the long view, essential to enlightened opinion and right conduct on the part of the citizens of a democracy." [15]

This same principle applies to mass demonstrations. For instance, a leader of a march of more than 2,000 college students protesting segregation and discrimination in front of a Baton Rouge, Louisiana, courthouse was arrested in 1964. It was said that the demonstration, though peaceful, might have led to a breach of the peace. The Supreme Court reversed his conviction. "A function of free speech [and free association] under our system of government is to invite dispute. It may indeed best serve its high purpose when it induces a condition of unrest, creates dissatisfaction with conditions as they are, or even stirs people to anger. Speech is often provocative and challenging. It may strike at prejudices and preconceptions and have profound unsettling effects as it presses for acceptance of an idea. That is why freedom of speech . . . is protected against censorship or punishment." [24]

However, the legality of a mass demonstration will probably depend upon the particular circumstances of the case. The Supreme Court in 1967 ruled that a group of 200 students were legally convicted under a "malicious trespass" statute when they marched onto a Florida jail grounds to protest the jailing of other students and the state's policy of segregated cells. The students had gone onto the jail property and refused to leave when the sheriff gave them a ten-minute warning. The state, the Court held, has the right to "preserve property under its control." [176]

2. Disclosure of Membership Lists

Some states (principally southern) have required the National Association for the Advancement of Colored People (NAACP) to disclose its membership lists, sometimes on the ground that the membership lists would be helpful in determining whether the NAACP was "conducting intrastate business in violation of the Alabama foreign corporation registration statute"; sometimes on the ground that the lists were necessary in an investigation of "suspected Communists" in the group.[49]

In these cases, the Supreme Court has held that the association had a constitutional right to remain in the state and to keep its membership lists secret. No one denied that "on past occasions revelation of the identity of its rank-and-file members has exposed these members to economic reprisals, loss of employment, threat of physical coercion, and other manifestations of public hostility." [96] The Court recognized the "vital relationships between freedom to associate and privacy in one's associations."

3. Loyalty Oaths

At one time or another, many states have required teachers and other public employees to take loyalty oaths. A Washington State oath read as follows: "I solemnly swear (or affirm) that I will support the Constitution and laws of the United States of America and of the State of Washington, and will by precept and example promote respect for the flag and the institutions of the United States and the State of Washington, reverence for law and order and undivided allegiance to the government of the United States."

The oath seems harmless enough. The trouble is, many very honest citizens have in fact refused to take it. Although the state loyalty oath was passed to try to keep Communists off the government payroll, it has succeeded instead in forcing law-abiding citizens to refuse jobs as teachers. For though the person devoted to overthrowing the government by force and violence may falsely take the oath, citizens whom no one would suspect of being Communists have been wary of hidden meanings in the language of the oaths.

The language in the Washington oath is so broad, in fact, that the Supreme Court struck it down on the grounds that it violated the due process clause of the 14th Amendment because it was too *vague*. A law whose language is not helpful in determining what is prohibited is unconstitutional. The Washington oath called for the promotion of respect for American "institutions." But just what institutions? And what kind of respect? The Court pointed out that "the oath may prevent a professor from criticising his state judicial system or the Supreme Court or the institution of judicial review. Or it might be deemed to proscribe advocating the abolition, for example, of the Civil Rights Commission, the House Committee on un-American Activities, or foreign aid." Similarly, what is meant by "undivided allegiance to the government of the United States"? Can the person who takes this oath make any criticism of United States governmental policies without violating his oath? The Court could not tell. In what way must an individual support the Constitution? And what does "respect for the flag" mean? Can a person advocate changing its color? In short, the oath was so vague it could not stand.[5]

In 1967, the Supreme Court moved a long way toward abolishing loyalty oaths altogether. When the University of Buffalo became part of the publicly owned State University of New York, Keyishian, an instructor in English, and a number of other teachers were required to sign certificates (the so-called "Feinberg certificates") swearing that they were not subversives. Just before the trial in the case, New York rescinded the requirement of signing the certificate; the law provided that each teacher be notified of various sections of the New York Education Law, one of which made it unlawful to utter "seditious words."[174] It was unclear whether the advocacy of "criminal anarchy" (outlawed in the Penal Law and defined in part as the "public display" of books teaching the doctrine of violent overthrow of government was a seditious utterance. The Supreme Court struck down the law in *Keyishian v. Board of Regents*[174] as too vague; the Court denied the power of a state to condition public employment by imposing unreasonable restrictions, such as making teachers liable for dismissal and possible criminal penalties if they violated laws vaguely worded. Asked the Court: "Does the teacher who carries a copy of the *Communist Manifesto* on a public street thereby advocate criminal anarchy? It is no answer to say that the statute would not be applied in such a case. We cannot gainsay the potential effect of this obscure wording on 'those with a conscience and scrupulous regard for such undertaking.' " The dangers of the teaching of violent overthrow are outweighed by the concern for free speech and association. Said the Court, "But even the Feinberg Law provision [the New York law making illegal the advocacy of sedition], applicable primarily to activities of teachers, who have captive audiences of young minds, are subject to these limitations in favor of freedom of expression and association; the stifling effect on the academic mind from curtailing freedom of association in such manner is manifest, and has been documented in recent studies."

Most loyalty oaths now are unconstitutional, either because their words are too vague or because they are too broad (that is, they would require persons to be fired from jobs because they are members of organizations to which they have a constitutional right to belong). Only if the oath requires the person taking it to swear that he is not a knowing and active member of a group which has as an unlawful purpose the overthrow of government by force and violence *and* that he does not support this unlawful goal, is the oath at present constitutional. Thus, a member of the Communist Party cannot be kept off a state government payroll solely because he is a member, if he is not knowingly a member, or if he is not an active member, or if he does not support the Party's unlawful goals.

In an unusual case in 1967, the Supreme Court held unconstitutional the action of the Georgia State Legislature in refusing to seat a member because they disbelieved the oath to which he *did* subscribe. Julian Bond, a Negro elected to the legislature, was refused his seat because of his political opinions, which the Legislature took to be too radical. Doubting the sincerity of his oath, the legislature excluded him. Bond appealed to the Supreme Court which awarded him his seat on the grounds that the state cannot deny a duly elected representative his office because of his political views. This marked the first time the Supreme Court's writ ran to the individual composition of a state legislature.[179]

4. The Right to Petition

Centuries ago in England, people were imprisoned merely for petitioning the King or Parliament to ask for changes in the form of government or in the laws. To prevent citizens from being afraid to ask for change, the Constitution guarantees the right to petition the government for the redress of grievances. Even so, occasionally people have been jailed; in 1918, for instance, some who petitioned Congress to repeal the espionage and sedition laws were thrown into federal prison, but their cases were never tested in court on constitutional grounds.

Criticism of a state court's handling of a case still pending, by sending a strongly worded telegram to the Secretary of Labor, is protected. The court cannot hold the sender in contempt of court, as a California court once tried to do.[12]

Although the thousands of letters and telegrams that pour into the White House and Congressional offices every year are the traditional form of petitioning the government (direct communication between citizen and legislature or executive) another very widespread and powerful form of petitioning is lobbying. Long ago organizations and special interest groups discovered that it was more effective politically to have in Washington paid agents who will visit Senators and Congressmen with the intent of influencing legislation. The name derives from the fact that the agents used to wait for legislators in the lobbies of the legislative chambers. As lobbying grew, the secrecy surrounding meetings between lobbyists and legislators gave rise to abuses like bribery. In an effort to curb the abuses and put legitimate lobbying on a sound basis, federal and state laws regulating lobbying were passed.

These laws have been held not to conflict with the freedoms guaranteed by the 1st Amendment because they are reasonable regulations to curb what would otherwise be serious interference with the legislative process.

Nevertheless, in one case, Rumely, the secretary of a group called the Committee for Constitutional Government, was found guilty of refusing to give Congress the names of those who purchased books which his organization had sold. The law under which he was convicted provided penalties for refusal to provide Congress with relevant documents "upon any matter" under congressional investigation. The Supreme Court reversed his conviction on the narrow ground that the House committee which was investigating him had not been given the power by the full House of Representatives to exact such information. But the Court hinted that if "lobbying activities" which were subject to Congressional power to control included regulation of "attempts to saturate the thinking of the community," then the rule giving the committee power to require disclosure would be unconstitutional.[157]

8   Crime and Liberty

Amendments 2-6, 8

Amendment 2

A well-regulated Militia, being necessary to the security of a free State, the right of the people to keep and bear Arms, shall not be infringed.

After the Revolution, there was a fear that a large army might not be controllable unless each person was guaranteed the right to use weapons. Hence the 2d Amendment. In practice the military forces have been controlled by political processes; today, many fear danger to the public because firearms are easily bought and sold. Federal and state laws which reasonably regulate the sale and possession of weapons are constitutional.

Amendment 3

No Soldier shall, in time of peace be quartered in any house, without the consent of the Owner, nor in time of war, but in a manner to be prescribed by law.

British practice before the Revolution was to the contrary: many colonists were forced to board and feed British soldiers. At any rate, the language seems clear enough and cases interpreting it have never come to the Supreme Court.

Amendment 4

The right of the people to be secure in their persons, houses, papers, and effects, against unreasonable searches and seizures, shall not be violated, and no Warrants shall issue, but upon probable cause, supported by Oath or affirmation, and particularly describing the place to be searched, and the persons or things to be seized.

This amendment guarantees an individual his privacy against governmental invasion only; a private person who unlawfully breaks into someone's home does not violate the 4th Amendment.

Lawful Arrests and Searches "Upon Probable Cause"

Normally, police need an arrest or search warrant before arresting a particular person or searching his belongings. The police could not arrest an entire crowd and hope to find their suspect among the group of people; nor could they search a house in the hopes they might find incriminating evidence if they did not have a *reasonable* belief that the particular thing they were looking for might be there.

A warrant issued by a magistrate is necessary because in requiring the government to show that there is "probable cause" to suspect a person or place the police are prevented from indiscriminate arrest, search, and seizure. "Probable cause" to believe (i.e., a reasonable belief) that a person committed a crime or that a certain kind of evidence will be found in a specific place cannot exist just because the police *say* they have probable cause. A statement to the magistrate that "I have good reason to believe and do believe that X has stolen property in his possession" is not good enough. Something more than a conclusion is necessary; facts must be set forth to support the conclusion. Thus, "I overheard X say he took the jewels" or "Y, who has never before been wrong, called me up and told me that X has the jewels" would both be sufficient to demonstrate probable cause, and a warrant for arrest or search and seizure could lawfully be issued.

Police may search a person's room, or body, or house, even without a warrant, if the search is made immediately following a lawful arrest. But the police must have sufficient information to believe their suspect guilty of a crime, they must tell the suspect who they are and ask permission to enter his home. They can break in only if refused permission. In one case federal narcotics agents first picked up a suspected narcotics dealer who told them that Blackie Toy was his supplier. Four hours later (at 6 o'clock in the morning) an agent arrived at Toy's laundry without a warrant. He requested his laundry, but it was too early and Toy refused. The narcotics agent then pulled out his badge, quickly identified himself, broke down the door, and chased after Toy, who was running back into his bedroom. The Supreme Court held the arrest clearly unlawful. The information the police had obtained was far too vague to justify what the police did; the mere say-so of a person who had never before been an informer was not good enough for an arrest without warrant four hours later.[168] Normally, an arrest warrant must be issued by a magistrate. Only when a person is caught in the act of a crime, or fleeing from the scene of a crime he just committed, may he be arrested without one.

Use of Unlawful Evidence

It was decided as long ago as 1914 that in *federal courts* evidence obtained unlawfully by police could not be used in the trial, even if this meant letting the defendant go free.[162] This "exclusionary rule," as it is called, is justified on the grounds that otherwise the guarantees of the 4th Amendment would be paper words. Said the Court: "If letters and private documents can be seized and held and used in evidence against a citizen accused of an offense, the protection of the 4th Amendment declaring his right to be secure against such searches and seizures is of no value, and, so far as those thus placed are concerned, might as well be stricken from the Constitution." If the illegally seized evidence cannot be introduced at the trial to help the state prove its case, the police will have no reason to search and seize illegally.

Not only is illegally seized evidence excluded, but so also is "the fruit of the poisonous tree"; any further evidence to which the police were led by reason of having illegally seized the first evidence is excluded. This is a fairly sweeping prohibition. Even if the later evidence is lawfully obtained, with scrupulous regard for the suspect's right, it cannot be used if the police were led to it by an earlier illegal search or seizure. Often, this prohibition will necessitate dropping a case against someone clearly guilty. The 4th Amendment is aimed at protecting the privacy of the guilty as well as the innocent. But even if we did not care about a criminal's privacy, it is of course not known whether he is guilty until after a *trial* at which evidence is to be used. The 4th Amendment, and the other amendments in the Bill of Rights, are for the protection of the *suspect,* and this means for the innocent as well as the guilty.

For a long time, however, *state* courts were not required to exclude illegally seized evidence, even though it was recognized that state police who made unreasonable searches and seizures did not act according to the due process of law as required by the 14th Amendment. "The security of one's privacy against arbitrary intrusion by the police—which is at the core of the Fourth Amendment —is basic to a free society," said the Court in 1949.[167] But without requiring exclusion of evidence, unreasonable searches continued.

Then, in 1957, Ohio police tried to get into the home of Miss Dollree Mapp without a search warrant. She called her attorney who said that if they did not have a warrant, she could refuse to admit them. So she refused and the police broke in anyway. They had said that they were looking for a person to question about a bombing in the town, and they thought he might be hiding in Miss Mapp's home. They handcuffed her and proceeded to search the entire house. Not only did they look in places where a person would normally hide, they also checked drawers, closet shelves, and boxes, where a person could not hide. They found no one, but they did come across some pictures which they claimed were obscene. So Miss Mapp was hauled off on a charge of possessing "lewd and lascivious books and pictures," a crime. At the trial, no search warrant was ever produced, and Miss Mapp was found guilty.

By 1961, she had appealed her case to the Supreme Court. And that Court reversed the conviction. In 1949 more than two-thirds of the states refused to exclude illegal evidence; by 1961 more than one-half the states were finally forced to adopt such rules because nothing else worked. Emphasizing the fact that the states themselves had come to exclude illegally obtained evidence, the Court observed in *Mapp v. Ohio*, "Nothing can destroy a government more quickly than its failure to observe its own laws, or worse, its disregard of the charter of its own existence." Miss Mapp went free.[85]

Wiretapping

"Tapping" someone's telephone in order to listen in on the conversation was declared permissible in 1928.[103] Six years later Congress made it illegal in the Federal Communications Act of 1934. Wiretapping is now unlawful whether done by private person, state police, or federal agent. Divulgence of remarks made during the conversation are excludable from evidence, unless one of the parties to the conversation consents.

The development of sophisticated means of electronic eavesdropping has led to serious legal problems. Today telephones can be made to transmit sounds even when on the hook. "Parabolic microphones" can pick up a discussion in an office across a busy street one hundred feet wide. The Federal Communications act does not apply to many of these devices, and so it may well be legal to listen in, uninvited, on anyone's private conversation. (This does not necessarily mean that a tape recording made with a parabolic microphone can be used at a trial; the privilege against self-incrimination might well be broad enough to require excluding such recordings.)

In a significant 1967 decision, the Supreme Court took

a step forward in the control of "bugging" devices. The police in New York under that state's "trespassory eavesdropping" statute had planted a microphone in the defendant's home and secured a conviction on the basis of evidence gathered by the microphone. The Court struck down the conviction, holding that the evidence should not have been admitted since the police had not obtained from the proper judicial authority a warrant specifying what was to be overheard.[178]

The Silver Platter

Until 1960, it had been thought that if state police stumble onto evidence that someone committed a *federal* crime while they were searching illegally for evidence that he committed a *state* crime, the evidence could be used in a federal trial. Since the federal authorities did not participate in the illegal search the evidence was said to be handed to them on a "silver platter." The Supreme Court tarnished the platter in 1960,[33] and the trick doesn't work anymore. (It doesn't work in reverse, either.)

Where the 4th and 5th Amendments Run into Each Other

Rochin was a dope peddler, who one morning in 1949 happened to have two capsules of narcotics lying on his night table. Three Los Angeles deputy sheriffs broke into his room, and during a struggle, Rochin swallowed the capsules. The police tried to pry his mouth open; being unsuccessful, they took him to a hospital and on the directions of one of the policemen, a doctor gave him a chemical to induce vomiting. It worked: among the contents of Rochin's stomach two capsules of morphine were found. On the basis of this evidence, Rochin was sentenced to sixty days imprisonment. The California Supreme Court denied a hearing. Two California justices dissented, saying that they thought such action by the police was close enough to coercing a confession (unconstitutional under the privilege against self-incrimination) to require excluding the evidence. "We find no valid ground of distinction between a verbal confession extracted by physical abuse and a confession wrested from defendant's body by physical abuse," the dissenters said.

Rochin appealed to the Supreme Court and found a more receptive audience. His conviction was upset, but on a different ground. "This is conduct that shocks the conscience," said Mr. Justice Frankfurter for the Court. "Illegally breaking into the privacy of the petitioner, the struggle to open his mouth and remove what was there, the forcible extraction of his stomach's contents—this course of proceedings by agents of government to obtain evidence is bound to offend even hardened sensibilities. They are methods too close to the rack and the screw to permit of constitutional differentiation." [118]

Amendment 5

No person shall be held to answer for a capital, or otherwise infamous crime, unless on a presentment or indictment of a Grand Jury, except in cases arising in the land or naval forces, or in the Militia, when in actual service in time of War or public danger;

The Grand Jury Clause

A grand jury is ordinarily composed of twenty-three members, sitting either for the purpose of investigating a particular person suspected of a crime, or for the purpose of investigating law-breaking in a particular area over a long period of time. The grand jury hands down an "indictment" or charge against a particular person when it is satisfied that there is probable cause to believe the person guilty. Rules of evidence before the grand jury are different from those during a regular trial, and the grand jury can hear evidence which might be excluded during trial. The grand jury's decision is by majority vote. If the grand jury fails to "return an indictment" against the suspect, he must be released if held in custody. The grand jury is considered a safeguard against moving too fast against someone suspected of a crime; two different juries passing on different questions must be convinced. Many consider the grand jury a nuisance, on the assumption that adequate safeguards surround the actual trial. Consequently, the grand jury has never been constitutionally required in *state* proceedings.[68] Many states, by virtue of their own constitutions, have grand juries, but others have abolished them, relying on an examination by a magistrate of the "probable cause" to hold a suspect.

Crimes punishable by fines of more than $1,000 or more than six months in jail, even if in a given case a lighter sentence is given, require indictment by a grand jury under the 5th Amendment. Members of the military forces—Army, Navy, Air Force, Marines, and Coast Guard—are not entitled to the civil grand jury. They are tried by court-martial proceedings. (The exception, "when in actual service in time of war or public danger," applies only to the militia; otherwise militiamen are entitled to 5th Amendment provisions.)

Amendment 5 (continued)

nor shall any person be subject for the same offense to be twice put in jeopardy of life or limb;

The Double Jeopardy Clause

A government, angry enough to go to the trouble, could continue to harass a person after he had been acquitted of a crime by trying him again and again. Moreover, should the government continue to prosecute, certainty of guilt or innocence would never be achieved, nor would respect for the judicial system be promoted. The double jeopardy clause stops a second trial whenever the defendant is acquitted, whether by jury or by a directed verdict. The government cannot appeal an acquittal. Whenever a jury says "not guilty" the defendant must be released. The clause also prohibits the government from retrying and resentencing a person who has already been found guilty and served his term.

Because state constitutions also provide against simple double jeopardy, few state cases have come to the Supreme Court. Complex problems have come up, however, and so far the full scope of the double jeopardy clause in the 5th Amendment has not been ruled applicable to the states.

For instance, in 1937 a man named Palko was indicted for first-degree murder in Connecticut, but the jury found him guilty of second-degree murder, and he was sentenced to life imprisonment. The state appealed the case on the grounds that there had been error in the trial court which had hurt the state's case. The second trial resulted in a conviction of murder in the first degree and the death sentence. The Supreme Court ruled that the outcome in the second case did not "shock the conscience" and consequently was not against due process. The death sentence stood.[105] So far, at least, this interpretation of double jeopardy has not been overruled.

Occasionally, a person will, by the same act, violate the laws of both the state and nation, as for instance, when someone robs a federally insured savings bank. It has been held that the federal government can try the suspect for the federal crime, even if a state jury has found him not guilty of the same act (made criminal by state law).[7] Similarly, a state may prosecute and impose an additional sentence on someone found guilty in a federal court.[1] This weird circumstance results because a federal system gives both federal and state sovereignties the power to protect identical interests.

Amendment 5 (continued)

nor shall be compelled in any criminal case to be a witness against himself;

"Pleading the 5th"

This clause finds roots in the fear of the inquisitorial methods employed by church courts four and five centuries ago. Confessions might well be false if they are beaten out of accused persons.

In any hearing in which testimony is required by law, a witness may refuse to answer any question, if the answer might tend to incriminate him in that proceeding or any future criminal proceeding. Although theoretically the witness is not the final judge of whether the answer *would in fact* tend to incriminate him, in practice he is. A mistake by a judge on that point may mean ultimately that the witness or defendant would go free, since the statement and all evidence that sprang from it might be excluded at the trial. Although the privilege against self-incrimination exists only for the benefit of the witness and is not to be used as a cover to protect other persons, in practice the witness is usually the final judge.

A person may refuse to answer questions in a state proceeding if there is a possibility of a later federal prosecution, and vice versa. However, if the state and federal governments grant the witness immunity from prosecution —that is, if they promise they will not prosecute him for any possible crimes which come to light as the result of his testimony—then the witness cannot refuse to testify. Once immunity is granted, he must testify even if he then is in danger of assassination by members of his gang for breaking his oath of silence. If he does refuse, he can be jailed for contempt of court; ordinarily, of course, nothing whatsoever can be done to a person who refuses to testify.

The problem of self-incrimination runs deeper than refusal to talk at trial or before a committee hearing. The privilege extends all the way to the first questioning of a suspect. What constitutes a coerced confession is a serious problem. Physical beating—the "third degree"—is obvious enough, and it still happens in some communities. But what about the confession signed after the police chief threatened that he would bring in the suspect's wife for questioning, when he had no intention of doing so? [119] What about the suspect who confessed while he was in the hospital under the influence of drugs and in severe pain, having just been shot in the liver? [71] Both confessions, said the Supreme Court, were coerced. The truth of the confession is irrelevant. There are so many ways in which "the defendant's will [can be] overborne" to induce a confession that in 1966 the Supreme Court laid down a series of guidelines for the police.

In *Miranda v. Arizona* a suspect was put in a special interrogation room, cut off from the outside world. He was never told that he had a right to remain silent and that he had the right to have a lawyer present to advise him during the interrogation. After questioning for two hours, Miranda signed a confession that he had committed the crime.

The Court tossed the confession out, and laid down a

series of procedures which the police must follow if confessions are to be allowed as evidence. The suspect must be given a full and *effective* warning of his rights. Unless the police can show that the suspect understood that he could keep quiet and that anything he said could be used against him, his confession must be excluded. The police must also advise him of his right to a lawyer and must tell him that if he cannot afford counsel they will have a lawyer appointed for him if he wants one.

Many police departments have bitterly criticized the *Miranda* case. Confessions, they say, are vital in obtaining convictions—*Miranda* will cause a cut in the number of confessions obtained and will raise the crime rate. Others do not agree that guaranteeing rights to suspects will have any bearing on how much crime is committed. David C. Acheson, special Assistant to the Secretary of the Treasury (Enforcement) and in charge of the Secret Service and Federal Bureau of Narcotics, has commented that "changes in court decisions and prosecution procedures have about the same effect on the crime rate as an aspirin would have on a tumor of the brain."

Another aspect of the privilege against self-incrimination occurs when a defendant refuses to testify at his trial. A natural inference perhaps is that the defendant has something to hide and is probably guilty. This is not true. The reason a defendant does not take the stand, usually, is because only if he does take the stand can information as to his past conduct be mentioned. A person with a *past* criminal record—though it does not say anything about whether the defendant committed the *present* crime— does make him look less trustworthy to the jury. Often prosecutors pointed out to the jury that the defendant did not take the stand and that that is suspicious conduct for a man who says he isn't guilty. The Supreme Court has ruled that such a comment is illegal under the privilege against self-incrimination, whether in state or federal court.[55]

Amendment 5 (continued)

nor be deprived of life, liberty, or property, without due process of law;

The Due Process Clause in Criminal Proceedings

The due process clauses of both the 5th and 14th Amendments forbid many governmental acts not specifically banned by the Bill of Rights. The accused has a right to be present at his trial and to have an unbiased judge. An Ohio statute once provided that the mayors of villages should be judges at trials concerned with violation of the liquor laws and that the mayor would receive a certain amount of the fine if the defendant was found guilty. Because of his obvious self-interest, such a judge cannot be unbiased, the Supreme Court ruled, and the law is invalid under the due process clause of the 14th Amendment.[143]

A statute which is vague is invalid. Many scores of state and federal statutes have been struck down because "void for vagueness." A conviction for a crime other than stated in the indictment is also void.

A legislative committee which has been authorized to conduct an investigation cannot ask questions unrelated to that investigation, as is sometimes done for the purpose of exposing the witness to social pressure and public ridicule.

The police cannot trick a person into committing a crime. If the police suggest a person commit a crime by bribing him, or tempting him in some other manner, a subsequent prosecution will fail. "Entrapment" is contrary to the due process of law.

Convictions based on perjured testimony, which the prosecutor knew to be false at the time of the trial but made no effort to have excluded, are unlawful.

A prisoner must be free from interference by prison officials in petitioning for habeas corpus.

A verdict of guilty at a trial at which no evidence was produced to support the finding violates due process.

In a sweeping 1967 decision the Supreme Court declared unconstitutional the procedures which most states had used for more than half a century in juvenile courts. Under the theory that a juvenile proceeding was not a criminal hearing (rather that the court was the protector of the youngster in trouble), thousands of juveniles had never received the right against self-incrimination, the right to counsel, to confrontation with witnesses, and many other rights which are (at least recently) taken for granted in regular criminal trials. When a 15-year-old Arizona lad was sentenced to a reformatory until he was 21 for making a lewd telephone call (the maximum sentence had this been a criminal trial was 2 months) he appealed and the Supreme Court reversed; from now on juvenile proceedings will require all the rights and protections accorded defendants at regular criminal trials.[180]

Many times people have been convicted under laws making criminal an act which they had no reasonable notice to know existed. This does not mean that in the usual case ignorance of the law is an excuse; it is not. But when a city passes an ordinance making it a crime for a person to remain longer than five days without registering with the police if he has committed a felony, a conviction for failure to register is a violation of due process if he had no way of knowing about the regulation and had been given no opportunity to comply.[79]

The Due Process Clause in Civil Proceedings

(See the 14th Amendment, p. 210.)

Amendment 5 (continued)
nor shall private property be taken for public use, without just compensation. (See the 14th Amendment, p. 207).

Amendment 6
In all criminal prosecutions, the accused shall enjoy the right to a speedy and public trial, by an impartial jury of the State and district wherein the crime shall have been committed, which district shall have been previously ascertained by law,

Criminal Prosecutions

Not all cases involving penalties are criminal cases. A person required to pay fifty dollars for an infraction of the revenue laws is not constitutionally entitled to 6th Amendment rights because the penalty is considered very minor. This does not mean he will not get a jury, for instance, but only that it would not be constitutional if he did not. For historical reasons, deportation proceedings and prosecutions for contempt of court for refusal to obey court injunctions are not classified as criminal cases even though the penalties are serious. Generally, however, all offenses of a serious nature, especially those involving moral fault, are entitled to the protection of this amendment.

Speedy and Public Trial

This clause has not been extensively dealt with by the courts. Delays in criminal proceedings are more than possible: they are a practical necessity. Many court calendars are crowded. To dismiss indictments against defendants because their trial has not begun within a short time period, like one week, one month, or even one year, would necessitate letting free many persons who are now awaiting trial. Nevertheless, the trial cannot be delayed indefinitely. An indictment, first issued in 1949, four years after the crime was supposed to have been committed, was finally dismissed by the Supreme Court in 1955. At that time, the trial had not begun and the defendant was still in jail and not allowed to find and interview witnesses.[156] The right to speedy trials applies to state as well as federal trials.

Except in certain aspects of cases involving national security, the defendant has a right to have the public attend. It is primarily the defendant's right; noisy or unruly members of the public can be removed from the courtroom.

Trial by Impartial Jury

In federal courts, the right to trial by an impartial jury includes all the rights which existed in the United States when the Constitution was written. The old English tradition sits with us still in this regard: the jury must consist of twelve persons, there must be a judge who has the power to instruct the jurors on what they are to do, and the jury verdict must be unanimous. The defendant may agree to less than twelve people or to a less than unanimous verdict, but that is his choice, not the United States Government's.

The 6th Amendment does NOT require jury trials in *state* courts, however. Although most state constitutions provide for jury trials in most cases, the jury can be abolished together or be composed of less than twelve men or need not have a unanimous verdict as far as the Constitution is concerned. A jury trial is not an element of due process or fair procedure.

But where a jury does sit, whether in state or federal courts, it must be impartial. Persons prejudiced against the defendant cannot be allowed to sit on the jury. In recent years, the Supreme Court has required that some verdicts be reversed and new trials begun, because newspaper stories and editorials concerning the case had heated up the population to such a frenzy that a fair trial in the location of the newspaper's circulation would have been impossible.

In one case, for instance, a television "interview" with a defendant in a murder trial was made with the active cooperation of the police department and broadcast on three different occasions within three days. More than 95,000 people in a community of 150,000 were estimated to have seen it. Three of the jurors had seen it, and two other jurors were deputy sheriffs of the Louisiana parish in which the crime happened. The Supreme Court reversed the verdict of guilty and ordered a new trial in another parish, where jurors would not have been exposed to the TV publicity.[116] What evidence the jury should hear and what should be excluded is a decision for the judge, not for a newspaper or TV. Where the judge is thwarted, the verdict falls.

In a more recent case, the prejudicing of the jury was even more blatant. Dr. Sam Sheppard was convicted in Cleveland in 1954 for the second-degree murder of his wife, who was found bludgeoned to death in their bedroom on July 4 of that year. Almost from the start of the investigation, newspapers—with bold headlines and editorials—stirred up the community. The county coroner called an inquest; Sheppard was subpoenaed and was searched and questioned in the view of several hundred spectators in a school gymnasium. From July 7 until July 30, while the police resisted arresting him, newspaper commentary was fiery. Stories proclaimed evidence existed which contradicted Sheppard's statements (but none was produced at the trial). On July 30, a front-page editorial screamed: "Why Isn't Sam Sheppard In Jail?" and was later titled, "Quit Stalling—Bring Him In." He was arrested that day. Not only did the papers attack Sheppard, but they ridiculed his lawyers' conduct of the case, and asked the local bar association to do something about the attorneys' attempts to change venue. A newspaper quoted a police detective calling Sheppard a "bare-faced liar," but the detective never appeared in court to testify. Indeed, much of the newspaper "evidence" would have been inadmissible in court—much of it was said to have been "leaked" to the press by the prosecution. Headlines continued: it took five volumes to hold the clippings of stories which accused Sheppard until his eventual conviction in December, 1954.

The trial judge did not improve the situation. Newspapermen were allowed the run of the courtroom—everytime the jury entered or left it was surrounded. The jury was allowed to make outside telephone calls. Reporters were allowed inside the bar, a few feet from the jury box —a space always reserved to the privacy of lawyers.

The trial itself began two weeks before a "hotly contested" election for a judgeship in which both the Chief Prosecutor and the trial judge were candidates. The judge refused to delay the trial until after the election.

It was too much. Said the Supreme Court, when it finally reviewed the case in 1966, 12 years after the conviction: "Indeed, every court that has considered this case, save the court that tried it, has deplored the manner in which the news media inflamed and prejudiced the public." [175] The Court's attack was directed not at the newspapers, however. The 1st Amendment's guarantees are not to be discarded. Noting the "carnival atmosphere at trial" and the judge's failure to control the courtroom and to curtail what publicity he could (for instance, out-of-court statements by court officials, lawyers, parties, witnesses), the Court reversed and ordered a new trial. After 10 years in prison, Sheppard was freed; at the new trial in the fall of 1966, under strict court control, he was acquitted.

Since the 1st Amendment forbids courts from attempting to silence newspaper, television, or radio commentary on trials, the issue of "fair trial vs. free press" is a complex one. What happens when the entire nation sees or reads about a crime? Could Lee Harvey Oswald have received a fair trial for the assassination of President John F. Kennedy?

Juries may be biased against the defendant in ways other than pure, personal prejudice. An angry mob may frighten a jury into rendering a verdict of guilty.[93] In a state where a pattern of racial discrimination persists in the selection of juries, so that Negroes are systematically excluded, the jury may be prejudiced against a Negro defendant on racial grounds. In both instances, the defendant's constitutional right to an impartial jury has been infringed.

Televising trials of felonies (such as murder, robbery, kidnapping, or embezzlement) also violates the Constitution. Even if no actual proof of harm is shown, the danger that the judge, jury, witnesses, and lawyers will act for the cameras and pay less attention to their duties is too great to permit cameras in the courtroom.[35]

Place of Trial

The defendant has the right to a "jury of the State and district wherein the crime shall have been committed." The boundaries of the district cannot be determined after the crime has been committed; they must be set forth beforehand by law. (The districts are usually counties.) But the government does not have the same right, and a person who thinks his trial will be jeopardized because of newspaper or TV publicity may ask for a "change of venue," a trial in another district in the state.

Amendment 6 (continued)
and to be informed of the nature and cause of the accusation;

Nature and Cause of Accusation

The defendant must be told of the charges against him, and the law which makes his act criminal must spell out exactly what is prohibited. To make it illegal "to make any unjust or unreasonable rate or charge in handling or dealing in or with any necessaries" is to put too heavy a burden on the defendant. Without a standard of what is unjust or unreasonable, it is difficult to prepare a defense. Also, the law borders on the ex post facto, since it is impossible to know before a court says so that any given rate is unjust.[148]

A defendant cannot be convicted of a crime which is different from that with which the grand jury has charged him in its indictment. A verdict for second-degree murder is valid even if the indictment charged first-degree murder, since it is a lesser related (or "included") crime. But a verdict of first-degree murder would not be valid against an indictment for second-degree murder.

Under this clause, an act can only be made a federal crime if Congress has passed a statute declaring it so. Judges do not have the power, as they once did in England, to declare and punish "common law crimes." Thus, a prosecutor must cite a statute which makes the act illegal; he cannot go to court, tell the judge that the act ought to be illegal, and let the judge decide whether it is. Since the common law exists only in the states, it is not open to a federal court to create a common law of crimes.[152] Whether a state prosecution for a crime not made punishable by statute would be invalid has not been clearly decided. Certainly if there is no statute prescribing the sentence for the act, it cannot be the basis for even a state prosecution.

Amendment 6 (continued)

to be confronted with the witnesses against him; to have compulsory process for obtaining witnesses in his favor,

Confrontation with the Witness

There are many exceptions to the right to challenge and cross-examine witnesses who testify against the defendant. This part of the 6th Amendment merely put in writing what had been recognized as a right in 1787; exceptions to the rule then are pretty much still exceptions now. For instance, a statement which a dying person makes can be introduced at the trial even though he obviously cannot be there. A person does not have the right to get the names of witnesses who testified against him at a grand jury.

It has been held that the reports of undercover agents, such as those who work for the FBI, can be introduced before administrative hearings (such as the Civil Service Commission) to determine the loyalty of the employee, without the informer's appearance in court. Once his identity is known his usefulness as a secret agent is destroyed. Cases like these arose during the early 1950's and were decided partly on the ground that since no one has a constitutional right to a government job, it was not a criminal punishment to dismiss a worker from his job following an administrative hearing in which the employee could not challenge his accusers. Nevertheless, since anything can be marked "secrecy necessary because national security requires it," the Supreme Court has found ways to overrule dismissals in which there was no right of cross-examination, though not on 6th Amendment grounds.

It is clear that if the witness appears in court, whether federal or state, the defendant or his attorney has an absolute right to question the witness and challenge his statements.

Compulsory Process Clause

This clause means, simply, that the government must make sure that the people whom a criminal defendant says will be helpful to him as witnesses will show up in court for the trial. The government can issue subpoenas, and people who refuse to come can themselves be convicted of a crime.

Amendment 6 (continued)
and to have the Assistance of Counsel for his defence.

Right to Counsel

Common law courts in England refused to let a person accused of a felony have a defense lawyer, even if he was willing and able to pay for his own private counsel. The original purpose of this clause was to reverse this rule.

Today, the "right to counsel" has been immeasurably broadened. Not only must a court let a person have his own lawyer, but every court—state or federal—must supply a defense attorney at state expense if the defendant is indigent or too poor to afford a lawyer.

The incorporation of the "right to counsel" clause in the due process clause in order to make it applicable to the states happened in three stages. In 1932, the Supreme Court ruled that in all cases involving the death penalty, a lawyer was absolutely necessary to insure that the rights of the defendant would be protected. If the defendant could not afford a lawyer, the state was told to assign counsel even if not requested by the defendant.[111]

Ten years later, the Supreme Court ruled that although it was not necessary to provide counsel in every criminal case, there might be cases in which "special circumstances" would make a lawyer essential to a fair trial.[10] "Special circumstances" include age, knowledge, and intelligence of the defendant. Very rarely in the next twenty-one years did the Supreme Court decide a case in which a "special circumstance" was not present.

Finally, in the landmark case of *Gideon v. Wainwright* in 1963, the Court ruled by a 9-0 vote that all indigent criminal defendants are entitled to lawyers at trial. Gideon had been convicted of a felony in a Florida state court. At the trial he asked for a lawyer, but the trial judge denied his request. From his jail cell, Gideon penciled a letter to the Supreme Court, asking for review of his case. The Court agreed and asked Abe Fortas (who was two years later appointed to the Supreme Court) to argue the case on Gideon's behalf. The attorney general of Florida asked the other attorneys general to file briefs with the court in opposition to Gideon. Instead, twenty-two states filed briefs siding with Gideon, and only three states went along with Florida's view that lawyers were not necessary.[50]

Said Mr. Justice Black for the Court: "Reason and reflection require us to recognize that in our adversary system of criminal justice, any person haled into court, who is too poor to hire a lawyer, cannot be assured a fair trial unless counsel is provided for him. This seems to be an obvious truth. Governments, both state and federal, quite properly spend vast sums of money to establish machinery to try defendants accused of crime. Lawyers to prosecute are everywhere deemed essential to protect the public's interest in an orderly society. Similarly, there are few defendants charged with crime, few indeed, who fail to hire the best lawyers they can get to prepare and present their defenses. That government hires lawyers to prosecute and defendants who have the money hire lawyers to defend are the strongest indications of the widespread belief that lawyers in criminal courts are necessities, not luxuries."

Gideon's case had a storybook ending. The Supreme Court ordered a new trial. This time, Gideon's defense attorney was quickly able to prove Gideon's innocence. Gideon had had to wait in jail; his attorney spent three days before the trial investigating. Gideon had not known how to conduct a cross-examination; his attorney did.

As a result of *Gideon v. Wainwright,* thousands of prisoners throughout the country sought new trials, and they got them. The ruling in the Gideon case was held to be retroactive: it extended even to people who had been convicted and exhausted their final appeals before the *Gideon* case arose. Some of these prisoners were freed altogether because their trials had taken place so long ago that none of the evidence or witnesses was available for a new trial.

Contrast with *Gideon* the result in *Mapp,* the illegally seized evidence case (p. 171). Prisoners were not allowed to go free if their convictions were final before *Mapp* was decided, even if evidence in their cases was admittedly seized unconstitutionally. Why the difference? Because the *Mapp* decision that evidence illegally seized should be excluded is a way to make the police obey the Constitution, not a decision that the evidence used tended to cast doubt on the correctness of the verdict. In *Gideon,* the absence of counsel does lessen the chance that the verdict was right. So everyone gets a new chance, whether conviction was final or not.

Even with the new deal given indigent defendants, the right to counsel clause is not exhausted. In the same *Mi-*

randa case which said that confessions were not valid unless the police advised the suspects of their right against self-incrimination (see p. 176), it was also decided that the suspect has the right to counsel even at the station house. If the suspect demands a lawyer upon being picked up in the middle of the street, the police must bring him in without questioning until a lawyer is secured. If the suspect says he is willing to forego his rights, he may certainly talk and the statements can certainly be used. But the hard problem still remains: how does the judge know whether the police gave the suspect *effective* advice?

Amendment 8
Excessive bail shall not be required, nor excessive fines imposed,

Bail and Fines

How much bail is excessive? No one really knows. Bail is money which a defendant must pay to the court if he wants to be released from jail before the trial begins. Failure to appear for trial means loss of the money. If $50,000 bail would be sufficient to guarantee that a defendant would show up at trial, then $100,000 bail in the same case would be excessive. But how can the judge tell whether $50,000 is sufficient? Since he usually cannot, there have rarely been cases in which the amount of bail was reduced by a higher court. Bail is not constitutionally required. The judge can refuse to set an amount at all if he thinks that the prisoner will "jump bail" and not show up for trial no matter what amount is fixed. But the decision must be made solely with regard to how much is necessary to insure that the defendant will be at trial. A decision to raise the price of bail because the defendant is supposedly dangerous is unconstitutional.

Excessive fines impose the same problem. Appellate courts do not have the power to review sentences; and the Supreme Court has rarely reduced the amount of a fine.

Neither of these provisions of the 8th Amendment apply to state court proceedings.

nor cruel and unusual punishments inflicted.

Cruel and Unusual Punishment

These words, like "necessary and proper" or "clear and present," are not considered independently of each other. They have become a formula. The Court "must draw meaning [of the clause] from the evolving standards of decency that mark the progress of a maturing society." The basic concept of the clause "is nothing less than the dignity of man." [141]

Until recently, the clause has not received much attention. In 1958, a soldier who had been court-martialed because he deserted the armed forces in time of war was to lose his citizenship as punishment. The Court reversed, saying that the penalty was "more primitive than torture," since it makes the person "stateless" and leads to "the total destruction of the individual's status in organized society." [141]

And until even more recently, the 8th Amendment had never been applied to the states. An 1890 case hinted that a state could not punish by "torture or a lingering death, such as burning at the stake, crucifixion, breaking on the wheel, and the like." [40] But the use of the electric chair is not one of these. When an electric chair failed to work on the first try, the prisoner made an unsuccessful appeal to the Supreme Court that another attempt would be cruel and unusual punishment.[44]

Finally, in 1962, the 8th Amendment was made applicable to the states. A California law made narcotics addiction a crime, punishable by a jail sentence, even if the addict had become addicted in another state and did not use, purchase, or possess narcotics in California. The Supreme Court pointed out that addiction as such is a disease, and that the state could not punish a person for addiction any more than it could put someone in jail for having leprosy. Punishment for disease is cruel and unusual.[117] The Court pointed out, however, that the fact that the state cannot *punish* does not mean that it cannot require the addict to be sent to a hospital to be cured. Infectious diseases which can spread rapidly in epidemic form, as well as diseases such as addiction which may cause the person to commit crime in order to get more narcotics, are not beyond the power of the states to deal with.

9   Rights Galore

Amendments 7, 9, 10

Amendment 7

In Suits at common law, where the value in controversy shall exceed twenty dollars, the right of trial by jury shall be preserved, and no fact tried by a jury, shall be otherwise re-examined in any Court of the United States, than according to the rules of the common law.

The 7th Amendment, which applies only to the federal government, did not introduce any novel ideas into American law. The English common law courts had twelve-member juries for civil cases as well as criminal cases, and this amendment sought only to preserve that right.

The right is a limited one. *Equity* courts and *admiralty* courts did NOT have jury trials. Whenever someone sued for an injunction, for instance, or claimed a breach of a maritime contract, the judge alone, and not a jury, would decide both the facts and the law.

This is still true today. Whenever a case comes up which in the old days would have had to go to a court of equity or admiralty, neither the plaintiff nor defendant is entitled to a jury trial. Although Congress *could* by law institute jury trials in these kinds of cases, it has not. So even though federal courts deal with common law, equity, and admiralty cases by the same procedures, only in the first type are jury trials required.

Sometimes the same case will involve both "legal" issues and "equitable" issues. Is a jury required or can it be dispensed with? The Supreme Court has recently ruled that the facts involved in the common law aspect of the case must first be tried to a jury; if there are any facts left over the judge can decide them.[8]

Central to the right of the jury trial is the requirement that the jury be composed of twelve people and that their verdict be unanimous. The jury must first resolve the disputed questions of fact (e.g., was the defendant negligent in the automobile accident? what was the intention of the person who signed the contract?) and then apply the law to the facts to reach a verdict. The judge must instruct the jurors as to how to go about deciding the questions of fact and how to apply the law. The meaning of the law is for the judge to decide.

The common law has a body of rules concerning what circumstances make it appropriate for an appellate court to review the jury's decision as to the facts in the case. Generally, appellate courts are not free to question the jury's findings but must accept them as indisputable facts. The Supreme Court usually must accept the facts as found, whether the case is from the state or federal courts, and must decide only whether the law was correctly interpreted, whether evidence was properly admitted, whether the judge properly instructed the jury, and any other legal points which counsel might have objected to in the lower court.

Although the Constitution does not require the states to follow these rules, many states do. This is not surprising, since the judicial systems of the states spring from the same traditions which gave birth to the federal judicial system.

Amendment 9

The enumeration in the Constitution, of certain rights, shall not be construed to deny or disparage others retained by the people.

It was feared that courts might infer that any rights NOT spelled out were not guaranteed. "If they listed the freedom of speech and all the others, why didn't they list the right to cook roast beef in the home?" went the argument. To avoid having to list every right which the people should enjoy (and to avoid the possibility that hundreds of rights would be missed), the 9th Amendment provides that even though not named in the Bill of Rights or Constitution, the people nevertheless enjoy these rights.

For 156 years, the Supreme Court never had occasion to find any rights which the government was trying to restrict protected by this amendment. Restrictions had always been knocked down (when they were found unlawful) by reference to other provisions. Then in 1947 in connection with the Hatch Act case (prohibition against federal employees from engaging in certain political activities, see p. 95), the Court acknowledged that the right to participate in politics was protected by the 9th Amendment, but concluded that the Congressional regulation was reasonable. Political activities are linked closely enough to the 1st Amendment that the Court's reference to the 9th Amendment might not have been significant.

The Court seemed to be taking a new look at the 9th Amendment in 1965, however. Connecticut had a statute on its books making it illegal for married couples to use contraceptive devices for birth control. A doctor and one of the directors of the Planned Parenthood League were convicted as accessories and fined for giving advice. The Supreme Court reversed the convictions and struck down the "anti-use" law.[58] For a number of reasons, the statute was said to be unconstitutional, but significantly, five Justices thought that the "right of privacy" had an important bearing on the case. A law making birth control illegal could only be policed by a drastic invasion of a married couple's privacy. The right of privacy, the majority thought, was protected by the 9th Amendment. Even more significant, this was not federal but state law, and the 9th Amendment, therefore, seems to extend to the states also, by being incorporated in the due process clause of the 14th Amendment.

Amendment 10

The powers not delegated to the United States by the Constitution, nor prohibited by it to the States, are reserved to the States respectively, or to the people.

The 10th Amendment was originally thought to be a statement of the obvious. If the branches of the federal government are not given certain powers, and if the Constitution does not prohibit the states from exercising these powers, then the states or the people alone can exercise them.

The amendment was not supposed to limit the powers of Congress, the President, or the courts. Nevertheless, for more than a century, the Supreme Court often interpreted the 10th Amendment as cutting down the power of Congress when it interfered with state law. Usually the cases concerned Congress' interstate commerce power. For instance, a law which prohibited the sale in interstate commerce of products made by the labor of children was struck down in 1918 on the grounds that since the states could regulate child labor within their borders, the federal government could not, even if the regulation was related to interstate commerce.[62] The case gave rise to a movement which put the Child Labor Amendment through Congress, but it was never ratified by enough states. The case itself was finally overruled by the *Darby* case [150] in 1941.

Today the 10th Amendment is rarely discussed by the Supreme Court. Because the supremacy clause says that all state laws are invalid if they conflict with acts of Congress, the 10th Amendment is no help to the states unless Congress had no power to pass the act in the first place. And if Congress had no power, either because Article I does not grant it or because some other amendment restricts Congress, then the 10th Amendment is unnecessary. As Chief Justice Stone said in *Darby:* "The [10th] Amendment states but a truism that all is retained which is not surrendered." It serves as a flag, to remind the federal government that its powers have theoretical limits.

10

Times Change, So Does Structure

Amendments 11, 12

Amendment 11

The Judicial power of the United States shall not be construed to extend to any suit in law or equity, commenced or prosecuted against one of the United States by Citizens of another State, or by Citizens or Subjects of any Foreign State.

The states had always thought they could not be sued by private individuals or companies, because of the doctrine of "sovereign immunity." In 1793 a man named Chisholm, a citizen of South Carolina, sued the state of Georgia for money owed him. He brought his suit in the Supreme Court because no other court would accept jurisdiction.[17] The Court's acceptance of jurisdiction greatly angered the states. They wanted to be sued in their own courts and then only when they agreed to be sued. Within two years the 11th Amendment was ratified (and three years later proclaimed) as part of the Constitution. This was the first of three times that the Supreme Court has been overruled by Constitutional amendment (the 13th Amendment and citizenship section of the 14th Amendment overruled *Dred Scott v. Sandford,* and the 16th Amendment overturned the decision in *Pollock v. Farmers' Loan & Trust Co.*).

A fundamental principle of international law has always been that a sovereign could not without consent be sued in the courts of another sovereign. Since the states each considered themselves sovereign, they did not want to be open to suit in the courts of another sovereign—the United States. Although it may seem foolish to find royal sovereignty a holdover in the states, there was a good practical reason for it. If the states did not consent to pay a money judgment, there was not much the federal courts could do. This may be a dismal view of human and institutional nature, but it is a real concern. Happily, many state legislatures and Congress, too, have passed laws allowing citizens to sue the government in a large variety of cases.

The 11th Amendment withdraws part of the jurisdiction given the federal courts by Article III. No state can be sued in a federal court unless another state or the United States is suing. Some states thought this meant that the Supreme Court could never review a case coming from the state courts if the state was a party to the suit. On the contrary, said the Court in 1821. If the state brings a person to trial in the state courts, and if he claims that the decision in the case was unconstitutional, then the Supreme Court can take the case on appeal, for the suit is not one which is "commenced or prosecuted"; it is merely the *continuation* of a suit already started.[20]

In certain cases, however, the 11th Amendment is not applied. If a state official engages in an unconstitutional act, the injured person can go to the federal courts for an injunction to have the state officer stopped. This is because a state official is considered not a part of the state for purposes of the 11th Amendment. Cities and counties and other subdivisions of the states can be sued in federal courts; only the states themselves are immune.

Amendment 12

The Electors shall meet in their respective states and vote by ballot for President and Vice-President, one of whom, at least, shall not be an inhabitant of the same state with themselves; they shall name in their ballots the person voted for as President, and in distinct ballots the person voted for as Vice-President, and they shall make distinct lists of all persons voted for as President, and of all persons voted for as Vice-President, and of the number of votes for each, which lists they shall sign and certify, and transmit sealed to the seat of the government of the United States, directed to the President of the Senate;—The President of the Senate shall, in presence of the Senate and House of Representatives, open all the certificates and the votes shall then be counted;—the person having the greatest number of votes for President, shall be the President, if such number be a majority of the whole number of Electors appointed;

The 11th Amendment was passed because the states did not want to change the structure of government as fast as the Supreme Court thought the Founding Fathers intended. The 12th Amendment, on the other hand, was adopted because the times had changed so fast that a new method of electing the President had to be found.

The Framers were wary of placing the choice even in the hands of the relatively few who met the property qualifications to vote for other public officers. They wanted the choice of the chief executive to be free of partisan politics, so it was given to a select body of distinguished men, of the highest moral and education qualifications. That was the plan. The "electors" (who when they meet are said be the "Electoral College") were to be chosen in each state by the legislature.

The Framers of the Constitution had disliked political parties and factions and they attempted to create a government which would make the rise of political parties impossible. This was perhaps the Convention's greatest misjudgment, for parties began to form even in Washington's Administration. By the election of 1800, the electors were no longer a group of highly distinguished citizens, but a group of men picked by each party and pledged to vote for their party's candidate.

Following the procedure outlined in Article II, the electors in 1800 cast two votes each, without saying which was for Vice President. The person with the highest number of votes was to be President. The Democratic party (the direct ancestor of the present party) had the majority of members in the electoral college, but the election resulted in a tie between Thomas Jefferson and Aaron Burr (since each Democrat cast one vote for Jefferson and one for Burr and the Federalists voted for two different men). The election was then thrown to the House of Representatives, as the Constitution stipulated. It took thirty-seven ballots before Jefferson was picked as President and Burr as Vice President.

The result of the election worried members of the majority party. If each elector had to cast two votes (each for different people) and could not specify which was for the President, and if the party had only one set of candidates, then there would be a tie every time and the House of Representatives would always take over. And if the House were controlled by the opposite party, as it was in 1800, the wishes of the majority of people could be thwarted. Or perhaps worse, suppose the Federalists, knowing that they would lose, had cast half their votes for Burr, whom the Democrats had wanted to be Vice President. With both Federalist and Democratic votes, Burr, rather than Jefferson, would have been President.

Times had changed. A party system which the Founding Fathers had not foreseen was doing funny things to the manner in which a President was supposed to be elected. So the 12th Amendment was passed in time for the 1804 election.

Now electors must specify which vote is for President and which is for Vice President. Thus the possibility of confusing the Presidential and Vice Presidential candidates has been ended. Today, a candidate must receive 270 out of the 538 electoral votes in order to be elected President.

In practice, the parties nominate single tickets, and electors are pledged to vote for the entire ticket of one party or the other. Split-ticket elections will probably never happen.

On election day in November, voters choose electors. Since electors are pledged to vote the way the majority in each state votes, the counting of the electoral votes by the President pro tem of the Senate on January 6 before a joint session of Congress generally produces no surprising results. Moreover, these days, computers predict the outcome of elections even before the polls close.

A troublesome flaw in the electoral system still exists, however. Even if all electors vote as pledged, they do not necessarily elect the man favored by the majority of voters. Benjamin Harrison in 1888 defeated President Grover Cleveland in the electoral college, even though Cleveland had received the greater number of popular votes.

This happened because the electors of each party run on opposing tickets. All those on the ticket of the winning party become electors, even though they did not get all the votes. Since the electors vote as pledged, the winning Presidential candidate in each state gets *all* the electoral votes of that state. Whether he gets 51 percent or 75 percent of the popular vote, the winning candidate gets 100 percent of the electoral votes and the loser takes nothing. So if the popular vote is concentrated in the right states, a candidate can become President even if he gets far less than a majority of the popular vote.

In fact, a candidate could win even if he got only twenty-four votes to his opponent's 35,000,000 votes. The twelve largest states have a combined total of 281 electoral votes, more than enough for election (New York, California, Pennsylvania, Illinois, Ohio, Texas, Michigan, New Jersey, Florida, Massachusetts, Indiana, and North Carolina). If because of heavy rains and bad weather on election day, only three people vote in each of these states, Candidate X would carry each state if he won two of the three votes (giving him twenty-four votes altogether). He would thereby win 281 electoral votes. Even if in the thirty-eight other states the weather was clear and everyone voted and they all voted for his opponent, the more than 35,000,000 votes would still give the loser only 257 votes. This is a bizarre example, of course, but because of the closeness of the 1960 election in many states, a shift of only 60,000 (out of nearly 70,000,000 votes cast) would have given Vice President Nixon the popular majority and Senator Kennedy the victory.

Amendment 12 (continued)

and if no person have such majority, then from the persons having the highest numbers not exceeding three on the list of those voted for as President, the House of Representatives shall choose immediately, by ballot, the President. But in choosing the President, the votes shall be taken by states, the representation from each state having one vote; a quorum for this purpose shall consist of a member or members from two-thirds of the states, and a majority of all the states shall be necessary to a choice.

If no person receives more than 270 electoral votes, the House of Representatives must choose a President on the same day in which the ballots are opened and counted. Each state gets one vote and at least thirty-four states must be present. The three candidates receiving the most votes in the electoral college are eligible to be chosen by the House and at least twenty-six votes are necessary to be elected.

After the 12th Amendment was passed, the only time the House ever chose a President was in 1824. The two-party system broke down and four candidates were nominated. John Quincy Adams, son of the first Federalist President, was elected, even though he had received fewer electoral votes than Andrew Jackson.

Amendment 12 (continued)

[And if the House of Representatives shall not choose a President whenever the right of choice shall devolve upon them, before the fourth day of March next following, then the Vice-President shall act as President, as in the case of the death or other constitutional disability of the President.—]

The 20th Amendment supersedes this section.

Amendment 12 (continued)

The person having the greatest number of votes as Vice-President, shall be the Vice-President, if such number be a majority of the whole number of Electors appointed, and if no person have a majority, then from the two highest numbers on the list, the Senate shall choose the Vice-President; a quorum for the purpose shall consist of two-thirds of the whole number of Senators, and a majority of the whole number shall be necessary to a choice.

The procedure for electing a Vice President, should Vice Presidential candidates fail to get a majority of the electoral votes, is the same as that for picking the President, except that the Senate rather than the House does the voting, and it must select a Vice President from the *two* highest candidates. Because candidates for both offices are nominated on the same party ticket and receive an equal number of votes in the electoral college, the Senate will usually never have to act unless the House must choose a President also. In 1836 Martin Van Buren received a majority of the electoral vote, but the vice-presidential candidate did not, so the Senate had to choose, the House did not.

Amendment 12 (continued)

But no person constitutionally ineligible to the office of President shall be eligible to that of Vice-President of the United States.

In 1960, some Republicans suggested that President Eisenhower run as Vice President in the coming election. He could not have run for President, because he already had two terms and the 22nd Amendment says that that is all one man can have. Since the 22nd Amendment made him "constitutionally ineligible" to run for the Presidency, this last sentence of the 12th Amendment made him ineligible to run for the Vice Presidency also.

11   Civil Rights Plus

Amendments 13-15

Amendment 13 (Section 1)

Neither slavery nor involuntary servitude, except as a punishment for crime whereof the party shall have been duly convicted, shall exist within the United States, or any place subject to their jurisdiction.

The 13th Amendment finally came out and said it: color is a pigment of the imagination.

For seventy years the brutality of slavery had survived in the United States. Only the brutality of a Civil War could abolish it. When the war had ended, the defeated rebels were in no position to delay the ratification of this amendment, which became effective in 1865.

The 13th Amendment applies only to persons, not to businesses or other organizations. The 13th Amendment makes no distinction among colors or religions or national origins. It does not differentiate between citizens and aliens. It means, purely and simply, that no one can be kept as a slave or be forced against his will to do work for another in any state, the District of Columbia, or any

United States territory, unless he has been convicted of crime and is serving a lawful jail sentence. This provision is directed toward the private individual, as well as the state and federal governments.

Human imagination is capable of anything. To abolish slavery did not mean that the eyes could not see color differences, and it remained for the 14th Amendment and eighty more years of history to make the Constitution truly color-blind.

Amendment 13 (Section 2)

Congress shall have power to enforce this article by appropriate legislation.

Because the 13th Amendment is "self-executing" (that is, it goes into effect without the need for Congressional legislation to support it) Section 2 of the amendment has come into play only rarely and in minor ways. Nevertheless, the section is important because it is the first time an amendment increased the powers of Congress. With the section, Congress can make slavery a federal crime and provide punishment—it could not have done so without Section 2.

Amendment 14 (Section 1, Clause 1)

All persons born or naturalized in the United States, and subject to the jurisdiction thereof, are citizens of the United States and of the State wherein they reside.

Prior to the Civil War, Negroes born in the United States could not become American citizens, even if they were free persons descended from free persons living in one of the original thirteen states at the time the Constitution was ratified.[30] A person was primarily a citizen of a state and only secondarily of the United States. With the passage of the 14th Amendment, the order of citizenship was reversed.

It is now possible to be a citizen of the United States, even though not a citizen of any state at all. Simply to be born in the United States is enough for national citizenship. The American citizen is automatically a citizen of any state in which he resides.

There is one exception. Those born in the United States but not "subject to the jurisdiction thereof" are not citizens. This is a limited class. A person born to a foreign ambassador living in the United States is not a citizen by virtue of birth; he is not subject to the jurisdiction because his parents are in diplomatic service. But children born in the United States to aliens, even if they are tourists on vacation, are United States citizens if their parents are not diplomats or foreign public officials.

The 14th Amendment also recognized the equal citizenship of those who immigrated and who were naturalized in accordance with federal law.

This clause makes national citizenship more significant than state citizenship and takes from the states the power to declare who shall not be a citizen of the state.

Only real persons can be citizens for purposes of the 14th Amendment. Corporations and associations cannot.

Amendment 14 (Section 1, Clause 2)

No State shall make or enforce any law which shall abridge the privileges or immunities of citizens of the United States;

Five years after this clause was passed, it became a "practical nullity" by a single blow from the Supreme Court. Louisiana passed a law establishing the Crescent City Live-Stock Landing and Slaughter-House Company, giving it a monopoly to carry on the livestock landing and slaughtering business in New Orleans and the surrounding area. The New Orleans butchers resisted, since it meant the closing down of their businesses. The butchers argued to the Court that the law was unconstitutional because, among other reasons, it abridged their privileges and immunities. But the court distinguished this clause from the privileges and immunities clause in Article 4 (see p. 118). There, the Court noted, the expression is "privileges and immunities of the citizens *in the several states.*" Here in the 14th Amendment, the words are *"citizens of the United States."* Conducting a slaughtering business is not a privilege and immunity of national citizenship. Only those privileges, said the Court in *The Slaughter-House Cases,* "which owe their existence to the Federal Government, its National character, its Constitution, or its laws" are privileges of national citizenship.[130]

Since the supremacy clause of Article 6 already made

unlawful any state interference with these privileges, the privileges and immunities clause was reduced to almost nothing. Nevertheless, a few privileges and immunities of national citizenship have been recognized, among them, the right to go freely from state to state, the right to vote in federal elections, the right to petition Congress for a redress of grievances, the right to engage in interstate commerce, the right to enter public parks and other public property, the right to use public navigable waters, and rights guaranteed under treaties.

Amendment 14 (Section 2, Clause 3)
nor shall any State deprive any person of life, liberty, or property, without due process of law;

The due process clause of the 14th Amendment, as we have already seen, has been constantly before the courts during the past half century. Its significance lies not alone in that unfair procedures in criminal proceedings are unconstitutional by its terms. The due process clause of the 14th Amendment, like its counterpart in the 5th Amendment, has been used in a wide variety of situations.

Substantive Due Process

In the early years of its history, the 14th Amendment seemed destined to be used only in cases of racial discrimination. In the *Slaughter-House Cases* the Court did not beat around the bush: "We doubt very much whether any action of a state not directed by way of discrimination against the negroes as a class, or on account of their race, will ever be held to come within the [scope] of this provision."

Four years later, in 1877, the Court refused to upset an Illinois law which regulated rates in the grain storage and transportation business. Arguing that the due process clause protected against unfair procedures only and not against the substance of legislation, Chief Justice Waite proclaimed in *Munn v. Illinois:* "We know that this [regulatory power] is a power which may be abused; but that is no argument against its existence. For protection against abuses by Legislatures the people must resort to the polls, not to the courts."

Within twenty years the Supreme Court completely reversed itself. The doctrine that the due process clause applies only to racial discrimination cases in which procedural unfairness occurred was thrown out the window. During those twenty years, as industry expanded, more and more states passed social and economic legislation to curb the harmful effects of the gigantic corporations which were being created. These corporations appealed to the Supreme Court for relief, on the theory that the due process clause forbade the states from passing laws which interfered with their property rights. The regulation of rates, working conditions, maximum hours of working time per week, and so on were all said to be property rights. Corporations were said to be "persons" within the meaning of the clause.

The Supreme Court agreed to it all, and the era of "substantive due process" was ushered in; it was to last until the middle 1930's, when President Roosevelt, after threatening to "pack" the Court by persuading Congress to allow six more Justices on the Bench, found a chastened Court turning back to its position in *Munn v. Illinois.* About the only thing that has remained is the definition of person: although a business corporation and other associations are not "citizens" they are "persons."

In Chapter 4 we saw the need for judicial review because otherwise Congress or the states could violate the Constitution willy-nilly. Now we see how the Court, given judicial review, can itself exercise a nonreviewable power.

During the time that the Court believed in the doctrine of substantive due process—the notion that certain kinds of economic and social legislation were bad—scores of state and federal laws were struck down. In effect, the words "due process of law" dropped out of the clause so that it read: "nor shall any state deprive any person of life, liberty, or property," with an emphasis on property.

Many of the laws which were voided dealt with improving working conditions and limiting the work week. In *Lochner v. New York,* a bakery owner contended that a New York law, which made it unlawful for anyone to require his employees to work for more than ten hours per day and sixty hours per week, unconstitutionally took away his property. The New York legislature had passed the law upon a wealth of medical evidence that the hot stuffy kitchens in bakeries were unhealthy. (Later labor laws were justified on the ground that unless the hours were limited and minimum wages fixed, workers could not escape sweat-shop conditions in the factories. This, indeed, may have been part of the justification of the bakery law.)

The Court found a flaw. The law, it said, interferes with the liberty of the workman to contract to work for longer hours (a liberty the workman surely did not want). Disregarding the medical testimony, the Court announced: "In looking through statistics regarding all trades and occupations, it may be true that the trade of a baker does not appear to be as healthy as some other trades, and is also vastly more healthy than still others. To the common understanding the trade of a baker has never been regarded as an unhealthy one. . . . It might be safely affirmed that almost all occupations more or less affect the health. There must be more than the mere fact of the possible existence of some small amount of unhealthiness to warrant legislative interference with liberty. It is unfortunately true that labor, even in any department, may possibly carry with it the seeds of unhealthiness. But are we all, on that account, at the mercy of legislative majorities?"

The Court was following the laissez-faire philosophy of the businessman of the day—that government should keep its hands off business and let a natural economic evolution take its course. Indeed, Darwin's theory of evolution came in part from the social and economic philosophy of Herbert Spencer, who in his book *Social Statics* advanced the proposition that in the "struggle for survival" some people would win and others would lose; that those who were poor, sick and starving had no right to expect to be rich, well, and fed, and even less right to combine together to force the legislatures to pass laws relieving them of their miseries.

To the position that the Court should follow such a

philosophy, Mr. Justice Holmes wrote one of the most classic dissents in the history of the Supreme Court. Replying to the majority in *Lochner,* he proclaimed: "This case is decided upon an economic theory which a large part of the country does not entertain. If it were a question whether I agreed with that theory, I should desire to study it further and long before making up my mind. But I do not conceive that to be my duty, because I strongly believe that my agreement or disagreement has nothing to do with the right of a majority to embody their opinions in law. . . . The 14th Amendment does not enact Mr. Herbert Spencer's *Social Statics* . . . A Constitution is not intended to embody a particular economic theory, whether of paternalism and the organic relation of the citizen to the state or of laissez faire. It is made for people of fundamentally differing views, and the accident of our finding certain opinions natural and familiar, or novel, and even shocking, ought not to conclude our judgment upon the question whether statutes embodying them conflict with the Constitution of the United States."

Today this dissent has by and large become the law. The cases in which both federal and state governments were held to have no power to regulate wages, working conditions, hours, and labor relations have all been overruled.

Similarly, under the so-called police power of the state the regulation of health, safety, and public morals by the states has been upheld. Included are a vast array of regulations concerning water supply, garbage, sewers, food, drugs, milk, gambling, liquor, automobiles, gasoline, storage, and laundries. The police power is also used to regulate the practice of the professions such as medicine, law, cosmetology, engineering, architecture, plumbing, and hundreds of others.

Eminent Domain

("nor shall private property be taken for public use without just compensation")

The words quoted above, the last clause in the 5th Amendment, are not specifically found in the 14th Amendment. But it has been held that state governments as well as the federal, must provide compensation when it takes private property.

The power of the government to confiscate land for public use is one of the oldest powers of government. Its legal name—"eminent domain"—stems from the recognition that the government has the greater right to land or other property when the public good requires it. Private property can only be taken for public use, but the legislature decides what a "public use" is. Courts are reluctant to review a pronouncement of the legislature that the taking of certain property is for public use.

The typical use of the eminent domain power is the taking of land in order to build state and federal highways, establish public parks and places of historic interest, and the use of water to generate electric power. The government has the right to take a part or all of your land, whether you are willing or not, whether you live on it or not, as long as you are paid in money the fair value of what you lost. Other kinds of direct takings have occurred in wartime, when the federal government requisitioned all sorts of products, from raw materials to cured pork and black pepper.

Sometimes the taking is indirect. If the government operates an airport close to a chicken farm, and the noise and lights of airplanes flying at low altitudes interferes with the farm's operation, property has been taken for which just compensation must be paid.[146] But not all such interferences are "takings" which require compensation. It is a matter of degree, to be decided, ultimately, by the courts.

The just compensation clause and the due process clause, though seemingly redundant, are not. The just compensation clause says that property can be taken for public use only if the government pays for what it gets. The due process clause says that even so, property may not be taken unless fair procedures are followed, such as allowing the person whose property is taken to be heard at the proceeding to determine the property's value.

Zoning

"Building zone laws are of modern origin. They began in this country about [1900]. Until recent years, urban life was comparatively simple; but with the great increase and concentration of population, problems have developed, and constantly are developing, which require, and will continue to require, additional restrictions in respect of the use and occupation of private lands in urban communities. Regulations, the wisdom, necessity and validity of which, as applied to existing conditions, are so apparent that they are now uniformly sustained [in 1825, or even in 1875] probably would have been rejected as arbitrary and oppressive. Such regulations are sustained, under the complex conditions of our day, for reasons analogous to those which justify traffic regulations, which before the advent of automobiles and rapid transit street railways, would have been condemned as fatally arbitrary and unreasonable. And in this there is no inconsistency, for while the meaning of constitutional guarantees never varies, the scope of their application must expand or contract to meet the new and different conditions which are constantly coming within the field of their operation. In a changing world, it is impossible that it should be otherwise." [160]

With the above words, the Supreme Court upheld the validity of zoning laws in 1926. Since that time, every city in the United States has passed regulations concerning the use to which land can be put. Businesses are excluded from some districts in order to create quiet, residential districts. Different kinds of businesses are put in different districts, those which pour forth smoke in one (or forbidden altogether), those which require closeness to railroad yards in another. Even residential districts are subdivided: on some only one- or two-story family houses are allowed; in others, these can be mixed with taller apartment dwellings. Zoning laws can be as complex as the conditions which call them into being. Regulations, unless clearly unreasonable or irrational, are not prohibited by the due process clause.

Due Process in Civil Proceedings

Just as due process requires fair procedures in criminal prosecutions, so it requires them in civil proceedings. This does not mean that all the common law rules of procedure which existed in the late 1700's are constitutional rights. They are not. The states are free to experiment. Yet certain fundamental rules remain.

A court does not have jurisdiction to hear a case if it has not obtained "jurisdiction over the person." This is usually easy enough—notice to the person in a method spelled out by law that a lawsuit has begun is sufficient. But a court in one state cannot simply send notice to a person in another state, without more, and have a legal right to proceed against him. Normally the courts of one state have jurisdiction over only those persons who live in the state or are *actually* present in the state. But there are exceptions. For instance, many states allow lawsuits against motorists who have driven in the state and then returned to their home states. In return for the use of the state highways, in other words, a state can allow a lawsuit in its own courts, if the visiting motorist causes an accident. Notice of the lawsuit sent through the mail is enough to get jurisdiction over the person. Laws of this kind are called "long arm statutes," because they reach into other states.

Similarly, long arm statutes are valid if they make a foreign corporation (organized under the laws of another state) suable in the state, as long as the corporation has done a sufficient amount of business in the state. This amount can be very small—mailing an insurance contract to a person living in the state might be enough. The situations involving the "presence" of a foreign company get exceedingly complex.

The fundamental requirements of due process are simple enough, however: notice to the person being sued and an opportunity to have his "day in court," whether it be judicial court or administrative agency. If a federal administrative agency issues orders and decides cases, federal courts must be empowered to review the legality of the agency decisions. This power of review extends to the acts of high executive officials, such as the Attorney General and the Secretary of State, as well as to the agencies themselves.

Amendment 14 (Section 1, Clause 4)

nor deny to any person within its jurisdiction the equal protection of the laws.

State Action

Although the 13th Amendment declared color a pigment of the imagination, it could not stop people from acting on that imagination, from seeing racial differences, and from making discriminations turn on the color of a man's skin. The equal protection clause was designed to end these discriminations and to make the Constitution "color-blind."

Yet the 14th Amendment only prevents "states" from denying equal protection of the laws. In 1875 Congress passed a law similar to the Civil Rights Act of 1964; the 1875 Act made it unlawful for any person to refuse another accommodations in an inn or hotel, among other things. Congress said in passing the law that it was acting under the power given to it in Section 5 of the 14th Amendment (see p. 224) to enforce the amendment. But, said opponents of integration, the 14th Amendment does not apply to actions taken by *private citizens;* therefore the Congress cannot make discrimination by private citizens unlawful.

In the *Civil Rights Cases* of 1883 the Supreme Court agreed. So the law has remained. Just as the Bill of Rights applied only to the federal government before the 14th Amendment was passed, so the 14th Amendment applies only to states and not to private persons or groups. (Because of these cases it was necessary for Congress in 1964 to use the commerce power to get at the same evils. See p. 57.)

So far, so good; but what kind of action is private and what kind is public or "state action"? Is a statute—i.e., an act of the state legislature—which discriminates the only kind of state action forbidden? Or are actions of state officials subject to the rule of the equal protection clause also? During the course of the past eighty years, the Supreme Court has increasingly enlarged the meaning of "state action." Today, the clause governs a wide number of diverse situations.

Arbitrary discrimination by *administrative officials* is unconstitutional under the equal protection clause. A San Francisco ordinance in 1886 made it unlawful to operate a laundry unless a license was obtained from the city board of supervisors. Yick Wo and Wo Lee, both Chinese laundrymen, had been denied licenses and were sent to prison for continuing to run their businesses. Arguing that their imprisonment was unconstitutional, they showed that almost all Chinese aliens who applied for licenses were turned down. Yet everyone else (except one) who applied was granted a license. There was no difference in terms of fire hazards or sanitary conditions between the laundries of those who received licenses and those who did not. The refusals were purely arbitrary; they sprang from the desire to discriminate against Chinese. Said the Court in ordering the city to grant licenses to the Chinese: "Though the law itself be fair on its face and impartial in appearance, yet, if it is applied and administered by public authority with an evil eye and an unequal hand, so as practically to make unjust and illegal discriminations between persons in similar circumstances, material to their rights, the denial of equal justice is still within the prohibition of the Constitution." [171]

Note what this case meant. For the purposes of determining what is "state action," even *city officials* are agents of the state. And the equal protection clause applies not just to citizens but to *any person* whatever, in this case, Chinese aliens.

State courts—whether local, county, or statewide—are agents of the state also. In 1945, a Negro couple bought a home in Missouri through a white real estate agent who did not reveal their identity because the property was covered with a "restrictive covenant." This was a contract saying that all the neighbors on the block mutually agreed not to sell to Negroes and that if any home was sold to a Negro the property would return to its original owners. Finding out that the new owners were Negro when they moved in, the neighbors went to court to block the sale. The trial court refused, but the Missouri Supreme Court agreed that the "restrictive covenant" was legally binding, and it ordered the couple out of the house. Three years later, the Supreme Court declared in *Shelley v. Kraemer* that state courts which enforce discriminatory contracts act unconstitutionally.

The Court agreed with the Missouri court that the restrictive covenant was legal. If the people who had signed the contract had voluntarily abided by it, there would have been no doubt that the refusal to sell to Negroes would have been perfectly lawful, insofar as the Constitution was concerned. But one of the signers did not abide by the contract, of course. He did sell the land. The other signers then went beyond merely private action; they asked a court to help. And a court, as an agent of the state, cannot order people out of houses because of the color of their skin. Racial discrimination by courts is therefore unconstitutional. Thus courts became color-blind, and the restrictive covenant died a sudden death in America. (Such covenants still exist, but since no court can enforce them, they aren't worth much.)

Legislatures, executives, and courts cannot discriminate under the 14th Amendment, then. But that is not all. In recent years a new doctrine has gained favor—if a *private* person or a group performs a "public function," then that person or group is an agent of the state also.

The public function can come up in two ways: either (1) the state helps out in the otherwise private endeavor; or (2) the private group does something which the state usually does. A restaurant in Wilmington, Delaware, was located inside an off-street parking lot building. The building was owned and operated by the Wilmington Parking Authority, a state agency. The restaurant was leased from the state by private persons, and refused to serve food to Negroes. The Court ruled that the refusal was unconstitutional because the state had a hand in the acitivity.[14]

Realizing that its connection with discriminatory activities may make them unconstitutional, a state in 1966 tried to take its hand out of running a public park. Senator Augustus O. Bacon left in his will in 1911 a park to the mayor and city council of Macon, Georgia, to hold for the use of white people only. When the city desegregated the park more than a half century later, the board of managers of the park sued in state court to have the city removed as trustee and to appoint private citizens so that the 14th Amendment would not apply to them. The Georgia Supreme Court allowed transfer of ownership, but the Supreme Court reversed. A park has a public character, the Court said, and when private individuals carry on a governmental function they become "instrumentalities" of the state and subject to the command of the equal protection clause. So the park remained integrated.[36]

Once, the town of Chicasaw, Alabama, owned entirely by the Gulf Shipbuilding Corporation, tried to prevent a Jehovah's Witness from handing out religious literature by refusing to let her on the sidewalk next to the post office. She was arrested under an Alabama law which makes it a crime to remain on private property after being told by the owner to leave. The Supreme Court upset the conviction: "Ownership does not always mean absolute dominion. The more an owner, for his advantage, opens up his property for use by the public in general, the more do his rights become circumscribed by the statutory and constitutional rights of those who use it."[87] In other words, the company town is still a town where the public lives, and neither the state nor the owners of the town can discriminate against the exercise of constitutional rights—in this case, the freedoms of speech and religion.[87]

The group taking "state action" may even be all the voters of the state. California had had a law on the books for many years which guaranteed the right to persons of all races and creeds to purchase property from private owners. In 1964 the voters in a statewide referendum passed a new law, repealing much of the old, now stating in effect that no private person could be compelled to sell property to those whom he did not wish to buy it. When a buyer protested this law, he claimed that the action of the voters was unconstitutional because they constituted the state and the state could not take away a statute which guaranteed equal protection of the laws. The California Supreme Court agreed, and so did the Supreme Court, and in 1967 the referendum was struck down.[182]

Segregation

All legislation involves some form of discrimination, because all laws divide things into classes: "This you can do and this you cannot do." The ticklish problem presented by the equal protection clause is to determine what is a *reasonable* classification.

Segregation—the enforced separation of the races—first came squarely before the Court in 1896, in the famous case of *Plessy v. Ferguson*. Plessy was arrested for violating a law which required whites and Negroes to sit in "equal but separate" railroad cars while traveling. Plessy was seven-eighths white. When he insisted on sitting in the "white only" coach, he was tossed off the train and into jail. The Supreme Court upheld the law, saying that the races could be separated as long as they were equally treated.

"We consider the underlying fallacy of [Plessy's] argument to consist in the assumption that the enforced separation of the two races stamps the colored race with a badge of inferiority. If this be so, it is not by reason of anything found in the act, but solely because the colored race chooses to put that construction upon it."

Dissenting, the first Mr. Justice Harlan replied: "Our Constitution is color-blind, and neither knows nor tolerates classes among citizens. . . . The destinies of the two races in this country are indissolubly linked together, and the interests of both require that the common government of all shall not permit the seeds of race hate to be planted under the sanction of law. . . . We boast of the freedom enjoyed by our people above all other peoples. But it is difficult to reconcile that boast with a state of the law which, practically, put the brand of servitude upon a large class of our fellow citizens, our equals before the law. The thin disguise of 'equal' accommodations for passengers in railroad coaches will not mislead anyone, or atone for the wrong this day done."

Fifty-eight years later, this dissent became law in *Brown v. Board of Education.* From 1896 to 1954, hundreds of laws were passed throughout the South and in other states requiring segregation of the races in almost every conceivable activity—schools, restaurants, theaters, hotels, transportation of all sorts, hospitals. Always the laws were justified on the grounds that they provided "separate but equal" facilities. Occasionally the Supreme Court ruled that Negroes must be admitted to white institutions because the facilities in the particular case were far from equal.[132]

Then in the early 1950's, cases arose from four different states—Kansas, South Carolina, Virginia, and Delaware—and the plaintiffs argued in all the cases that *segregated schools are by their very nature unequal,* that no matter what the state does, segregation is not within the equal protection of the laws. The Supreme Court agreed, and the wall of separation between white and black began to crumble.

"Today," said Chief Justice Warren in a unanimous opinion for the Court, "education is perhaps the most important function of state and local governments. Compulsory school attendance laws and the great expenditures for education both demonstrate our recognition of the importance of education to our democratic society. It is required in the performance of our most basic public responsibilities, even service in the armed forces. It is the very foundation of good citizenship. Today it is a principal instrument in awakening the child to cultural values, in preparing him for later professional training, and in helping him to adjust normally to his environment. In these days, it is doubtful that any child may reasonably be expected to succeed in life if he is denied the opportunity of an education. Such an opportunity, where the state has undertaken to provide it, is a right which must be made to all on equal terms. . . . To separate [Negro schoolchildren] from others of similar age and qualifications solely because of their race generates a feeling of inferiority as to their status in the community that may affect their hearts and minds in a way unlikely ever to be undone. . . . We conclude that in the field of public education the doctrine of 'separate but equal' has no place. Separate educational facilities are inherently unequal." [13]

In a companion case, decided the same day, the Court also held that segregation by the federal government in Washington, D.C., schools, was unconstitutional under the 5th Amendment, because it deprived Negroes of liberty without due process of law. "In view of our decision that the Constitution prohibits the states from maintaining racially segregated public schools, it would be unthinkable that the same Constitution would impose a lesser duty on the federal government," the Chief Justice wrote. [11]

There remained the problem of how long the states should have to work out new laws and procedures, build new schools, hire more teachers, work out new school districts, and plan new transportation routes in order to carry out the decision in the *Brown* case. The next year, the Court decided the second *Brown* case, saying that necessary changes to bring about integration must be done "with all deliberate speed."

The catalogue listing the failures of the state governments to carry out the law of the Constitution is not for this book. "Massive resistance" programs were begun. One Virginia county abolished public schools altogether. Parents who sent their children to private schools received tax concessions and tuition funds—until the Supreme Court saw through the scheme in 1964. [57] Private schools were not obliged to accept Negroes, and few Negroes could afford them or meet their entrance requirements anyway.

Legal device after legal device was used, and the Court had its hands full—and will continue to have its hands full for years to come—hearing cases involving segregation and the equal protection clause. In dozens of decisions, the Court has struck down segregation in public parks, public housing projects, public beaches, municipal golf courses and swimming pools, courtrooms, transportation facilities, and playgrounds.

Segregation has meant more than separation of the races in physical places. As late as 1967, 16 states forbade inter-marriage between white and non-white: these were the so-called "miscegenation" statutes. A test case was brought to the Supreme Court in that year when a Negro wife and white husband, who had been married in Washington, D.C., returned to their home state of Virginia and were convicted under the Virginia law. They were sentenced to one year in jail but given a suspended sentence for 25 years if they would leave Virginia. They did and brought suit to declare their conviction unlawful; the Supreme Court of Appeals of Virginia turned them down. Laws of this type had been defended under the equal protection clause by arguing that the white person was equally as guilty as the Negro (or the Chinese, Japanese, or Indian). The Supreme Court reversed in a unanimous decision. Said the Chief Justice: There was "patently no legitimate overriding purpose independent of invidious racial discrimination which justifies this classification . . . We have consistently denied the constitutionality of measures which restrict the rights of citizens on account of race." [181]

In 1958 the governor and legislature of Arkansas even argued that they were not bound by the decisions of the Supreme Court in *Brown* and other cases. In a rare opinion, signed by *each* of the Justices individually, the Supreme Court thundered back that this was constitutional nonsense.[23]

Nevertheless, as long as administrators, executives, and legislatures refuse to follow, the Court's decisions remain unenforced. Here, as everywhere, the Court stands, in Professor Howe's phrase, "on the edge of futility." The force of public opinion usually causes people to go along, but in the explosive issue of race relations, where feelings and emotions are deep, where local ways have been fixed by a century of tradition, public opinion may resist. When that happens, we must trust to the good sense of the American people to come eventually to peace with its Court, its law, and its Constitution.

Apportionment of State Legislature

For more than sixty years, the sizes of election districts

within most states were highly unequal. For instance, Colebrook, Connecticut, with a population of 592, and Hartford, Connecticut, with a population of 177,397, each elected two representatives to the state legislature. In New Jersey, one district had 35,000 people; another, 905,000. In California, one district had 297 times as many people as another.

Although most state constitutions required that districts be apportioned strictly on the basis of population and that new censuses and redistricting should be made every ten years, the states disregarded their own constitutions. As a result, the majority of the state legislatures were elected by a substantial minority of the people in almost every state. The rural districts which once had as many people living in them as the city districts, but which by the 1960's had far fewer people, still sent as many representatives to the state assembly and senate as did the much more populous city districts. The rural interests were thus able to control at least one or both houses of the state legislatures. In state after state, legislation which was supported by a majority of the people in the state was defeated by a majority in the legislature which represented a minority of the people. In Michigan, for example, the legislature blocked the appointment of state officials named by a governor of the opposite party for more than ten years.

The Supreme Court had uniformly dismissed almost all reapportionment cases before the 1960's. Only where certain special conditions existed did the Court decide the case—as when the city of Tuskegee, Alabama, changed its shape from a square to a twenty-eight-sided figure in order to exclude Negroes who lived away from the center from voting (see p. 225). But usually the Court refused even to hear the cases, stating that they presented "political questions" with which a court should not meddle.

By the 1960's the minority groups had become so entrenched in the state legislatures that there seemed no way to press for reform. The legislature itself would not redistrict; no legislator wants to draw a line which would turn him out of office. The state courts would not help. Congress would not act for a variety of political reasons: the House of Representatives was not apportioned according to population itself; Senators and Representatives did not want to upset the status quo in their home states. As urban problems continued to mount—slums, air pollution, crime, health—state legislatures were not politically equipped to provide effective help.

In 1964, the Supreme Court decided the first of a series of cases concerning state legislative reapportionment, and struck down the legality of the state systems under the equal protection clause (not on the ground that the state constitutions demanded redistricting, for the Supreme Court has no power to decide any question concerning state constitutions other than whether any particular provision clashes with the federal constitution).

"Legislators represent people, not trees or acres. Legislators are elected by voters, not farms or cities or economic interests. As long as ours is a representative form of government, and our legislatures are those instruments of government elected directly by and directly representative of the people, the right to elect legislators in a free and unimpaired fashion is a bedrock of our political system. . . . The Equal Protection Clause demands no less than substantially equal state legislative representation for all citizens, of all places as well as of all races." So saying, the Court struck down Alabama's legislative districting system in *Reynolds v. Sims*. In a series of sweeping cases [54], [83], [120] the Court invalidated the apportionment in state after state. The remedy: apportionment of *each* house of each legislature on a "one man, one vote" basis. To date, more than forty states have begun redistricting under federal court order; the whole process of state politics is being remade.

The states had answered the Court with the so-called federal analogy: the states send the same number of Senators to the United States Senate, even though unequal in size, and the method of electing the President is without sole regard to population. Therefore, why couldn't counties within a state, no matter what their population, each send a representative to the state senate, at least? The answer is that the analogy is not so good. Counties and other subdivisions of the state do not have any sovereign powers; they are administrative units subject to control by the state. The states, on the other hand, are not mere administrative units with respect to the United States. Their lines cannot be redrawn by Congress. Congress cannot legislate in areas reserved to the states.

Because the federal analogy does not hold, it does not follow, as some people have suggested, that the United States Senate should now be reapportioned on a "one man, one vote" basis. Twice the Constitution spells out the guarantee to each State of two Senators. The Senate is a body in which the states themselves are represented. It is the House of Representatives which must be elected by districts substantially equal in size of population within each state.

Aliens

Even though they are not citizens, aliens are also protected by the equal protection clause. Legislation which unreasonably discriminates against them is unconstitutional. Because Congressional power to declare those aliens who can and cannot become citizens is beyond judicial review (see pp. 60–1), sometimes clashes occur between state and federal law.

An Ohio law which forbids aliens to own or operate poolrooms was upheld because the business was shady enough that it seemed proper to keep out aliens.[19] A Washington state law which made it unlawful for aliens to own land was upheld on the grounds that the Congressional classification could be adopted by the states.[135] At the time, 1923, Japanese, Chinese, and Malayans were ineligible for citizenship, though they could live in the United States. It was feared in Washington that ownership of land by aliens might result in aliens buying up the state.

On the other hand, states cannot deny the right to work in ordinary occupations. An Arizona law requiring employers with more than five employees to maintain a work force at least eighty percent of which must be citizens was struck down. Because it was a device to keep aliens from working, it violated the equal protection clause.[142] Similarly, state laws which prohibit aliens from commercial fishing, even when the aliens are ineligible for citizenship, are unconstitutional.[134]

Criminal Procedures

There have been a number of decisions involving criminal procedures under the equal protection clause. Perhaps the most well known is *Griffin v. Illinois*, in which the Supreme Court ruled that defendants too poor to buy transcripts of their trial could not for that reason be denied the right to have their cases reviewed by a higher appellate court. The rule in Illinois had been for defendants at their own cost to give the trial records to the higher court. This was held to be an unconstitutional discrimination between rich and poor.[56]

Amendment 14 (Section 2, Clause 1)

Representatives shall be apportioned among the several States according to their respective numbers, counting the whole number of persons in each State, excluding Indians not taxed.

After the Civil War, the former slaves had become citizens, and the southern states were given the right to add these people into the hopper in order to figure out how many representatives the states could send to Congress.

"Indians not taxed" were excluded, but the meaning of the term was never clear. Does it mean Indians who did not actually pay taxes or those whom neither the states nor federal government tried to tax? Does it mean only those Indians not taxed by the state or those not taxed by anyone? Indians are now subject to federal taxation; since 1940 they have been included in the federal census which computes the statistics for determining how many seats in the House should go to each state. So this particular phrase seems to have fallen into disuse.

Amendment 14 (Section 2, Clause 2)

But when the right to vote at any election for the choice of electors for President and Vice-President of the United States, Representatives in Congress, the Executive and Judicial officers of a State, or the members of the Legislature thereof, is denied to any of the male inhabitants of such State, being twenty-one years of age, and citizens of the United States, or in any way abridged, except for participation in rebellion, or other crime, the basis of representation therein shall be reduced in the proportion which the number of such male citizens shall bear to the whole number of male citizens twenty-one years of age in such State.

This provides a method of forcing states to guarantee the right to vote. If the vote is denied to those entitled to it, the state's delegation to Congress can be reduced in proportion to the number of citizens denied the right to vote. Although plenty of people have been denied the right to vote in our history since then, this provision has never been used. As a method of force, it has so far failed because members of Congress have found it politically inadvisable to suggest to their fellow members that perhaps they do not belong, since their states have been unconstitutionally denying the vote to citizens.

At the time the amendment was ratified in 1868, women were not destined to have the vote for fifty-two years. So the figuring was done on the basis of "male inhabitants."

Amendment 14 (Section 3)

No person shall be a Senator or Representative in Congress, or elector of President and Vice President, or hold any office, civil or military, under the United States, or under any State, who, having previously taken an oath, as a member of Congress, or as an officer of the United States, or as a member of any State legislature, or as an executive or judicial officer of any State, to support the Constitution of the United States, shall have engaged in insurrection or rebellion against the same, or given aid or comfort to the enemies thereof. But Congress may by a vote of two-thirds of each House, remove such disability.

This section was passed to punish the officials in the United States and separate state governments who aided the Confederacy during the Civil War. On June 6, 1898, Congress suspended the operation of Section 3 as to all rebels prior to that date. Since that time no one has come within its terms. Presumably it would apply to a person convicted of treason or espionage who sought political office.

Amendment 14 (Section 4)

The validity of the public debt of the United States, authorized by law, including debts incurred for payment of pensions and bounties for services in suppressing insurrection or rebellion, shall not be questioned. But neither the United States nor any State shall assume or pay any debt or obligation incurred in aid of insurrection or rebellion against the United

States, or any claim for the loss or emancipation of any slave; but all such debts, obligations and claims shall be held illegal and void.

This section was passed to assure citizens and foreigners alike who had loaned money to the United States to finance the Civil War that the United States would recognize and pay off all its debts. Although the Civil War debt has been paid off, the clause is not dead; it still forbids Congress from borrowing money one day and then refusing to pass appropriations to pay it back the next.

The last sentence of Section 4 was inserted to stop payment of debts incurred by the South on behalf of the rebellion. It was further notice to the people of the country that the debts were accumulated in a dishonorable cause.

Amendment 14 (Section 5)
The Congress shall have power to enforce, by appropriate legislation, the provisions of this article.

After the Civil War, Congress passed a number of laws, making it a crime for private citizens to discriminate on the basis of race. In the *Civil Rights Cases*, the Supreme Court said that these laws were beyond the power of Congress under the enforcement clause, since the 14th Amendment only prohibits state discriminations. Citizens acting privately do not constitute state action. That is why the Civil Rights Act of 1964 proclaimed private discriminations illegal under the commerce clause and not under the 14th Amendment. The commerce clause is a positive power, enabling Congress to regulate. The enforcement clause is at best a negative one, enabling Congress to stop state-made discriminations.

In recent years, the power of Congress to enforce the amendment has been broadened by a wider interpretation of what actions are attributable to the states. Although murder by private citizens cannot be made a crime by Congress under this clause, Congress can outlaw murders of civil rights advocates who are attacked *jointly* by state policemen and private citizens, for then the private individuals are acting with the state in depriving persons of life without due process of law.[155]

Amendment 15 (Section 1)
The right of citizens of the United States to vote shall not be

denied or abridged by the United States or by any State on account of race, color, or previous condition of servitude.

Southern states were not scared by the threat in the 14th Amendment, nor did Congress make a move to reduce southern representation in Congress because Negroes were being denied the right to vote. Instead, in 1870 the 15th Amendment was ratified, directly denying the United States and any state from preventing any person from voting. For the next century, many states sought ways to avoid the impact of the amendment.

One of the earliest devices was the "grandfather clause." A literacy test was required of all voters. But a special exemption was granted to all persons who were eligible voters on January 1, 1867, and descendants of such voters. This exemption excluded Negroes, who were not eligible in many states until the 15th Amendment was ratified in 1870. So illiterate whites voted; illiterate Negroes did not. Another device was to require Negroes to register during a ten-day period about six months before the election; if they did not, they would lose their right to vote forever. Whites did not have to register at all. These devices were struck down by the Supreme Court, although the last, not until 1939.[60, 81]

Still another way to prevent Negroes from voting is to redraw the lines of the voting district so that they suddenly live outside. When Tuskegee, Alabama, carved itself into a twenty-eight-sided figure to dry up the Negro vote, the Court called foul and refused to permit it.[53]

Meanwhile, one of the great American political techniques had been developed—the primary election. Candidates within the same party run against each other in the primary and the winner of that election receives the party's nomination for the position which he is seeking. Usually, only Democrats vote in Democratic primaries and only Republicans in Republican primaries. The primary is, however, a district-wide or state-wide election. The Constitutional Convention had not contemplated primaries, of course, and many states began to use them as a way to discriminate between the races.

Texas passed the White Primary Law, allowing only whites to vote in the primary. This effectively took away the Negroes' right to vote, since whoever won the Democratic primary in Texas, as in most southern states at that time, won the election. Texas defended on the ground that a primary was not an election and the 15th Amendment protects the right to vote in *elections* only. The Supreme Court in 1927 was willing to agree that the primary was not an election, but the law was struck down anyway on the basis of the equal protection clause.[100]

So Texas repealed the White Primary Law and passed another. This time the executive committees of the political parties were given the authority to determine who should vote in the election. Texas reasoned that the 14th Amendment prohibited only the *states*, not private political parties, from discriminating. When the executive committee did what was expected and excluded Negroes, the same Negro voter who had protested before came forward to sue again. Again the Supreme Court struck down the law. When the state delegates its authority the way Texas did, the executive committee becomes an agent of the state, and under the 14th Amendment cannot deny equal protection of the laws.[99]

After its defeat in the Court, Texas amended its law so that all the voters in the Democratic party could decide whether or not to exclude Negroes. For a time this worked. The Court had reasoned that when all the people in a private party, and not just the executive committee, decide to discriminate, then this is private discrimination and neither the 14th nor 15th Amendments forbids it.[59]

The belief that the 15th Amendment did not cover primaries lingered until 1944. In that year the Supreme Court took another Texas case. Three years before, the Court had recognized the fact that primaries were true elections, whether or not the Founding Fathers had ever heard or conceived of them.[147] A changed membership on the Court was now ready for the fourth Texas primary case, and this time racial discrimination was hit hard. When political parties organize primary elections under cover of state statute, they become "instrumentalities" of the state, no matter whether the executive committee or the entire membership speaks. "Constitutional rights would be of little value if they could be thus indirectly denied," wrote the Court in *Smith v. Allwright*.

One Justice dissented, not so much because he thought

that the Texas Democratic party should be able to discriminate but because he thought the Court was acting too hastily in overruling a decision handed down only nine years before. "The reason for my concern," he wrote, "is that the instant decision overruling that announced about nine years ago tends to bring adjudications of this tribunal into the same class as a restricted railroad ticket, good for this day and train only."

Replying to his criticism, the majority said, "In reaching this conclusion we are not unmindful of the desirability of continuity of decision in constitutional questions. However, when convinced of former error, this Court has never felt constrained to follow precedent. In Constitutional questions, where correction depends upon amendment and not upon legislative action, this Court throughout its history has freely exercised its power to reexamine the basis of its constitutional decisions. This has long been accepted practice, and this practice has continued to this day. This is particularly true when the decision believed erroneous is the application of a constitutional principle. . . . Here we are applying . . . the well-established principle of the 15th Amendment, forbidding the abridgment by a state of a citizen's right to vote."

The final blow was struck in 1953, and again in Texas. In one county, a private political club known as the Jaybird Democratic Association ran candidates in its own primary in May. It had no official connection with the Democratic party, it did not organize primaries under state laws, it did not use state voting machinery or state funds. For sixty years, with only one exception, the winner of the Jaybird primary would run unopposed in the July Democratic primary and win the November election. Needless to say, Negroes were excluded from voting in this pre-pre-election. In *Terry v. Adams,* the Supreme Court found the Jaybird party too closely tied to the whole election process to let its discrimination stand.[136]

Two other discrimination techniques have also fallen. One is the literacy test, in which a person must be able to "understand and explain" the Constitution of the United States to the voting registrar before being certified. It seemed that whenever Negroes tried, even if they were college-educated, they failed, and whites were usually never asked. The tests were not really aimed at literacy, and the Supreme Court looked behind its stated purpose and struck it down.[27]

The other technique is the poll tax: in order to vote, a person had to pay a certain amount of money to the state. The poll tax was known to those who wrote the Constitution and they gave it sanction in Article 1. But times had changed, and the poll tax was being used to keep poor Negroes from voting. In 1966 it, too, was overturned [64] (though on a 14th, not 15th, Amendment basis).

Amendment 15 (Section 2)
The Congress shall have power to enforce this article by appropriate legislation.

Congress has passed sections of the Civil Rights Acts of 1957, 1960, and 1964 under this clause. The Acts give the federal government the right to go to federal court to prevent state officers from discriminating in both federal and state elections.

12 Taxes, Senators, Liquor, and Women

Amendments 16-19

Amendment 16
The Congress shall have power to lay and collect taxes on incomes, from whatever source derived, without apportionment among the several States, and without regard to any census or enumeration.

During the Civil War, Congress passed an income tax law which few doubted was constitutional. When that law lapsed and Congress passed another in 1894, however, the Supreme Court struck it down.[110]

The law had laid a uniform tax on all incomes from "professions, trades, employments, or vocations." The Constitution in Article I, Section 2, Clause 3 (see p. 36) and Section 9, Clause 4 (see p. 78) said that "direct taxes" could not be uniform (a tax in which each person in the country pays the same amount or the same percentage is a uniform tax). Rather, direct taxes had to be paid by the states in proportion to their population. The apportionment for this kind of tax was too cumbersome, so the Congress preferred to tax "indirectly."

In 1895, because of the Court's ruling, income taxes became direct taxes, and in order to levy them, Congress would have to do so according to the apportionment. To get around this ruling, the 16th Amendment was ratified in 1913, allowing Congress to tax incomes without apportionment. This was no new power, however; even without the amendment Congress had the power to tax incomes.

As a result, a series of "internal revenue codes" have been passed. The federal tax code itself is more than 1,000 pages long, and the regulations of the Treasury Department concerning the administration of the tax laws amount to tens of thousands of pages. A special tax court and regional tax offices were established to handle the huge amount of litigation which arose. A specialized field of law—tax law—was created and many lawyers spend their entire working days on federal tax problems of large corporations. Today, the federal government receives more than $100 billion from income taxes; almost the entire federal budget is dependent on the income tax to finance government programs and operations.

Amendment 17 (Clause 1)

The Senate of the United States shall be composed of two Senators from each State, elected by the people thereof, for six years; and each Senator shall have one vote. The electors in each State shall have the qualifications requisite for electors of the most numerous branch of the State legislatures.

In 1789, only a small percentage of the citizens of each state could vote. Usually, only white adult males with a certain amount of property were qualified to vote for representatives to the state legislatures (and hence for Representatives to Congress). During the next 120 years, voting rights expanded enormously. The original system by which the state legislatures chose Senators came under increasingly heavy attack.

The attack was not due solely to the issue of voting rights. Frequently, deadlocks in the two houses of the state legislatures prevented the state from sending any Senator to Washington. Also, the state legislatures were often the captives of special interest groups, such as the railroads and steel and oil companies. These groups forced the legislatures to elect to the Senate men who were sometimes nothing more than agents of the companies themselves. (These were the "railroad Senators" and the "steel Senators.")

The 17th Amendment, ratified in 1913, tended to change that. Special interest Senators have sometimes been elected since then, but it is far more difficult for a private pressure group to put their candidate over on the people than it was to put him over on the few score state legislators.

Amendment 17 (Clause 2)

When vacancies happen in the representation of any State in the Senate, the executive authority of such State shall issue writs of election to fill such vacancies: *Provided,* That the legislature of any State may empower the executive thereof to make temporary appointments until the people fill the vacancies by election as the legislature may direct.

When vacancies occur in the House of Representatives, the governor of the state must call for an election. The 17th Amendment does not fully follow this procedure for Senators. The governor must call for a new election, unless the state legislature otherwise by law allows the governor to appoint someone to the Senate for a short time (as most state laws do permit). In practice, a person is appointed to the Senate until the next scheduled election or until the appointee's term of office expires. At that point he must bow out or run for election.

Amendment 17 (Clause 3)

This amendment shall not be so construed as to affect the election or term of any Senator chosen before it becomes valid as part of the Constitution.

Just to make sure that no one tried to cause a Senator trouble by claiming that his position in the Senate was unconstitutional because he had been elected by the legislature rather than the people of the state, the last part of the 17th Amendment specifies that those elected before the ratification of the amendment were entitled to their seats.

Amendment 18 [(Section 1)

After one year from the ratification of this article the manufacture, sale, or transportation of intoxicating liquors within,
the importation thereof into, or the exportation thereof from
the United States and all territory subject to the jurisdiction
thereof for beverage purposes is hereby prohibited.]

For seventy-five years before this "prohibition" amendment was ratified, those opposed to alcohol had actively
campaigned against the use of liquor anywhere, anytime.
Although Maine went "dry" in 1842, no real chance for
success came until the First World War, when many re-
trictions were put on liquor under the wartime powers of
Congress. The Anti-Saloon League, playing on the fact
that the people were already being deprived of liquor and
that voters would probably not object to putting these de-
privations on a constitutional level, pressed a hard fight
for the prohibition of liquor, whether manufactured, sold,
or transported. In 1919, they were successful.

A large measure of their success was due to the fact
that during wartime it was patriotic to be clean-living, to
the fact that the opposition was not well organized, and
to the fact that the small, vocal opposition came from
urban areas where large clusters of recent immigrants had
settled. To be on the side of Prohibition was to favor real
"Americanism."

The breweries and retail stores were given one year to
wind up their businesses; the amendment went into effect
in 1920.

Note that the amendment said that intoxicating liquors
were prohibited only if used for "beverage purposes."
This meant that wine and other liquors could be used for
religious or medicinal purposes.

Amendment 18 [(Section 2)

The Congress and the several States shall have concurrent
power to enforce this article by appropriate legislation.]

The Volstead Act, prescribing all sorts of criminal penalties for violations of this amendment, quickly went into
effect. Liquor inspectors ran into buildings and houses
searching for distilleries, and tapped telephone conversations. This had the effect of giving rise to a number of
cases involving the 4th Amendment, but it did not give

rise to much enforcement. In spite of the initial enthusiasm for the new, moral America, the enforcement procedures were exceedingly ineffective. Congress was stingy with funds; the states were uncooperative; the public got tired of having to drink its liquor illegally in "speakeasies" and underground bars. Disrespect was being heaped on the federal courts, whose orders were constantly being disobeyed.

Amendment 18 [(Section 3)

This article shall be inoperative unless it shall have been ratified as an amendment to the Constitution by the legislatures of the several States, as provided in the Constitution, within seven years from the date of the submission hereof to the States by the Congress.]

This section fixed a reasonable time-period in which the amendment had to be ratified to go into effect. It prevented the possibility that the amendment would lurk in the shadows of state legislative corridors for decades and suddenly be ratified by the final three-fourths, when earlier states would have changed their minds. Some succeeding amendments have also specified a time limit.

Amendment 19

The right of citizens of the United States to vote shall not be denied or abridged by the United States or by any state on account of sex. Congress shall have power to enforce this article by appropriate legislation.

As far back as the 1830's, women had asked for equal suffrage with men. The tempo of women's movements picked up when Wyoming granted women full voting rights upon its admission into the Union in 1890. From then until 1920, twenty-eight additional states granted women equal voting rights with men. At that point the 19th Amendment took over, and women were free to vote in all states. Many people feared that women would become masculine if allowed to vote. Although there can be no doubt that the amendment greatly aided women in pressing for wider legal and social rights, it is questionable whether the amendment alone is responsible for the increasingly equal treatment of women in America.

13   Mopping Up

Since 1933, six unrelated amendments have been adopted
—two in 1933, and one each in 1951, 1961, 1964, and
1967. Generally, these amendments have corrected weak-
nesses in the structure of the federal government and extended still further the right to vote.

Amendment 20 (Section 1)

The terms of the President and Vice President shall end at
noon on the 20th day of January, and the terms of Senators
and Representatives at noon on the 3d day of January, of the
years in which such terms would have ended if this article
had not been ratified; and the terms of their successors shall
then begin.

This "lame duck" amendment ended a source of irrita-
tion brought about by a chance in technology. It took
many weeks for Congressmen and Senators to travel from
their home states to the national capital in 1789. So the
date set for President Washington's inauguration was
March 4, at which time the terms of members of Congress would also begin. But since Congressmen have
two-year terms, and since each Congress began in December, this meant that Congressmen (and Senators)
who had been defeated or who had not run for reelection
in November would continue to serve until March.

By the 1930's methods of transportation and communication were much improved. The 20th Amendment, ratified in 1933, shortened the waiting period for new Presidents, Senators, and Representatives. Under the first section of the amendment, the terms of all Congressmen
elected in November, 1932, would end on January 3,
1935, rather than March 4 of that year. Similarly, Sena-
torial terms that were to expire on March 4, 1935, March

4, 1937, and March 4, 1939, ended on January 3 in each of those years. New Senators and Representatives took office on the same day that the old terms ended. The last Presidential inauguration on March 4 was President Roosevelt's first in 1933. His second inauguration took place January 20, 1937.

Amendment 20 (Section 2)

The Congress shall assemble at least once in every year, and such meeting shall begin at noon on the 3d day of January unless they shall by law appoint a different day.

Not only did new Congressmen and Senators have to wait four months before they could take office, but those whom they had defeated could remain active in Congress. Since each new session began the first Monday in December, defeated members of Congress actually took part in a Congress to which they did not belong. The period between the first Monday in December and March 4 was known as the "lame duck" period. The 20th Amendment, Section 2, eliminated this period by providing that each new session of Congress shall begin on the same day as the new members' terms of office. (The First Session of the 90th Congress began on January 10, 1967, because Congress by law decided to begin a week later.)

Amendment 20 (Section 3)

If, at the time fixed for the beginning of the term of the President, the President elect shall have died, the Vice President elect shall become President. If a President shall not have been chosen before the time fixed for the beginning of his term, or if the President elect shall have failed to qualify, then the Vice President elect shall act as President until a President shall have qualified; and the Congress may by law provide for the case wherein neither a President elect nor a Vice President elect shall have qualified, declaring who shall then act as President, or the manner in which one who is to act shall be selected, and such person shall act accordingly until a President or Vice President shall have qualified.

Suppose a President-elect were to die before January 20. Or suppose no President is chosen by January 20, perhaps because the leading candidate had failed to get a majority of the votes in the electoral college and the

House of Representatives had failed to decide. Or suppose it was found that the President-elect was not fully qualified to be President, perhaps because he was too young, or had not lived long enough in the United States. None of these possibilities has ever occurred, but the Constitution made no provision and the 20th Amendment provides for such eventualities, just in case.

If the President-elect dies, the Vice President becomes President. In the other situations named above, the Vice President becomes Acting President and must step aside when a President is properly elected. In case there is no available Vice President, Congress is given power to decide who should become Acting President to wait for the President to be properly chosen. The line of succession is the same as that spelled out by Congress under its power to legislate in Article 2 (see pp. 89–90).

Amendment 20 (Section 4)

The Congress may by law provide for the case of the death of any of the persons from whom the House of Representatives may choose a President whenever the right of choice shall have devolved upon them, and for the case of the death of any of the persons from whom the Senate may choose a Vice President whenever the right of choice shall have devolved upon them.

Suppose the House of Representatives must pick a President, and one of the leading contenders dies. Must the election proceed with the remaining candidates or can a replacement candidate be found? The 20th Amendment gives Congress the power to decide this question as well as what should happen if a Vice Presidential candidate dies while the Senate has responsibility for choosing.

This still leaves open the serious question of what happens if a President becomes sick or injured and unable to perform the duties of his office. Should the Vice President become President? Who is to determine whether a President is really unable to function? (See the 25th Amendment, see p. 207).

Amendment 20 (Sections 5 and 6)

Sections 1 and 2 shall take effect on the 15th day of October following the ratification of this article.

This article shall be inoperative unless it shall have been ratified as an amendment to the Constitution by the legislatures of three-fourths of the several States within seven years from the date of its submission.

The 20th Amendment was ratified by February, 1933.

Amendment 21 (Section 1)

The eighteenth article of amendment to the Constitution of the United States is hereby repealed.

Prohibition, the "noble experiment," was a flop. Businessmen who were supposed to go out of business went underground and the underworld of gangsters and racketeers opened up secret breweries and smuggled huge amounts of liquor into the United States. The net result of the enormous "bootleg" industry (so-called because illegal liquor was supposed to be hidden in the legs of long boots) was to make gangsters and racketeers fabulously rich. Organized crime received a boost from which it still profits today.

The plain fact was that people wanted liquor. When a law is so uniformly ignored that the attempts of the government to enforce it are laughed at, the law must go. So the 18th Amendment was swept aside by "repeal," the 21st Amendment, in 1933.

Amendment 21 (Section 2)

The transportation or importation into any States, Territory, or possession of the United States for delivery or use therein of intoxicating liquors, in violation of the laws thereof, is hereby prohibited.

Even before national Prohibition, the states had always been free to prohibit the manufacture, sale, or use of liquor.[70] The 21st Amendment left up to the states the decision as to whether to be wet or dry. By the 1960's, all states at one time or another became wet again. Almost all states retain laws regulating the sale of liquor to minors.

Amendment 21 (Section 3)

This article shall be inoperative unless it shall have been ratified as an amendment to the Constitution by conventions in the several States, as provided in the Constitution, within seven years from the date of the submission hereof to the States by the Congress.

The convention method of ratification has been used only once. It was called for in connection with the 21st Amendment to make sure that the amendment would quickly be ratified. The state legislatures were dominated by rural interests whom many thought might want to retain the 18th Amendment. By electing delegates to state conventions, however, the voters could exact pledges from candidates to vote for the proposed amendment. That happened. The amendment was passed by Congress in February, 1933, and sent to the states. Three-fourths of the states had ratified by December.

Amendment 22 (Section 1, Clause 1)

No person shall be elected to the office of the President more than twice, and no person who has held the office of President, or acted as President, for more than two years of a term to which some other person was elected President shall be elected to the office of the President more than once.

George Washington began a 144-year tradition when he refused to run for a third term in 1796. Franklin D. Roosevelt put an end to the "unwritten law" that Presidents should serve no more than eight years when he was elected to third and fourth terms in 1940 and 1944. To make the old tradition a part of the Constitution, this amendment was proposed by Congress in 1947 and ratified in 1951.

The 22nd Amendment makes ten years the maximum term any person can serve as President. If a Vice President serves more than two years of another person's term as President, he is eligible for reelection only once. President Lyndon B. Johnson, who served fourteen months of President Kennedy's term, is eligible to be reelected twice.

Amendment 22 (Section 1, Clause 2, and Section 2)

But this Article shall not apply to any person holding the office of President when this Article was proposed by the Congress, and shall not prevent any person who may be holding the office of President, or acting as President, during the term within which this Article becomes operative from holding the office of President or acting as President during the remainder of such term.

This article shall be inoperative unless it shall have been ratified as an amendment to the Constitution by the legislatures of three-fourths of the several States within seven years from the date of its submission to the States by the Congress.

The 22nd Amendment was worded to allow President Truman to run for reelection in 1952 if he chose to. He did not, and this section is now obsolete.

Amendment 23 (Sections 1 and 2)

The District constituting the seat of Government of the United States shall appoint in such manner as the Congress may direct:

A number of electors of President and Vice President equal to the whole number of Senators and Representatives in Congress to which the District would be entitled if it were a State, but in no event more than the least populous State; they shall be in addition to those appointed by the States, but they shall be considered, for the purposes of the election of President and Vice President, to be electors appointed by a State; and they shall meet in the District and perform such duties as provided by the twelfth article of amendment.

The Congress shall have power to enforce this article by appropriate legislation.

Residents of certain parts of Maryland and Virginia lost their right to vote in federal elections in 1802 when they became part of the District of Columbia. Because the District is not a state and has neither Senators nor Congressmen to represent its citizens in Congress, residents of Washington, D.C., had no voice in the election of the President.

The 23rd Amendment ratified in 1961, remedied this situation. The District, with a population of almost 1,000,000, larger than each of the thirteen smallest states, is now entitled to three electors—the maximum allowed the least populous states.

Amendment 24 (Sections 1 and 2)

The right of citizens of the United States to vote in any primary or other election for President or Vice President, for electors for President or Vice President, or for Senator or Representative in Congress, shall not be denied or abridged by the United States or any State by reason of failure to pay any poll tax or other tax.

The Congress shall have power to enforce this article by appropriate legislation.

The elimination of the poll tax was brought about to "provide a more direct approach to participation by more of the people in their Government." A constitutional amendment was thought necessary because Congress had no power to alter the qualification which the states laid down concerning who should have the vote. The amendment was ratified in 1964.

Many people had argued before its adoption that the 15th Amendment prohibited poll taxes in both federal and state elections. They therefore thought that the 24th Amendment was unnecessary. Some even thought it was dangerous. Since the 24th Amendment only covered federal elections and still left the states free to collect poll taxes on state elections, they feared that if a case involving the constitutionality of the state poll tax were then to come to the Supreme Court, the Court would have to rule that the 15th Amendment did not prohibit the state tax. If the 15th Amendment did, it would also prohibit the federal poll tax, and in that case, why was the 24th Amendment necessary? These fears proved groundless in 1966, when the Court did take such a case, and ruled that under the 14th Amendment (thus avoiding the 15th Amendment problem) poll taxes in state elections were unconstitutional.[64]

Amendment 25 (Section 1)
In case of the removal of the President from office or his death or resignation, the Vice President shall become President.

The 25th Amendment is the most recent addition to the Constitution. Proposed by Congress to the states in July, 1965, it was ratified by the 38th state in February, 1967. The amendment is the outcome of extensive Congressional hearings which followed in the wake of President Kennedy's assassination.

The original provisions of Article II did not make clear whether the Vice President was to become Chief Executive when the President died or was merely to become an Acting President. In 1841, Vice President Tyler assumed the Presidency when William Henry Harrison died one month after taking office. Since that time, no one has disputed that succeeding Vice Presidents are really Presidents. This section is more than an affirmation of an historical custom, however. The next sections create a new constitutional officer, the "Acting President," and Section 1 was written to ensure that when a President *dies* (as opposed to becoming sick), the Vice President will become President, as he has in the past.

Amendment 25 (Section 2)

Whenever there is a vacancy in the office of the Vice President, the President, shall nominate a Vice President who shall take the office upon confirmation by a majority vote of both houses of Congress.

Article II and the 12th and 20th Amendments did not provide for filling the Vice Presidential slot when he resigns (as John Calhoun did in 1832), or when he succeeds to the office of President (as happened in 1841, 1850, 1865, 1881, 1901, 1923, 1945, and 1963), or when he dies in office (as happened in 1812, 1814, 1853, 1875, 1885, 1899, and 1912). Altogether, there have been some thirty-eight years in our nation's history when there has been no Vice President. During all of this time, no President has ever died or resigned. But the situation has always been uneasy, especially since the person who would succeed to the Presidency would probably be a person in his seventy's or eighty's (since usually only persons of that age become Speaker of the House and President pro tempore of the Senate).

This section provides the method of filling the gap. Since as a matter of practical politics the Presidential candidate usually chooses his running mate, allowing the President to pick the Vice President makes sense. When a Presidential nominee names the Vice Presidential candidate, however, he must bear in mind that the ticket has to appeal to the entire country. Once a President is in office, he may not choose a Vice President on the same basis, there being no election pressure. So an additional vote—that of both houses of Congress—is required.

Amendment 25 (Section 3)

Whenever the President transmits to the President pro tempore of the Senate and the Speaker of the House of Representatives his written declaration that he is unable to discharge the powers and duties of his office, and until he transmits to them a written declaration to the contrary, such powers, and duties shall be discharged by the Vice President as Acting President.

Nothing in the Constitution or the 12th or 20th Amendments spelled out what could happen should the President become too physically or mentally sick to shoulder the burdens of office. It has been said that President Wilson's wife took a large hand in running the White House for more than a year after World War I when he was too ill to work.

What finally crystallized the drive for this amendment was the assassination of President Kennedy. Had the bullet not killed him, but only paralyzed him, no one knows what Vice President Johnson's role would have been, if any. In an age when nuclear war can be started, fought, and concluded in less than half an hour, it is vital to have a President who can act.

Under this section, the Vice President would become Acting President (but not President) when the President notifies him and Congress in writing that he is too ill to go on. The Vice President assumes the full powers and duties of the Presidential office, until the Chief Executive recovers his strength.

Amendment 25 (Section 4, Clause 1)

Whenever the Vice President and a majority of either the principal officers of the executive departments or of such other body as Congress may by law provide, transmit to the President pro tempore of the Senate and the Speaker of the House of Representatives their written declaration that the President is unable to discharge the powers and duties of his office, the Vice President shall immediately assume the powers and duties of the office of Acting President.

If the President is too ill even to write (or he refuses to write though he is mentally ill), the Vice President can still become Acting President. When he and a majority of the Cabinet officers declare that the President is too ill to act, the Vice President becomes Acting President immediately. (This section also allows Congress to name some agency other than the Cabinet to determine the extent of the President's disability. It has already been suggested that Congress create a Commission on Presidential Disability for this purpose.)

Amendment 25 (Section 4, Clause 2)

Thereafter, when the President transmits to the President pro tempore of the Senate and the Speaker of the House of Representatives his written declaration that no inability exists, he shall resume the powers and duties of his office unless the Vice President and a majority of either the principal officers of the executive department or of such other body as Congress may by law provide, transmit within four days to the President pro tempore of the Senate and the Speaker of the House of Representatives their written declaration that the President is unable to discharge the powers and duties of his office. Thereupon Congress shall decide the issue, assembling within 48 hours for that purpose if not in session. If the Congress, within 21 days after receipt of the latter written declaration, or, if Congress is not in session, within 21 days after Congress is required to assemble, determines by two-thirds vote of both houses that the President is unable to discharge the powers and duties of his office, the Vice President shall continued to discharge the same as Acting President; otherwise, the President shall resume the powers and duties of his office.

When a President regains his health he reassumes the powers and duties of his office within four days. Normally the Vice President and executive officers (or another body of men, if Congress has so provided) will not protest. But it is possible that a President who has become mentally ill may think he is fit to govern when in fact he is not. In that case his written declaration that he is no longer disabled can be overridden. The final decision must be made by Congress. If two-thirds of both houses have not voted within three weeks that the President is still unable to govern, he resumes his office.

This section has been severely criticized on the grounds that three weeks is far too long in our world to wait in doubt. An Acting President might be afraid to act, knowing that within three weeks he will no longer have the power. Or, he might act too hastily, in an attempt to do what he can while he still has the power.

Furthermore, Section 4 leaves unresolved the question of what happens once Congress by a two-thirds vote determines that the President is unfit to resume his official powers and duties. Can the President simply write another letter, saying no inability exists, and must Congress then vote again? Is there a reasonable time-period after a Congressional vote during which a disabled President would not be allowed to write? Would the Supreme Court decide these questions or leave it up to Congress? No one knows.

14 Interpreting The Future

"The life of the law has not been logic," said Oliver Wendell Holmes; "it has been experience." He did not mean that logic had no part to play in the judicial process. He did mean that the experience of past generations has proved the testing ground for what definitions will work and what will not. New circumstances give rise to new experiences and new tests. Some constitutional clauses dry up—the contract clause is one. It has a very limited role in modern society because lawyers have learned how to avoid it, and judges have learned to squeeze from other clauses the protections guaranteed by the contract clause. Some of these other clauses seem destined to go on and on as formal sources from which constitutional decisions can be drawn—the due process clauses, for instance. Others are maturing—the equal protection clause. Still others are just beginning to grow—the 9th Amendment's protection of the right to privacy.

Just as the clauses grow and expand in meaning and use, so each case decided by the courts has an impact far broader than its specific facts. Each case forces those opposed to find some *other* way of achieving their objectives. Those who favor segregation used to find it easy to enforce their policies: simply pass a law declaring lunchrooms, and hospitals, and schools segregated. When the Court says that these laws are unconstitutional, there are other devices to which segregationists can resort. But each of these devices is tested in turn. Each different case spells out the limits of lawfulness of all forms of segregation. Over the long course of decades, the courts help shape and fashion constitutional rules to meet many circumstances.

The school segregation cases are a good evidence of the Supreme Court's modern role. In the past, the Court usually has decided a case with reference only to the particular individuals involved in the dispute. Increasingly, however, the Court at times stands ready to consider cases which involve large social and political policies bearing on the freedom of the individual, and to decide these cases in favor of the individual. Though the school children were harmed by segregated classrooms, many were far more harmed by the ruling that segregation is unconstitutional. The strife and turmoil which followed *Brown v. Board of Education* indicates that many communities were strained to the breaking point. Negro children and families have been physically injured. The closing down of Negro schools without corresponding expansion of the pace of integration has meant that many Negroes have had less schooling than they would have received before *Brown*. In one Virginia county, schools were closed down for a total of four years.

The decision and its consequences make clear that the Supreme Court, through its decisions involving the Constitution, is an agency promoting social change. When there is absolutely no other institutional means for bringing about change, the Court stands ready to effect it. In the segregation cases, none of the southern states were politically inspired to repeal segregation laws; the Negro had no political power. Because many southerners in

Congress were chairmen of important committees which could block civil rights bills, and because southern Senators used the filibuster to prevent such bills from being voted on, the national legislature was not politically equipped to act either. That left the Supreme Court.

Because the Court has been instrumental in bringing about changes does not mean that it has acted beyond its legitimate scope of power. Often, the very purpose of a lawsuit is to ask for a change, and the Court cannot avoid the hard questions by refusing to decide them. In this regard, consider the reapportionment cases. For many years the Court had done just that, refused to consider or pass on the lawfulness of malapportioned state legislatures. The minority in power in each state would not rearrange the voting districts, because it would be voting itself out of office. Congress refused to help, in part because Congressional seats were themselves not equally apportioned in each state, and also because the national legislators did not want to upset the political balance in their home states. The popular majorities in each state, therefore, were stymied. The only way they could get the districts redrawn was to appeal the constitutional question to the Supreme Court.

In both the segregation and reapportionment cases, the states learned a lesson which they should have known all along. You can always be a little bit unjust and get away with it, because there is always play in the joints of a free society, but if you go too far, you will be slapped down and the slap will sting. For sixty years the states had ignored their own constitutions, which declared that districts should be apportioned according to population only. If the states had been more circumspect and had not flagrantly flaunted their own laws, perhaps "one man, one vote" as *federal* law would never have been declared. But the enormity of the states' lawlessness demanded severity.

Similarly, it should not have been a surprise that the interstate commerce power was used by Congress to enact civil rights laws to secure, primarily for Negroes, a step toward all-too-long suppressed equality. Nor should it have been a surprise that the Supreme Court would sustain such legislation under a clause which seemingly deals with business and trade rather than with justice and equality. For it was the very coming together of the American people into an increasingly single nation— brought on by the development of national markets after World War II—that helped spark the Negroes' awareness of what life might be like, that helped urge others to protest with the Negro, that provided funds, and that caught the attention of news media and eventually the people, the government, and the world. It was a burgeoning economy that made it possible to start a revolution. As the nation became interdependent, no people could be downcast, without casting down the delicately tuned economy. At least, so it can be—and was—amply and successfully argued.

From the perspective of 175 years, it is apparent that a majority almost always has more than one way of reaching its desired goals. There are almost always alternatives. It is also apparent that as circumstances change, majorities change, and so do goals and desires. Few people would dismantle today's technology and industry and return to the "pastoral" life envisioned by President Jefferson. Because our national life has shifted focus from farm to city, our laws and power centers have had to shift also. The 90th Congress has immense powers, compared to the 1st Congress. The problems which Congress must solve through legislation have likewise multiplied, undoubtedly beyond the stretch of imagination of the most visionary member of the 1st Congress. Without the problems, there would not be the power.

If the states have lost power with respect to Congress, because problems have become nationwide, the states today exercise a far greater power over their citizenry than decades ago. Think of the licenses and registration procedures necessary for anything from automobiles to voting. Think of the innumerable laws which the hundreds of municipal agencies promulgate and enforce. Think of the tangle of government agencies, bureaus, and departments. It is estimated that in the New York metropolitan area there are more than 1,400 different "governments" each with their power to plan, to administer, to regulate.

And if Congress and the states have changed, so have

the courts and the Executive. Today state and federal courts are clogged with cases. Some local courts have a backlog as great as four years. The Federal Executive has grown to be an employer of millions. It sends rockets to the moon, administers agencies which look after automobile safety, the wheat crop, the future of the Grand Canyon, and still worries about the mail service.

Looming up between each, between the Congress and courts, between the President and Congress, and between the Congress and the states, stand the federal administrative agencies. These organs of government operate "in between" the law: they write regulations to plug loopholes, they prosecute offenders of the law, they watch over their respective industries, technologies, and activities to ensure that the law will be more smoothly administered than were it left to the already too-busy Congress and courts.

Through it all, the people go about their daily tasks. Have increased governmental regulations and laws meant a decrease in our freedom of action? Some people think so. It is no doubt a nuisance to fill out income tax forms (and no doubt a nuisance, to some, to have to pay taxes). The investor cannot speculate so freely with the Securities and Exchange Commission watching over his significant transactions. Rates of commercial carriers are regulated. Business does not operate without an eye toward the rules of the National Labor Relations Board. It is true that in many areas of life, our actions are restricted by what legislatures, courts, and agencies deem lawful and proper.

As individuals, however, and as families, our freedom is immeasurably greater than that of our Revolutionary forebears. Law, science, commerce, and culture have combined to give us far greater living standards, far greater education, far more ways in which to occupy our lives. Our freedom to speak and publish, to worship and associate as we please, is greater today than ever before, if only because there are more ways in which to speak, to print, to worship, and to associate, and because there are more of us to do it. Should we be suspected of crime, our freedom against arbitrary governmental power is far more secure today than it ever was.

Of course, freedom can be increased. The methods and institutions of government can be improved. New developments in technology and commerce always mean new problems, new dangers, and new promises. Pollution of our air and waterways has reached the danger point. Industrial refineries, automobiles, and dozens of other causes contribute to the national smog, harmful to life and property. Electronic devices now in operation can overhear conversations miles away. Computers are capable of coordinating and storing vast amounts of data about vast numbers of people. Possible invasions of privacy might defeat us as much as smog, traffic fatalities, poverty, and crime.

It is impossible to guess with any degree of accuracy how these problems will be attacked and how they will be solved. It is obvious, however, that as the people of America begin to attack these and other problems, the Constitution will figure in the argument, as it always has. For instance, if pollution is a national problem, it can be argued that Congress should play a paramount role. Undoubtedly many laws to curb pollution could be justified under the commerce clause, but perhaps a new power will evolve, a federal power to remedy national health and safety hazards. As Congress develops more and more power, more and more problems are brought to it for solution. Since the states are increasingly incapable of solving their own problems (such as poverty and crime), many people argue, Congress must provide the answers. At the same time, however, the Supreme Court has begun to develop the constitutional doctrine of "one man, one vote." If the enforcement of this principle shifts power centers within the states, if the states are led to reconsider their constitutions and their governmental structure, they may organize themselves more efficiently and thereby ease the burden which Congress increasingly shoulders.

The future and the Constitution are not fixed. Just as future events will call for new approaches to interpretation of our fundamental law, so the Constitution, through interpretations of the past, will continue to shape our evolving history.

TABLE OF CASES

NOTE ON CITATIONS

The cases cited in this table can be found in any standard law library. Since 1876, the opinions in cases decided by the Supreme Court have been published in the official volumes known as *United States Reports* (abbreviated "U.S."). Thus, *Abbate v. United States,* 359 U.S. 187 (1959), means that the case of *Abbate v. United States* can be located in volume 359 of the *United States Reports* at page 187, and that the case was decided in 1959.

Prior to 1876, the Supreme Court decisions were published in volumes bearing the name of the Reporter of Decisions of the Supreme Court, the officer in charge of coordinating and preparing the decisions for publication. For instance, *Barron v. Baltimore* (7 Pet.) 243 (1833) means that the case appears at page 243 of the seventh volume of Richard Peters. To make the citations uniform in the following table of cases, all such old cases will contain a double citation. Thus, *Barron v. Baltimore,* 32 U.S. (7 Pet.) 243 (1833), indicates that 32 U.S. and 7 Pet. are equivalent. The reporters and abbreviations of their names, from 1790 on, are Alexander James Dallas (Dall.), reporter from 1790 to 1800, William Cranch (Cr.), 1801-1815, Henry Wheaton (Wheat.), 1816-1827, Richard Peters (Pet.), 1828-1842, Benjamin Howard (How.), 1843-1860, Jeremiah Black (Bl.), 1861-1862, and John William Wallace (Wall.), 1863-1875. Cases heard during the October term, 1875, appear in 91 U.S., and the reporters' names were dropped thereafter.

An extra citation may appear following some cases in this table. This means that a rehearing was held, that the case was returned to the Court for further proceedings, or that a new case stemming from the old dispute had arisen.

The name of the Justice who wrote the majority opinion follows each citation in this table. (A few cases bear the notation "per curiam," meaning that the Court as a whole wrote the opinion, rather than an individual Justice. Usually a per curiam opinion is a short paragraph.) The letters "C.J." after some names indicate Chief Justice. Following each name is the vote in the case ("U" meaning unanimous, as far as the official reports indicate). Occasionally, the vote will total less than nine. This is because a Justice may have resigned or died shortly before the case was decided, or because he may have been involved in the case before he was appointed to the bench or did not participate in the oral argument and thus took no part in the decision, or because (in the early cases) the Court consisted of less than nine Justices.

Cases are included in this table only if they have been referred to in the text. This is by no means meant to be an exhaustive listing of all Supreme Court cases involving the Constitution.

Cases are arranged alphabetically except for a few which were decided after the hard-cover edition had been written. These recent cases are appended under the heading "Recent Cases" (beginning at p. 295) and are referred to in the text by their footnote numbers.

(NUMBERS IN BRACKETS REFER TO PAGES IN THE TEXT.)

1. *Abbate v. United States,* 359 U.S. 187 (1959). Brennan, 6-3. The defendants, upon their guilty pleas, were convicted in an Illinois court of conspiracy to destroy property of another and served three months in jail. Subsequently, they were tried for the same act, conspiracy to destroy communications facilities operated by the United States, a federal crime. The Supreme Court held this second conviction not to be a violation of the 5th Amendment double-jeopardy clause.

2. *Abrams v. United States,* 250 U.S. 616 (1919). Clarke, 7-2. Abrams and four others were convicted in federal court of violating the Espionage Act by circulating pamphlets designed to incite factory workers to strike and to stop manufacturing munitions essential to United States activities in World War I. The Supreme Court upheld their conviction, saying the 1st Amendment was not violated, even though the ultimate intent of the propagandists was to prevent United States interference with the Russian Revolution and not to prevent United States prosecution of the war with Germany. [140, 153]

3. *Adamson v. California,* 332 U.S. 46 (1947). Reed, 5-4. At his trial, Adamson refused to take the stand to testify in his behalf, in accordance with his privilege to refuse to incriminate himself. The prosecutor commented on the fact that the defendant did not take the stand, asking the jury to consider that such conduct seemed likely to come only from a guilty person. Adamson was convicted and he appealed, claiming a deprivation of liberty without due process. The Supreme Court affirmed, saying that the 14th Amendment

did not incorporate the no-comment rule, which the 5th Amendment makes binding on the federal courts. This case was overruled by *Griffin v. California.* [139]

4. *Aptheker v. Secretary of State,* 378 U.S. 500 (1964). Goldberg, 6-3.
Aptheker, editor of a journal of the United States Communist Party, was denied a passport and the right to travel abroad, under a section of the Subversive Activities Control Act of 1950. The Supreme Court reversed the lower court's determination that the Act was constitutional as applied to Aptheker, holding that the right to travel was an essential part of the liberty guaranteed by the due process clause of the 5th Amendment; the Court examined the statute on its face and found it to be overly broad, restricting as it did the right of travel of anyone who was a member of an organization found to be subversive. [149]

5. *Baggett v. Bullitt,* 377 U.S. 360 (1964). White, 7-2.
Washington State required a loyalty oath of its employees. The oaths were broadly written, containing a declaration by the affirmant that he would promote "by precept and example . . . respect for the flag and the institutions of the U.S. and the State of Washington." A second oath required the person to swear he was not subversive, defined in part as one "who commits, attempts to commit, or aids in the commission or advocates, abets, advises or teaches by any means any person to commit, or aid in the commission of any act intended to overthrow, destroy, or alter, or to assist in the overthrow, destruction, or alteration . . . of the government of the U.S., or of the State of Washington . . . by revolution, force, or violence." The Supreme Court reversed the district court's dismissal of the suit seeking an injunction against enforcement, holding that the oaths were too vague to afford the takers due process of law under the 14th Amendment. [164-5]

6. *Barron v. Baltimore,* 32 U.S. (7 Pet.) 243 (1833). Marshall, U.
The Bill of Rights (prior to the passage of the 14th Amendment) applied only to the federal government. The city of Baltimore could destroy Barron's wharf business by drying up the dock water for a public reason and need not pay him for what it took. [136]

7. *Bartkus v. Illinois,* 359 U.S. 121 (1959). Frankfurter, 7-2.
Bartkus was tried and acquitted in federal court for the crime of robbing a federally insured savings bank. Later, on substantially the same evidence, he was convicted in an Illinois state court for the state crime of robbing a bank. The Supreme Court rejected his contention that the cooperation of state and federal officials resulted in double jeopardy under the 5th Amendment and that the prior acquittal necessitated a bar to trial under 14th Amendment due process. [176]

8. *Beacon Theatres v. Westover,* 359 U.S. 500 (1959). Black, 5-3.
   In a complex civil antitrust suit, issues of law and equity were presented. The judge ruled that he would try in equity the issues common to both claims and a jury would sit only for the purely legal issues. The Supreme Court reversed, holding that the district judge acted beyond his discretion, since issues which should be tried before a jury cannot be deprived of a jury hearing under the 7th Amendment merely because they also are common to an equity suit. Hence the issues common to equity and legal proceedings must be tried to a jury and only the purely equitable issues can be tried to the judge alone. [192]

9. *Beauharnais v. Illinois,* 343 U.S. 250 (1952). Frankfurter, 5-4.
   The defendant was convicted in state court for distributing anti-Negro pamphlets in violation of a "group libel" law, prohibiting exhibition in a public place of any publication exposing "citizens of any race, color, creed or religion to contempt, derision, or obloquy." He appealed, the Supreme Court affirmed. The law is not vague, does not violate the 1st and 14th Amendments, and no clear and present danger need be shown since libel is not protected speech. [157]

10. *Betts v. Brady,* 316 U.S. 455 (1942). Roberts, 6-3.
    Betts was refused a lawyer to represent him at state expense, when he requested counsel at his trial for robbery, saying he was too poor to afford a lawyer. The Supreme Court affirmed his conviction, holding that the 14th Amendment does not incorporate the 6th Amendment's provision of right to counsel in criminal trials unless there are special circumstances. This case was overruled by *Gideon v. Wainwright.* [187]

11. *Bolling v. Sharpe,* 347 U.S. 497 (1954). Warren, C.J., U.
    The district court for the District of Columbia had refused to admit Negro schoolchildren to the white-only public schools. The Supreme Court reversed, saying that segregation was a deprivation of due process under the 5th Amendment. [217]

12. *Bridges v. California,* 314 U.S. 252 (1941). Black, 5-4.
    Bridges, an officer of a union, sent a telegram to the Secretary of Labor, in which he called the decision of a California judge involving the union "outrageous" and announced an intention not to let the state court enforce its order. A Los Angeles newspaper in an editorial just as strongly announced that the judge would make a "serious mistake" if he refused to enforce the order and granted a new trial instead. Bridges and the newspaper were held in contempt and

convicted by the state court. The Supreme Court reversed; it did not find that the telegram or editorial tended to interfere with justice by intimidating the judge. Freedom of speech is broad, and it cannot be assumed that judges are so weak they will be swayed by out-of-court statements. [167]

bition was a form of regulation, and that Congress had the authority to deal with lotteries in such a manner. [59]

17. *Chisholm v. Georgia*, 2 U.S. (2 Dall.) 419 (1793). Jay, C.J., 5-1.
Chisholm sued Georgia for money owed. Claiming it could not be sued without consent, Georgia took no part in the suit. The suit was brought to the Supreme Court because Article III gave original jurisdiction to the Court in all cases in which a state is a party. The Court held it had jurisdiction to hear disputes between an individual citizen and his state and awarded Chisholm the money. This case was overruled by the 11th Amendment. [195]

18. *Civil Rights Cases*, 109 U.S. 3 (1883). Bradley, 8-1.
An Act of Congress made it unlawful for hotels, restaurants, theaters, and other privately owned facilities to discriminate against any persons on account of race. The Court reversed a conviction under the law, holding it unconstitutional, since it was based on the 14th Amendment, which forbids only states from denying equal protection of the laws, not private individuals. This case made it necessary for Congress to resort to the commerce clause in the 1960's to achieve the same ends that the Reconstruction Congresses sought. [211, 224]

19. *Clarke v. Deckebach*, 274 U.S. 392 (1927). Stone, U.
A treaty with Great Britain guaranteed the right to "merchants and traders of each nation" to "enjoy the most complete protection and security for their commerce." An Ohio law prohibited issuance of licenses to aliens to operate pool halls. The Supreme Court held that the law did not violate the treaty and that it was not an unreasonable discrimination and thus did not violate the equal protection clause. [221]

20. *Cohens v. Virginia*, 19 U.S. (6 Wheat.) 264 (1821). Marshall, C.J., U.
The Court had exercised appellate jurisdiction from the start under the Judiciary Act of 1789 to hear cases on appeal from the final state judgment in which a state rules that its own laws are superior to the federal Constitution, laws, or treaties. The 11th Amendment, passed in 1795, said states could not be sued in federal courts by their own citizens. Here, Virginia had convicted Cohens of selling lottery tickets, a state crime. Cohens argued that the tickets were issued by the city of Washington, D.C., under an act of Congressional authorization. On appeal, the Virginia Supreme Court argued that the Supreme Court of the United States could not hear the case since it was between a citizen and his state. The Court rejected the argument, reasoning that the

11th Amendment meant only that a citizen could not begin a suit against his state in federal court. An appeal is not the beginning of the suit. Otherwise, no citizen could ever protest his conviction in a state criminal case, no matter how unconstitutionally the state had acted. Having decided in favor of its own jurisdiction, the Supreme Court held for Virginia, since the Act of Congress had not said the tickets had to be sold outside Washington, if a state objected. [106, 196]

21. *Coleman v. Miller,* 307 U.S. 433 (1939). Hughes, C.J., 7-2.
The Kansas senate ratified the Child Labor Amendment, years after it had originally rejected it. The secretary of state of Kansas certified that the state had ratified. Mandamus was sought to have him strike the certification from the record, on the grounds that a state could not ratify what it earlier rejected. The Supreme Court dismissed the suit (thus, in effect, affirming the state Supreme Court's denial of mandamus), holding that ratification was a political question which Congress and the state legislatures alone could settle. The certification stood. (The amendment failed to pass, and the change in the Court's view toward interstate commerce questions in the late 1930's made the amendment unnecessary.) [124]

22. *Cooley v. Board of Wardens, Port of Philadelphia,* 53 U.S. (12 How.) 299 (1851). Curtis, 7-2.
The interstate commerce clause does not prohibit the states from making laws that affect commerce among the states as long as the laws only regulate those aspects of commerce which do not require a national uniformity of regulation. The regulation of pilots on riverboats is a local matter and Pennsylvania can constitutionally require local pilots to be aboard. National uniformity here is unnecessary. [52]

23. *Cooper v. Aaron,* 358 U.S. 1 (1958). Per curiam, and a signed opinion by all nine Justices.
The governor and other high officials of Arkansas refused to carry out the desegregation orders of the federal courts, pursuant to the Supreme Court's decision in *Brown v. Board of Education.* They claimed that they were not constitutionally bound to the Supreme Court's adjudication. The governor used National Guard troops to prevent Negro schoolchildren from entering the schools. Because the school board, which had attempted to abide by the Supreme Court ruling and integrate the schools, was rebuffed by the executive, legislative, and judicial authorities of the state, the board asked the Court to delay its integration order, urging that otherwise more violence might occur. The Supreme Court rejected the contention of the board that be-

cause some state officials resisted the board's good faith attempt to comply, it should be excused now from having to comply. Any state officer who wars against the Constitution violates his Article 6, Clause 3, oath to support it. The Supreme Court is the final adjudicator of constitutional questions. [218]

24. *Cox v. Louisiana,* 379 U.S. 559 (1965). Goldberg, 5-4.
Cox was arrested and convicted for disturbing the peace, obstructing public passages, and picketing near a courthouse, when he led a demonstration of more than 2,000 Negro students to within 101 feet of a Baton Rouge courthouse, with the approval of the police chief, and then spoke, urging a lunch counter sit-in, at which point tear gas was turned on the crowd. Cox was arrested the next day. The Supreme Court reversed the conviction on all three counts, though upholding the statute which proscribed picketing in front of a courthouse. The statute used the phrase "near a courthouse," and Cox urged that this was unconstitutionally vague. The Court rejected this argument, but held with Cox that "near" could be defined by the police officer in charge in a given situation, and when the police chief allowed him to conduct his demonstration, he was not "near" a courthouse for the purposes of the statute. Otherwise, he would have been entrapped by the police, a violation of the 14th Amendment due process clause. [163]

25. *The Daniel Ball,* 77 U.S. (10 Wall.) 557 (1871). Field, U.
A vessel that travels on navigable water entirely within one state but carries goods bound for destinations out of state is subject to interstate commerce laws of Congress, since the goods have begun to move in commerce between the states. Hence, it was unlawful for "The Daniel Ball," which plied the waterways in Michigan, to refuse to register under Congressional laws. [53]

26. *Dartmouth College v. Woodward,* 17 U.S. (4 Wheat.) 519 (1819). Marshall, C.J., 5-1.
New Hampshire tried to take control of Dartmouth College, which had been granted a charter by the King. The Court held that New Hampshire had no power to take over the private institution, since the charter was like a contract, which could not be impaired by the state under the contract clause. [81]

27. *Davis v. Schnell,* 336 U.S. 933 (1949). Per curiam.
The Boswell Amendment to the Alabama Constitution provided that only persons who can "understand and explain" any article of the United States Constitution to the satisfaction of the board of registrars could vote.

No standards were laid down to guide the board, and the Supreme Court affirmed the lower court's decision that this arbitrary power to exclude people from voting was a violation of the 14th Amendment. [227-8]

28. *DeJonge v. Oregon,* 299 U.S. 353 (1937). Hughes, C.J., 8-0. DeJonge spoke at a meeting of the Communist Party in Oregon. That state had a criminal syndicalism law, making the advocacy of industrial or political revolution by unlawful means a crime. The Supreme Court reversed the conviction; it ruled that since the only reason DeJonge was convicted and sentenced for seven years was his speech at the meeting (there being no evidence that he advocated violence), the law as applied to his act was unconstitutional, an abridgement of his freedom of speech under the 1st and 14th Amendments. [162]

29. *Dennis v. United States,* 339 U.S. 162 (1950) and 341 U.S. 494 (1951). Vinson, C.J., 6-2. Dennis and ten others were convicted of violating the Smith Act of 1940, which made conspiracy to overthrow the government by force or violence unlawful. The defendants were convicted particularly of having conspired to organize the Communist Party to advocate the overthrow of the government. They appealed on the ground that the Act was unconstitutional because it abridged their freedoms of speech and association and because the statute was vague. The Supreme Court rejected all arguments and the convictions were affirmed. The holding in this case was narrowed by the later cases of *Yates, Scales,* and *Noto.* [155]

30. *Dred Scott v. Sandford,* 60 U.S. (19 How.) 393 (1857). Taney, C.J., 7-2 (each Justice wrote a separate opinion). Dred Scott was a Negro slave belonging to a United States Army surgeon. He was taken to Illinois (a free state) from Missouri (a slave state) in 1834, and two years later to a place in the Territory of Louisiana north of the Missouri Compromise line (hence free). In 1838 he was taken back to Missouri and continued in bondage for nine years. In 1847, after having been sold to a New York citizen, Scott brought suit in Missouri, claiming on the basis of past decisions that once having lived in free states and territories, he was entitled to freedom. Taney ruled that the Missouri Compromise, enacted into federal law by Congress, was unconstitutional, insofar as it prohibited a person from holding property (slaves) in certain territories, because it was against due process to make a property right depend on location. So living in the Territory of Louisiana did not confer freedom. (Nor did living in Illi-

nois, because, said the Court, slave status depended on the state of residence, which was Missouri, even though Scott lived temporarily in Illinois.) Taney also went further than he had to and ruled that a Negro could not become a citizen of the United States, and that no state could confer national citizenship upon him (though a state could confer state citizenship). Although no majority agreed with Taney's reasons, six Justices agreed that the case should be remanded to the lower court with instructions to dismiss the case. The whole argument, which led to the Civil War, came to and end with the 13th and 14th Amendments. [202]

31. *Duncan v. Kahanamoku,* 342 U.S. 833 (1945) and 327 U.S. 304 (1946). Black, 6-2.
Following the Japanese attack on Pearl Harbor, the governor of Hawaii put a United States Army general in Hawaii in charge of the government. Military courts were substituted for civil courts and Duncan, a civilian employed by the Navy, was convicted in one of the military courts for assault. The Supreme Court ruled that the military government was unlawful and that the suspension of habeas corpus, which the military government had ordered, was unconstitutional when it remained suspended beyond the length of time necessary for restoring order. In Hawaii, that period was not very long. [76, 91]

32. *Elfbrandt v. Russell,* 384 U.S. 11 (1966). Douglas, 5-4.
Elfbrandt, an Arizona teacher, refused to take the state loyalty oath because she could not discover its full meaning and scope. It required her to swear her allegiance to state and nation; a state law provided that anyone who after taking the oath joined the Communist Party or any other organization which had for one of its purposes the overthrow of the government by force could be removed from his job and prosecuted for perjury. The Supreme Court held the law unconstitutional, finding an abridgement of freedom of association, since it forbade a person from being a teacher in the public schools even if he did not support the illegal aims of the organization to which he belonged. This made the law too broad, since one can belong to any organization as long as he does not support any illegal purposes. [156]

33. *Elkins v. United States,* 364 U.S. 206 (1960). Stewart, 5-4.
State police illegally came across evidence that Elkins was involved in a federal crime. The police turned the evidence over to federal officers, who brought Elkins to trial in federal court. The Supreme Court reversed the

conviction, holding that evidence illegally obtained by
state officials, even if federal officials had no hand in its
gathering, must be excluded at trial. This case spelled
the demise of the "silver platter" doctrine. [173]

34. *Erie Railroad Co. v. Tompkins,* 304 U.S. 64 (1938).
Brandeis, 6-2.
Tompkins was injured by the railroad while he was
walking along its Pennsylvania track. He sued in New
York, where the company was incorporated, in a federal district court, which took jurisdiction because of
the diversity of citizenship. The lower courts applied
the federal rule of negligence, which resulted in a verdict for Tompkins. The Supreme Court reversed, saying that in diversity cases, there is no federal common
law, and that federal courts must use the state common
law. [112]

35. *Estes v. Texas,* 381 U.S. 532 (1965). Clark, 5-4.
Estes was convicted of fraud, a felony, in a state trial
at which television cameras beamed the proceedings to
home viewers. The Supreme Court reversed and ordered a new trial, holding that to televise a trial is a
denial of due process, since the cameras might tend to
make the participants be less diligent in the carrying
out of their courtroom duties (it was feared that they
would play to the cameras instead). [184]

36. *Evans v. Newton,* 382 U.S. 296 (1966). Douglas, 6-3.
A park administered by a public body discriminated
against Negroes. Fearing that the discrimination would
be struck down under the equal protection clause, the
city officials tried to divest themselves of control and
place the operation of the park in private hands, to
carry out the intent of the person who had willed the
park to the white citizens of the city. The Supreme
Court ruled that the device would not work; any discrimination would be a violation of the equal protection clause and the Court refused to let the city divest
itself of control. [214]

37. *Everson v. Board of Education,* 330 U.S. 1 (1947).
Black, 5-4.
New Jersey state law authorized local school districts to
make rules concerning transportation of schoolchildren.
A board of education reimbursed parents of children
who used public buses to and from both public and
parochial schools. A taxpayer sued the board of education, claiming that the reimbursement of parents of
children attending parochial school was unconstitu-

tional under the establishment clause of the 1st Amendment. The Supreme Court upheld the board, saying that the clause cannot be used to put religions at a disadvantage. [141, 147]

38. *Ex parte Endo,* 323 U.S. 283 (1944), Douglas, U.
The government conceded that Miss Endo was a loyal citizen, but ordered her detained under the wartime acts designed to protect the United States against sabotage. On an appeal from a denial of a petition of habeas corpus, the Supreme Court held that where loyalty is conceded, it was unconstitutional to detain a citizen, since the wartime restrictions, intended to guard against sabotage, were not necessary in her case. [68]

39. *Ex parte Garland,* 71 U.S. (4 Wall.) 333 (1867). Field, 5-4.
An Act of Congress declared that no attorney could practice before the federal courts, even if previously allowed to, unless he first took an oath stating he had never engaged in conduct hostile to the United States. The Act was aimed at lawyers who sided with the Confederacy. Garland had been pardoned by the President for his activities on behalf of the Confederacy and when he was excluded from practice, the Supreme Court declared the act unconstitutional because it was like a bill of attainder: it punished for past conduct a named class of persons, and insofar as it punished for acts not unlawful at the time, it was an ex post facto law as well. [92]

40. *Ex parte Kemmler,* 136 U.S. 436 (1890). Fuller, U.
Kemmler was sentenced to death for murder after conviction by a jury. The sentence called for execution by electrocution. Kemmler filed a petition of habeas corpus, claiming that electrocution was a cruel and unusual punishment, contrary to the 8th Amendment as incorporated by the 14th Amendment. The Supreme Court affirmed the sentence—the electric chair is not cruel and unusual.

41. *Ex parte McCardle,* 73 U.S. (6 Wall.) 318 (1868) and 74 U.S. (7 Wall.) 506 (1869). Chase, C.J., U.
The Supreme Court had held that it had jurisdiction to hear a habeas corpus appeal from a lower court involving the lawfulness of the military arrest of McCardle, a southern newspaper editor. This jurisdiction was based on The Reconstruction Act. After the Supreme Court heard argument, but before it handed down a decision in the case, Congress repealed the Act granting jurisdiction, and the Court ruled that it had no authority to decide the case, its jurisdiction having been removed.

The decision of the lower court thus stood as the final ruling—against McCardle. [115]

42. *Feiner v. New York,* 340 U.S. 315 (1951). Vinson, C.J., 6-3.
Feiner, a university student, was arrested for speaking to a crowd of people, after he had made derogatory remarks about the President, the mayor and other officials, and after the police had asked him several times to stop because they noticed the crowd growing restless. Feiner appealed his conviction, charging that the police had suppressed his political opinions, contrary to the 1st and 14th Amendments. The Supreme Court upheld the conviction, holding the police empowered to prevent public riot before it happens. [190]

43. *Fletcher v. Peck,* 10 U.S. (6 Cr.) 87 (1810). Marshall, C.J., U.
A grant by a state legislature of the title of public lands to private persons is as binding as a contract, and the state, under the contract clause, could not a few years later take back the land. Hence, a person who refused to pay the persons from whom the land was purchased could not escape his contract by claiming that the title was clouded with the possibility that the state would recover the land. [81]

44. *Francis v. Resweber,* 329 U.S. 459 (1947). Reed, 5-4.
The defendant had been convicted of murder in the first degree and was sentenced to death. He was placed in the electric chair and the switch was thrown, but because of a malfunction, the power was not great enough to kill him. He made an appeal to the Supreme Court claiming that to try to execute him again would be double jeopardy and cruel and unusual punishment. The Supreme Court held against him on both grounds. [190]

45. *Freedman v. Maryland,* 380 U.S. 51 (1965). Brennan, U.
Freedman refused to submit his motion picture to the Maryland Board of Censors for approval prior to its public showing. Conceding that the picture would have been given a license had he applied for it, he was convicted. The Maryland Supreme Court sustained the conviction and the Supreme Court reversed, holding the censorship law to be unconstitutional because of its procedures, since it placed a prior restraint on the showing. The Court ruled that in order to be upheld, a censorship law must (1) put the burden of showing a film enjoinable on the state, (2) make the state either issue a license within a stated, brief time period or get a court injunction against the film, and (3)

give an assurance that a court will determine the case promptly on its merits. [150]

46. *Frothingham v. Mellon*, 262 U.S. 447 (1923). Sutherland, U.
   Mrs. Frothingham sued the Secretary of the Treasury to prevent him from paying out funds of the United States in accordance with the Maternity Act. She claimed that Congress had no power to spend federal money to help mothers and that she was injured by having to pay increased taxes to support the Act. The Supreme Court dismissed her suit, holding that she had no "standing" to sue, since her only injury was as a federal taxpayer and like the millions of taxpayers, was too slight to justify the suit if any injury at all, in fact, could be found. [104]

47. *Gallagher v. Crown Kosher Supermarket*, 366 U.S. 617 (1961). Warren, C.J., 6-3.
   Massachusetts law forbade opening of stores on Sundays (except for sale of kosher meat until 10 A.M.). The store had been operating on Sundays (and done one-third of its weekly business) without interference, but then the state enforced the law, prohibiting it from doing business on Sunday. Suing for an injunction to stop the state from enforcing the law (the police chief had arrested and prosecuted the store's manager), the store lost its case in the Supreme Court, which reversed the lower court's finding that the blue laws were an "unbelievable hodgepodge." The law was a constitutional exercise of the state's police power and was not invalid under the 1st and 14th Amendments. [147]

48. *Gibbons v. Ogden*, 22 U.S. (9 Wheat.) 1 (1824). Marshall, C.J., U.
   The acts of the New York legislature, granting an exclusive monopoly to two men to navigate the waters of New York with steamboats were unconstitutional as against the interstate commerce clause insofar as they prevented steamboats, licensed by Congress to carry on a coastal trade, from navigating the New York waters. [51]

49. *Gibson v. Florida Legislative Investigation Committee*, 372 U.S. 539 (1963). Goldberg, 5-4.
   Gibson was ordered to appear before the Committee and to bring membership lists of the Miami branch of the National Association for the Advancement of Colored People, of which he was president. The chairman of the Florida Committee said the inquiry would be directed toward Communist activities in various fields, such as education and race

relations. Gibson refused to produce the membership lists, though he did answer all questions put to him and volunteered to answer any questions concerning membership on the basis of his personal knowledge. He refused to produce the lists, because he thought their use by the Committee would deprive the members of their freedom of association. He was convicted of contempt, sentenced to prison, and fined. The Supreme Court reversed the contempt conviction; there was no evidence to show that the NAACP was Communist-oriented; it had tried for years to prevent Communists from joining; since the subject of the inquiry was Communism and no one charged the NAACP, Gibson could refuse to disclose the list. [164]

50. *Gideon v. Wainwright,* 373 U.S. 335 (1963). Black, U.
Gideon was convicted of petty larceny in Florida, after the court refused to appoint counsel for him; he was indigent. The Supreme Court reversed the conviction, holding that the 6th Amendment as incorporated in the 14th, guarantees the right of counsel to all criminal defendants and that the state must appoint counsel if the defendant cannot afford one. This case overruled *Betts v. Brady.* [187]

51. *Ginzburg v. United States,* 383 U.S. 463 (1966). Brennan, 5-4.
Ginzburg was convicted of having violated the postal statutes by mailing obscene material. The Supreme Court upheld the conviction, holding in part that when it is unclear whether the work is obscene, evidence that the defendant meant to "pander to prurient interest" would go toward sustaining the conviction. [160]

52. *Gitlow v. New York,* 268, U.S. 652 (1925). Sanford, 7-2.
The New York State criminal anarchy statute prohibits the publication of pamphlets advocating the overthrow of organized government by violence. Gitlow was convicted and appealed to the Supreme Court on the grounds that the statute was arbitrary and unreasonable and that the 14th Amendment makes the 1st Amendment applicable to the states. The Supreme Court agreed for the first time that the 1st Amendment was incorporated in the 14th, but disagreed that the statute was unreasonable and under the *Schenck* doctrine (*Schenck v. United States*), the conviction stood. [153]

53. *Gomillion v. Lightfoot,* 364 U.S. 339 (1960). Frankfurter. U.
Tuskegee, Alabama, carved itself up into a twenty-eight-sided figure, in order to exclude Negroes who lived on the city borders from voting in municipal elections. The Supreme Court had on many previous occasions refused to review cases involving the fairness of state legislative districts,

on the grounds that these were political questions, but this time the Court ruled that scheme was a clear violation of the equal protection clause, because its only purpose was to disfranchise Negroes. [225]

54. *Gray v. Sanders, 372 U.S. 368 (1963).* Douglas, 8-1.
Georgia organized its voting districts for primaries for United States Senator and for statewide offices on a county-unit basis. Plaintiffs sought an injunction and the Supreme Court held that the county-unit system, in which each county was given equal representation in the voting, was unconstitutional under the equal protection clause, since the counties were of varying population sizes. [220]

55. *Griffin v. Illinois, 351 U.S. 12 (1956).* Black, 6-3.
The defendant Griffin failed to take the stand in his criminal trial. The judge instructed the jury that it could consider his failure to take the stand while it deliberated on its verdict. The Supreme Court reversed the jury verdict of guilty, holding that neither judge nor prosecutor could comment on the defendant's failure to take the stand, the rule stemming from the 5th Amendment's prohibition against self-incrimination, as incorporated by the 14th Amendment. This case overruled *Adamson v. California.* [178]

56. *Griffin v. Illinois, 351 U.S. 12 (1956).* Black, 6-3.
Illinois allowed appeal of a criminal conviction only if certain documents were prepared by the defendant; preparation usually required use of a stenographic transcript of the trial proceedings. These were costly and only those indigent defendants sentenced to death were given a transcript free. Griffin appealed and the Supreme Court reversed, holding that the denial of transcripts to all defendants was a deprivation of due process and of equal protection of the laws. The right to appeal cannot be made to turn on wealth. [222]

57. *Griffin v. Prince Edward School Board, 377 U.S. 218 (1964).* Black, U (two Justices disagreed in part).
Prince Edward County, Virginia, in an attempt to avoid the ruling in *Brown v. Board of Education,* closed down its public schools and gave tax subsidies and tuition grants to parents who sent their children to private schools which accepted whites only. Other Virginia counties kept their public schools open. The Supreme Court held that the action of the county was a violation of the equal protection clause, since Prince Edward County schoolchildren were treated differently than children of other counties since they must go to private schools or none, solely because of the race issue. The Supreme Court allowed an injunction against the tax and tuition subsidies and permitted the federal district

court to require the county to levy taxes to open the public
schools on an integrated basis. [217]

58. *Griswold v. Connecticut*, 381 U.S. 479 (1965). Douglas, 7-2.
Defendants, a doctor and a member of the Connecticut
Planned Parenthood League, were convicted of giving out
birth control information to a married couple under a statute which forbade the use of contraceptives. The Supreme
Court held the statute unconstitutional, since it was an invasion of the married couple's right to privacy, under the 9th
Amendment as made applicable to the states by the 14th,
and therefore the conviction could not stand, since it cannot
be a crime to give out information about something which
is not itself a crime. This was the first case involving the 9th
Amendment to declare a right protected against state invasion. [193]

59. *Grovey v. Townsend*, 295 U.S. 45 (1935). Roberts, U.
Following its defeat in *Nixon v. Herndon* and *Nixon v.
Condon*, the Texas Democratic Party passed a resolution at
a state convention, allowing only white persons to vote in
party primaries. When Grovey, a Negro, was not permitted
to vote, he sued and lost in the Supreme Court. The party
as a whole had voted to refuse to give the vote to Negroes;
this, said the Court, was substantially different from the executive committee. The whole party could not be considered
an instrument of the state under the 14th Amendment. This
case was overruled by *Smith v. Allwright*. [225]

60. *Guinn v. United States*, 238 U.S. 347 (1915). White, C.J., U.
Oklahoma required its citizens, as a condition to voting in
state elections, to be able to read and write any section of
the state constitution. But the so-called grandfather clause
exempted all persons and their descendants who were entitled to vote on January 1, 1867, a time at which no Negroes
were allowed to vote, because the 15th Amendment had not
yet been passed. The Supreme Court ruled the requirement
unconstitutional under the 15th Amendment, as a denial, on
the basis of race, of the right to vote. [225]

61. *Hague v. Congress of Industrial Organizations*, 307 U.S. 496
(1939). Roberts, 5-2.
Assemblies on public grounds were prohibited by a Jersey
City, N.J., ordinance, unless a permit was first secured from the Director of Public Safety. Mayor Hague
used this ordinance to refuse to allow the Congress of Industrial Organizations to assemble and to distribute leaflets.
The Supreme Court held the ordinance unconstitutional;
since union membership was protected by the National
Labor Relations Act, the discussion of labor relations and

union organization was an issue of national citizenship and is protected against state interference by the 14th Amendment due process clause. [151]

62. *Hammer v. Dagenhart,* 247 U.S. 251 (1918). Day, 5-4.
The Keating-Owen Act of 1916 prohibited sales of commodities in interstate commerce produced by factories which employed children under fourteen years of age. The father of two underage children brought suit against Hammer, the United States District Attorney in North Carolina, to prevent him from stopping the children from working. The lower court enjoined Hammer, who appealed to the Supreme Court, which affirmed, holding that Congress could not constitutionally prohibit sales in interstate commerce of child-made goods. This case was overruled by *United States v. Darby.* [194]

63. *Harisiades v. Shaughnessy,* 342 U.S. 580 (1952). Jackson, 6-2.
Harisiades, a Greek citizen, was ordered deported, pursuant to the Alien Registration Act of 1940, for being a member of the Communist Party, even though at a time before a federal law made membership a crime. The Supreme Court affirmed the deportation order, holding it neither a denial of due process nor a criminal punishment barred by the ex post facto prohibition in Article I, Section 9. [61]

64. *Harper v. Virginia Board of Elections,* 383 U.S. 663 (1966). Douglas, 6-3.
Virginia had a poll tax for state elections, requiring each person before he qualified to vote to pay a small fee. The plaintiffs claimed they were indigent and therefore were barred from voting. The Supreme Court struck down the poll tax, holding it to be a violation of the equal protection clause. [228, 239]

65. *Heart of Atlanta Motel, Inc. v. United States,* 379 U.S. 241 (1964). Clark, U.
Approximately 75 percent of the motel's customers were from out of state. It refused rooms to Negroes, in violation of the Civil Rights Act of 1964, which made such refusal, where the business was engaged in interstate commerce, a crime. The motel contested the Act, asserting Congress had gone beyond its commerce power, but the Supreme Court upheld the Act, finding the business to be engaged in interstate commerce and an antidiscrimination requirement to be a regulation of such commerce. [58]

66. *Hirabayashi v. United States,* 320 U.S. 81 (1943). Stone, C.J., U.

An executive order permitted military commanders to declare nighttime curfews for persons of Japanese ancestry. Hirabayashi, a United States citizen, resident of Seattle, defied the order and was convicted in federal court. The Supreme Court affirmed, holding the executive order, which had been ratified by Congress prior to Hirabayashi's arrest, to be within the war power and not a violation of due process. [67]

67. *Humphrey's Executor (Rathbun) v. United States*, 295 U.S. 602 (1935). Sutherland, U.
Humphrey was reappointed to the Federal Trade Commission by President Hoover in 1931 for a term of seven years. Nearly two years later, President Roosevelt removed him from the office because he wanted to substitute his own men in order to carry out his policies. Humphrey having died, Rathbun, the executor of his estate, sued for salary. The Supreme Court held that the estate was entitled to the salary: the President could not remove a commissioner of the FTC at will since when Congress established the commission, it was to be an independent agency of the government, and that under the Act establishing it, removal was limited to "inefficiency, neglect of duty or malfeasance in office," none of which was Humphrey guilty. [94]

68. *Hurtado v. California*, 110 U.S. 516 (1884). Matthews, 7-1.
Defendant was charged by the district attorney in a California court with murder, but there was no grand jury indictment. He was convicted and sentenced to death. Appealing to the Supreme Court, he contended that the 14th Amendment due process clause made a grand jury an essential part of criminal trial proceedings. The Court disagreed—whether to have grand juries in state judicial proceedings is a matter of state constitutional law, not federal. It is not unfair to dispense with such preliminary proceedings. [174]

69. *Illinois ex rel. McCollum v. Board of Education*, 333 U.S. 203 (1948). Black, 8-1.
Religious teachers came into the public schools once a week to give religious instruction to those whose parents consented to it. Children who did not attend the religious classes were sent to another classroom to do other work. The Supreme Court held such a "released time" program to be a violation of the establishment clause of the 1st Amendment, since tax-supported public schools were used for religious purposes. [142]

70. *In re Rahrer*, 140 U.S. 545 (1891). Fuller, C.J., U
Rahrer, an agent of Missiouri liquor dealers, sold beer and whiskey in Kansas, which had a law outlawing all liquor sales. Congress in 1890 had passed the Wilson Act, making

any shipment of liquor into a state subject to the laws of
that state, even if the liquor was shipped and remained in its
original package. Rahrer was convicted of violating the
Kansas law. He claimed in his appeal that the Wilson Act
was unconstitutional because it delegated commerce power
to the states. If the Wilson Act were unconstitutional, Kansas could not prohibit him from selling liquor in its original
package because of prior Supreme Court rulings (the "original package" doctrine). But the Supreme Court found no
improper delegation, and the conviction was affirmed. [51,
236]

71. *Jackson v. Denno*, 378 U.S. 368 (1964). White, 5-4 (each of
four dissenting in part).
Jackson made a confession while he was in a hospital awaiting an operation. He was suspected of murder and had himself been shot in the liver and lost blood; while being questioned he was given drugs and refused water preparatory to
the operation. At the trial he stated he could not remember
the questioning at the hospital, saying he had been in pain.
The judge allowed the confession in evidence and instructed
the jury first to consider whether the confession was voluntary or not. If it found the confession involuntary it was to
disregard it and determine guilt or innocence on the basis of
other evidence. If it found the confession voluntary, it was
to assess its truth and reliability as part of its consideration.
Jackson was convicted and he filed a habeas corpus petition
on the grounds that the New York method of allowing the
confession to go to the jury was contrary to the due process
clause. The Supreme Court agreed, reversed and ordered a
new trial. The judge must first decide whether the confession was voluntary; if he decides it is, it can go to the jury;
if not, the jury cannot hear it. If it goes to the jury, the jury
can still disregard it if it thinks the confession involuntary.
[177]

72. *Joseph Burstyn, Inc. v. Wilson*, 343 U.S. 495 (1952). Clark,
U.
The motion picture "The Miracle" was shown in New York
for eight weeks when its license was withdrawn on the com-
plaint that it was "sacrilegious." The Supreme Court ruled
that a statute permitting a state to forbid a showing of a sacrilegious movie was unconstitutional since the standard was
far too vague to justify restrictions on the expression of
ideas. Movies are as entitled to 1st Amendment protection as
are books and newspapers. [159]

73. *Katzenbach v. McClung*, 379 U.S. 294 (1964). Clark, U.
McClung's restaurant, unlike the motel in *Heart of Atlanta
Motel, Inc. v. United States*, was not patronized by out-of-
state customers. It did purchase 46 percent of its food from a
local merchant who in turn purchased it from out of state.
McClung refused to serve Negroes—a violation of the Civil

Rights Act of 1964, if he was engaged in interstate commerce. The lower court found no interstate commerce but the Supreme Court reversed, sustaining the constitutionality of the Act, finding that although McClung's contribution to interstate commerce might be small, it was not when considered along with the contribution to interstate commerce of all similarly situated restaurants. [58]

74. *Kingsley Pictures Corp. v. Regents,* 360 U.S. 684 (1959). Stewart, U.
The movie "Lady Chatterley's Lover" was denied an exhibition license under the New York statute prohibiting the showing of a motion picture in which adultery is "presented as being right and desirable for certain people under certain circumstances." The Supreme Court reversed, holding that the statute as applied violates the 1st and 14th Amendments freedom to advocate ideas. [159]

75. *Knauer v. United States,* 328 U.S. 654 (1946). Douglas, 6-2.
Knauer's citizenship was revoked when it was discovered that before his naturalization, at the time he swore allegiance to the United States, and subsequently, he was a thoroughgoing Nazi and follower of Adolph Hitler. The Supreme Court affirmed the revocation, but held that the standard of proof is strict, and that it would reexamine the facts to determine whether Knauer took the oath falsely. One of the reasons for the strict test is that naturalized citizenship is not a second-class citizenship. Hence naturalized citizens are as free to criticize the United States as native-born citizens and a court should not be hasty in depriving a person of his freedom to speak. [60]

76. *Korematsu v. United States,* 323 U.S. 214 (1944). Black, 6-3.
An executive order, based on an Act of Congress, required all persons of Japanese ancestry to leave California after the outbreak of war. Korematsu was a United States citizen who refused to leave. He was convicted; the Supreme Court affirmed. The order was valid under the Congressional war power; since there was some evidence that some citizens of Japanese descent were disloyal and since the danger was great and time short, the order to evacuate all was permissible. [67]

77. *Kovacs v. Cooper,* 336 U.S. 77 (1949). Reed, 5-4.
A Trenton, N. J., ordinance outlaws sound trucks and other loudspeakers on public streets. The Supreme Court held that this ordinance does not go beyond the state's legitimate police power to protect itself from unwanted noises. The ordinance is not a violation of the 1st and 14th Amendments since the citizen at home is part of a "captive audience" and

cannot escape the "loud and raucous" noises which the ordinance forbade. Since there are other ways of communicating ideas, a total ban of sound trucks is not unconstitutional. [151]

78. *Kunz v. New York*, 340 U.S. 290 (1951). Vinson, C.J., 8-1.
A New York City ordinance gave the police commissioner the power to grant licenses to those wishing to speak on religious matters on public streets, but set no standards to be employed by the commissioner in determining to whom permits should be issued. Kunz ridiculed certain religions, lost his permit, spoke anyway, and was convicted, fined $10, and the Supreme Court reversed; the complete discretion of the commissioner rendered the ordinance unconstitutional since the 1st Amendment forbids arbitrary power to impose prior restraints on religious speech. [151]

79. *Lambert v. California*, 355 U.S. 225 (1957). Douglas, 5-4.
Lambert was convicted of failure to register with Los Angeles police. A city ordinance required such registration when the person had been previously convicted of a felony and remained in the city longer than five days. The Supreme Court reversed, on the grounds that since the defendant had no actual knowledge of the ordinance and there was no showing by the state that there was even a probability of knowledge, the conviction was a violation of due process. [180]

80. *Lamont v. Postmaster General*, 381 U.S. 301 (1965). Douglas, 8-0.
An unsolicited copy of a publication from Communist China was sent to Lamont, and the Post Office Department sent him a notice that by authority of the Postal Service and Federal Employees Salary Act of 1962 it would destroy the mail unless he specifically requested it. The Act gave the Secretary of the Treasury the authority to determine what was Communist "political propaganda" and allowed the Post Office to destroy such works. Lamont, a publisher, filed suit to enjoin enforcement of the Act, on the grounds that his freedom of speech was restricted unconstitutionally since since he had to request each piece of mail and it would not be sent freely to him. Since Congress had decided that mail should be delivered, it could not make the method of delivery turn on the contents of the envelope or the country of origin. This recognition of the right to receive publications marked the first time the Supreme Court struck down a federal statute as contrary to the 1st Amendment. [63]

81. *Lane v. Wilson*, 307 U.S. 268 (1939). Frankfurter, 6-2.
An Oklahoma statute said that all citizens qualified to vote in 1916 who failed to register in a certain twelve-day period would be perpetually disfranchised, except those who could

vote in 1914. Negroes were not allowed to vote in that year because of a "grandfather clause" which had been declared unconstitutional by the Supreme Court in *Guinn v. United States* in 1915. Hence Negroes had twelve days in which to register or forever lose their vote; whites need not register. The Supreme Court reversed the lower court, which had held against the plaintiffs, Negroes, suing for damages. The law was a violation of the equal protection clause. [225]

82. *Lochner v. New York*, 198 U.S. 45 (1905). Peckham, 5-4.
A New York statute made it unlawful for bakeries to work their cooks more than sixty hours a week. Lochner was convicted of requiring an employee to work longer. The Supreme Court agreed with the bakery company that the law was unconstitutional since it interfered with the freedom of the employer to contract with the worker. The case has been overruled, and today the hours in almost all types of work are regulated. [205-6]

83. *Lucas v. Colorado General Assembly*, 377 U.S. 713 (1964). Warren, C.J., 6-3.
Under an amendment to the Colorado constitution, approved by the people of the state, the Colorado senate was to be apportioned in such a manner that counties with one-third of the state's population would elect a majority of the members. The state House was apportioned on a population basis. The Supreme Court ruled that the plan was unconstitutional, notwithstanding the fact that it was approved by the people, since apportionment on a strict population basis is a federal constitutional requirement under the equal protection clause. A popular vote cannot void the United States Constitution. [220]

84. *Luther v. Borden*, 48 U.S. (7 How.) 1 (1849). Taney, C.J., 5-1.
Which of two opposing state governments is the legitimate one is a political question, not a judicial one, and the Supreme Court will not decide. It will however, follow the decisions of the President, Congress, and state courts. Since the Rhode Island courts decided the original Rhode Island government was the lawful one, in the face of a rebellion Rhode Island could declare martial law and arrest those who were aiding the rebellion, and the fact that the plaintiff was in league with the rebels was a defense to his charge that defendants trespassed on his property. [121]

85. *Mapp v. Ohio*, 367 U.S. 643 (1961). Clark, 6-3.
Police broke into Miss Mapp's home without a warrant in search of a suspect involved in bombing incidents. They found no suspect, but did find some allegedly obscene pic-

tures for possession of which Miss Mapp was convicted under a state obscenity law. She appealed to the Supreme Court, claiming her right of privacy had been unconstitutionally invaded by the police, because they failed to get a warrant and otherwise conform to the 4th Amendment. The Supreme Court reversed her conviction, holding for the first time that the 4th Amendment was incorporated in the 14th, and applied against the states as well as the federal government. [171-2, 188]

86. *Marbury v. Madison*, 5 U.S. (1 Cr.) 137 (1803). Marshall, C.J., U.

A person who is appointed to a federal court is entitled to the judicial office once the Senate approves and the President signs his commission. But the section of the Judiciary Act of 1789 allowing the plaintiff to ask the Supreme Court for a mandamus to force the Secretary of State to deliver the commission is unconstitutional, since Article III does not allow the Supreme Court to act as a trial court (original jurisdiction), except in two special situations. The Court will not decide a constitutional question if it can avoid it; hence the Court first had to decide whether Marbury was entitled to the office. Since the Court could not order the remedy the suit was dismissed. [107]

87. *Marsh v. Alabama*, 326 U.S. 501 (1946). Black, 5-3.

The defendant was convicted for a violation of the Alabama trespass statute after she had failed to stop passing out religious literature and to leave the streets of Chicasaw, a company-owned town, the managers of which had warned her that she could not distribute without a permit and that they would not issue her one. The Supreme Court reversed the conviction, holding that a trespass statute could not be used to deny 1st Amendment rights, and that a person could not be ordered off the streets of a town, even if privately owned, when the only objection is to religious literature. [214]

88. *McCulloch v. Maryland*, 17 U.S. (4 Wheat.) 316 (1819). Marshall, C.J., U.

Maryland tried to tax the national bank. Since Congress has power under the necessary and proper clause in Article I, Section 8, to enact those means of government which are reasonably calculated to achieve lawful ends, such as regulation of commerce and coining of money, the national bank was constitutional. Futhermore, since federal law and the institutions created by it are supreme under Article 6, and since "the power to tax involves the power to destroy," Maryland's attempt to tax a federal body was unconstitutional. [70, 124]

89. *McNabb v. United States*, 318 U.S. 332 (1943). Frankfurter, 7-1.
The McNabbs, Tennessee mountaineers, were accused of killing a federal official of the Alcohol Tax Unit of the Bureau of Internal Revenue, while he was investigating sales of whiskey on which taxes had not been paid. They were taken to a federal building and instead of being first brought before a United States commissioner or judge, were kept locked up and questioned for more than five hours at a stretch, from 3 A.M. Thursday morning until 2 A.M. Saturday morning. They were convicted on the strength of confessions, and on appeal the Supreme Court reversed, not because the confessions were involuntary and therefore unconstitutional, but because the whole proceeding (including the fact that Congressional law required the accused to be brought before a United States commissioner or judge) was thoroughly uncivilized. The Supreme Court has the supervisory power to review, establish, and maintain rules of evidence in federal courts. Although the decision did not rest on the Constitution, but on the relationship of the Supreme Court to lower federal courts, the substance of the case has become part of later cases decided on constitutional grounds, both as to state and federal governments. [137]

90. *Memoirs v. Massachusetts* (A Book Named "John Cleland's Memoirs of a Woman of Pleasure" v. Attorney General of Massachusetts), 383 U.S. 413 (1966). Brennan, 6-3.
This was a civil injunction against a book on the grounds of obscenity. The Massachusetts Supreme Judicial Court held that a patently offensive book which appeals to prurient interest need not be unqualifiedly worthless before it can be held obscene. The Supreme Court reversed on that point, finding the book not unqualifiedly worthless. [158-9]

91. *Miranda v. Arizona*, 384 U.S. 436 (1966). Warren, C.J., 6-3 (with one of the majority dissenting in part).
Miranda and other defendants were arrested and instead of first being warned of their right to counsel, and of the fact that if they talked what they said could be used in court against them, were interrogated until they confessed. The Court held the proceedings to be violations of the 5th and 6th Amendments as made applicable to the states by the 14th, and laid down sweeping rules which can be summarized by saying any conviction which results from interrogation in which the police do not first inform suspects of the above rights and provide counsel for indigent suspects at the questioning stage will be reversed. [177-8, 189]

92. *Missouri v. Holland*, 252 U.S. 416 (1920). Holmes, 7-2.
A treaty with Great Britain provided for restrictions on the hunting and selling of migratory birds, and required each

nation to pass laws to outlaw hunting and selling. Congress did so, and the state of Missouri protested, saying it had a property right in the birds and Congress had no power to pass the law. The Supreme Court held that even if the law, standing by itself, was unconstitutional (since the Constitution gave Congress no power to pass such laws), it was valid when passed pursuant to a treaty, since the Constitution does not forbid such a treaty and the treaty called for the law. Under the necessary and proper clause the law must stand. [125]

93. *Moore v. Dempsey*, 261 U.S. 86 (1923) Holmes, 7-2.
A number of Negroes, assembled in a church, were fired upon by a crowd of white men. In the disturbance one of the white men was killed. Many Negroes were hunted down and shot that night and another white man was killed, for whose murder the defendants, Negroes, were indicted and convicted. They charged in a petition for habeas corpus that their conviction was a violation of due process, claiming that the trial was mob-dominated, that a son of one of the defendants' lawyers was run out of town, that newspapers inflamed public opinion, that the key witnesses were whipped and tortured until they said what the prosecution wanted, that Negroes were excluded from the jury, that their lawyer, appointed by the court, was given no time to prepare the case and called no witnesses (though he could have), that the trial lasted only forty-five minutes and the jury took five minutes to bring in a guilty verdict, and that the governor of the state was warned not to commute their death sentences or they and some other Negroes coming on to a later trial would be lynched. The federal district court dismissed the petition and the Supreme Court reversed, holding that if the district court found the facts to be true the defendants must be released. [184]

94. *Munn v. Illinois*, 94 U.S. 113 (1877). Waite, C.J., 7-2.
"When the owner of property devotes it to a use in which the public has an interest, he in effect grants to the public an interest in such use, and must to the extent of that interest, submit to be controlled by the public, for the common good, as long as he maintains the use." Thus the Illinois Act regulating use and conditions of grain warehouses and fixing prices was not a taking of property without due process under the 14th Amendment. [82, 204-5]

95. *Muskrat v. United States*, 219 U.S. 364 (1911). Day, U.
Congress passed an Act allowing certain Indians to sue the United States to test in federal court the validity of prior acts of Congress relating to Indian lands. The Supreme Court dismissed the suit, holding that the Court cannot judge an Act of Congress as an abstract question. Here

there was no "case or controversy," merely a citizen not claiming any injury, asking the Court to consider whether a law was valid. The results in this case has been somewhat modified by the Federal Declaratory Judgments Act, allowing the federal courts to hear cases in which real controversies are present, in advance of the injury. [104]

96. *NAACP v. Alabama,* 357 U.S. 449 (1958). Harlan, U.
The National Association for the Advancement of Colored People is a New York corporation, which opened an Alabama office without qualifying to do business there. It was required to designate a place of business and an agent to receive legal summonses. Alabama filed suit to oust it from the state, alleging the NAACP was causing Alabama irreparable harm. The state court ordered the association to cease doing business and to cease trying to qualify. The organization then asked for the restraining order to be dissolved and the court, on the state's motion, ordered many records of the organization, including membership lists, to be produced in court. The NAACP gave over many records, but not the lists, and was held in contempt and fined $100,000. The Supreme Court reversed the judgment, holding the order to produce membership lists a requirement which would jeopardize the organization's right to pursue its lawful ends privately; hence the order was invalid since it would tend to suppress liberty of the association to advance its political ideas, a right protected by the 14th Amendment. [164]

97. *Near v. Minnesota,* 283 U.S. 697 (1931). Hughes, C.J., 5-4.
Near's newspaper, *The Saturday Press,* was enjoined from further publication under a Minnesota statute which provided for the abatement of defamatory periodicals. *The Saturday Press* had charged public officials with misconduct. The Supreme Court reversed the conviction and held the statute unconstitutional. The abatement of a periodical is the prior restraint of future issues, and this is the heart of censorship which is prohibited by the 1st and 14th Amendments. [152]

98. *New York Times Co. v. Sullivan,* 376 U.S. 254 (1964). Brennan, U.
The New York Times lost a $500,000 verdict in Alabama and appealed to the Supreme Court, protesting that the device of using a civil damage suit was actually a way that the state could infringe on its 1st Amendment freedom of press. The newspaper had carried an ad which had some minor mistakes of fact, and the police commissioner, not named in the ad, sued on the theory that his reputation had been injured. The *Times'* staff had seen nothing to indicate that the advertisement carried any mistakes on its face and so it was run without being checked for accuracy. The Supreme

Court reversed the judgment, holding that public officials cannot sue for libel unless actual malice is proved and that there was no malice shown here. The case was dismissed. [158]

99. *Nixon v. Condon*, 286 U.S. 73 (1932). Cardozo, 5-4.
After the Supreme Court voided the Texas white primary statute (see *Nixon v. Herndon*), Texas passed another law, permitting the executive committees of political parties to determine who could vote in primaries. The Democratic Party Executive Committee allowed only white persons to vote. Nixon again brought suit, and again won. When the state delegates authority to a party executive committee, the committee becomes an agent of the state for purposes of the 14th Amendment, and the discriminatory action of the party was a violation of the equal protection clause. [226]

100. *Nixon v. Herndon*, 273 U.S. 536 (1927). Holmes, U.
A Texas statute declared it unlawful for a Negro to vote in a primary election. The Supreme Court, while declining to say that a party primary was an election within the meaning of the 15th Amendment, held nevertheless that such a statute violates the equal protection clause of the 14th Amendment. [226]

101. *NLRB v. Jones & Laughlin Steel Corp.*, 301 U.S. 1 (1937). Hughes, C.J., 5-4.
The National Labor Relations Board had found the company guilty of engaging in unfair labor practices, unlawful under the National Labor Relations Act. The company had discriminated against its employees who were members of the union and was trying to prevent them from organizing. The company failed to abide by the order of the NLRB. The Supreme Court ruled that the Act was constitutional, since regulation of labor is within Congress' interstate commerce power, as long as the businesses regulated by the Act affected interstate commerce. [56]

102. *Noto v. United States*, 367 U.S. 290 (1961). Harlan, U.
Convicted of violating the membership clause of the Smith Act, Noto's conviction was reversed by the Supreme Court because the evidence was insufficient to prove that the Communist Party advocated forcible overthrow of the government at the present time, not as abstract doctrine but as an incitement to action. Present advocacy, not an intent to advocate in the future, is necessary. Witnesses testified that Noto was in the Party and believed in its doctrines, but no evidence showed that Noto was going to take violent action or that he had advocated others to do so. [156]

103. *Olmstead v. United States,* 277 U.S. 438 (1928). Taft, C.J., 5-4.

Olmstead was the leader of a conspiracy to violate the National Prohibition Act. Telephone messages were received by Olmstead's company, and these conversations were intercepted by federal officials. The officers tapped the phones outside Olmstead's offices, used the evidence in court, and obtained a conviction. Olmstead appealed, claiming that wiretapping was a violation of the 4th and 5th Amendment. He lost. The Court found no searching or seizing, no entry into a residence or place of business, no coerced confession. The result of the case was reversed by Congress in 1934 with the passage of the Federal Communications Act, and the Court has been whittling away at the constitutional result ever since. But the case itself has never been completely overruled. [172]

104. *O'Malley v. Woodrough,* 307 U.S. 277 (1939). Frankfurter, 7-1.

A part of the federal Internal Revenue Code of 1932 provided that federal judges appointed after 1932 should be taxed on their incomes like all other income earners. A federal judge sued to recover taxes he paid, asserting that because the Constitution says his salary could not be reduced while he was a judge he could not be taxed, for a tax was a reduction. The Supreme Court held against him, ruling that since the Act declared that the salary of a judge appointed after the Revenue Code was passed would be taxed there was no diminution of salary. Judge Woodrough was appointed to a United States Court of Appeals in 1933. This is not the same as taxing for the first time a person who was *already* a judge, an act which had been declared unconstitutional by the Court in 1920. [103]

105. *Palko v. Connecticut.* 302 U.S. 319 (1937). Cardozo, 8-1.

Palko was convicted of second-degree murder. The state appealed his conviction on the grounds that the trial court had made errors of law prejudicial to the state. Connecticut's highest court ordered a new trial, and this time Palko was sentenced to first-degree murder (carrying the death penalty). He appealed on the grounds that the order for new trial made him liable to double jeopardy. The Supreme Court affirmed his conviction, holding that there had been no double jeopardy, since the first trial had contained errors. (It is doubtful that if a state today attempted to retry a person who was acquitted by a jury the Supreme Court would not find this unconstitutional, because this part of the 5th Amendment is incorporated in the 14th Amendment— even though this would probably require overruling *Palko*). [139, 175-6]

106. *Passenger Cases* (Smith v. Turner), 48 U.S. (7 How.) 283 (1849). McLean, 5-4.
The transportation of passengers between the states is an activity involving interstate commerce requiring national uniformity; a state law requiring payment of a fee for each passenger when a ship comes to port is a local regulation of interstate commerce and is therefore unconstitutional under the doctrine of *Cooley v. Board of Wardens*. [58]

107. *Pennsylvania v. Wheeling & Belmont Bridge Co.*, 54 U.S. (13 How.) 518 (1852), 59 U.S. (18 How.) 421 (1856). McLean, 7-2.
Virginia authorized a bridge to be built over the Ohio River at Wheeling. In a suit brought in the Supreme Court under its original jurisdiction by Pennsylvania against the bridge company, a special master appointed by the Court found the bridge to obstruct navigation on the river because it was too low for some boats to pass under. This was an interference with the commerce of Pennsylvania, since boats carried goods along the Ohio to Pennsylvania canals and railroads. The bridge company was ordered to change the structure into a drawbridge. But Congress then passed a law declaring under its commerce power that the bridge was lawful and the Court ruled in the second case that its order in the first case could not be enforced. [28, 51, 100]

108. *Pierce v. Society of Sisters*, 268 U.S. 510 (1925). McReynolds, U.
Oregon law required that every child between the ages of eight and sixteen attend public school. The Society of Sisters, a corporation which operated a number of private Catholic schools, brought suit. The Supreme Court held that the Oregon law "unreasonably interferes with the liberty of parents and guardians to direct the upbringing and education of children under their control." Furthermore, the law would destroy property rights protected by the 14th Amendment. [145]

109. *Plessy v. Ferguson*, 163 U.S. 537 (1896). Brown, 7-1.
A citizen of Louisiana, with one-eighth "African blood," was arrested for refusing to leave a segregated white car. He appealed his conviction on the grounds that the state statute, providing for segregation in railroads, denied him equal protection of the law. The Supreme Court affirmed, saying the 14th Amendment was not intended to guarantee "social equality," and that the customs and traditions of the state made the law reasonable. Overruled fifty-eight years later in *Brown v. Board of Education*. [215]

110. *Pollock v. Farmers' Loan & Trust Co.*, 157 U.S. 429 (1895) and 158 U.S. 601 (1895). Fuller, C.J., 5-4.

Taxes on real estate and personal property are direct taxes and cannot be levied except by apportionment among the states. Therefore, taxes on the income from such property are direct and require an apportionment also. Hence, said the Supreme Court, the federal income tax statute of 1894 was unconstitutional, since it did not provide for an apportionment and since it is doubtful that Congress would have wanted the rest of the Act—taxing incomes from professions and employment—to stand alone. In 1913, the 16th Amendment overruled this case. [228]

111. *Powell v. Alabama*, 287 U.S. 45 (1932). Sutherland, 7-2.
Powell and eight others, Negroes, were convicted of rape of two white girls. They were too poor to afford counsel, were represented by none, in a courtroom with a hostile public. They were sentenced to death. The Supreme Court reversed the conviction, holding that in capital cases, the state must appoint counsel, because almost no defendant can properly defend himself. This case was absorbed by the broader ruling of *Gideon v. Wainwright*. [187]

112. *Prize Cases* (The Brig "Amy Warwick," The Schooner "Crenshaw." The Barque "Hiawatha," The Schooner "Brilliante"), 67 U.S. (2 Bl.) 635 (1863). Grier, 5-4.
Private vessels owned by foreigners and citizens of Virginia were seized by armed United States ships after President Lincoln declared a blockade of southern ports at the outbreak of the Civil War, even though Congress had not made a formal declaration of war. Held, even though some owners had not been aware of the existence of actual hostilities, a state of war existed; that being so, neutrals must respect a blockade; not only were the rebellious vessels lawfully captured, but so were the neutral foreign vessels, since one failed to leave the blockade within the fifteen-day period allowed and the other tried to crash through the blockade. Some of the property of one of the southern vessels was returned to its owner, since he had bought and paid for it before a state of war began and since he was a New Yorker, and thus not an enemy. [91]

113. *Reid v. Covert*, 354 U.S. 1 (1957). Black, 6-2.
Wives of members of the United States armed forces were tried for murder of their husbands in court-martial proceedings and not by civil courts with juries. The court-martial trials were based on the Uniform Code of Military Justice. The Supreme Court reversed and ordered new trials, holding that in capital cases the 6th Amendment forbids trial of civilians by court-martial in time of peace overseas. The Constitution follows the flag. [66]

114. *Reynolds v. Sims*, 377 U.S. 533 (1964). Warren, C.J., 8-1.

This was a suit by Alabama taxpayers, who charged that the state legislature was unconstitutionally apportioned, since it was based on a 1900 census and the districts bore no relation to the population size. The Supreme Court held that a legislature not apportioned according to population was a violation of the equal protection clause, because legislators represent people, not cows, acres, or trees. Both seats of the state legislature must be apportioned according to population, and the federal analogy (the United States Senate is not districted according to population but according to states, so the states ought to allow their counties representation in the state Senates on a similar basis) was rejected. [219]

115. *Reynolds v. United States,* 98 U.S. 145 (1879). Waite, C.J., U.
An Act of Congress declared polygamy a crime. Reynolds, a Mormon, was convicted of having two wives in the territory of Utah. He argued that this was allowed by his religion and that under the 1st Amendment his religious practices could not be forbidden. The Court held his conviction lawful, distinguishing between religious beliefs and acts which interfere with other people. Since Congress had declared that polygamy was an act against peace and good order, disruptive of American society, the 1st Amendment did not prevent it from being made illegal. Opinions are protected, but an action cannot be justified on the grounds that a religion disapproves of the law against it. [147]

116. *Rideau v. Louisiana,* 373 U.S. 723 (1963). Stewart, 7-2.
A televised interview of the defendant Rideau was played three times to the citizens of the parish in which he was to be tried for kidnapping and murder. Rideau admitted both in the interview. He was convicted by jurors; some of them had seen the program and some of the jurors were deputy sheriffs. The conviction was affirmed by the state Supreme Court, but the United States Supreme Court reversed. The showing of the interview was prejudicial and a denial of due process, since no one advised Rideau to be silent during the interview and since in a real sense his trial took place, as far as the people of the parish were concerned, when the film was televised, and not before the judge and jury. A new trial was ordered in a changed venue. [182]

117. *Robinson v. California,* 370 U.S. 660 (1962). Stewart, 6-2.
Under a California statute, Robinson was convicted of being a dope addict, even though there was no evidence that he had brought narcotics into the state, had purchased them or sold them or used them within the state. The Supreme Court reversed, holding the conviction to be "cruel and unusual" punishment, since the evidence proved only that the defendant had the disease of addiction. A disease as such is

not punishable, although the state can order such persons to a hospital to receive treatment. This case incorporated for the first time part of the 8th Amendment into the 14th Amendment. [190]

118. *Rochin v. California,* 342 U.S. 165 (1952). Frankfurter, U. Police officers saw Rochin swallow a pellet of narcotics, which they wanted to seize as evidence. They caused him to vomit up the narcotics. The Supreme Court reversed the conviction because the action was contrary to the 4th Amendment as incorporated in the 14th; it offended due process because it "shocked the conscience." [139, 174]

119. *Rogers v. Richmond,* 365 U.S. 534 (1961). Frankfurter, 7-2. Questioned for six hours about a robbery, Rogers continued to deny committing it. Then the police chief told him his wife would be brought in. After another hour, the chief told Rogers he would be "less than a man" if he did not confess to spare his wife the trouble. The wife had arthritis, so Rogers confessed and was convicted. A habeas corpus petition in the federal district was granted on the grounds that the confession was coerced, but the Court of Appeals reversed again because the district court went outside the records of the state court and decided the facts again. The Supreme Court denied certiorari. The district court then dismissed the petition, the Court of Appeals affirmed, and this time the Supreme Court granted certiorari and reversed, holding that there was sufficient evidence of "overbearing petitioner's will to resist," and this question is unrelated to whether the confession is true. [177]

120. *Roman v. Sincock,* 377 U.S. 695 (1964). Warren, C.J., 8-1. The districts electing the majority of Delaware's state Senate and House seats consisted of 22 percent and 18.5 percent, respectively, of the state's total 1960 population. Under a 1963 state constitutional amendment, the representation was changed; now two-thirds of the Senate was elected from 31 percent of the population and a majority of the House from 28 percent of the population. There was no state initiative or referendum procedure. The Supreme Court found the state constitutional provisions a violation of the equal protection clause and remanded the case to the district court to consider whether under general equitable principles an election should be called under the unconstitutional scheme anyway in order not to disrupt the state. [220]

121. *Roth v. United States,* 354 US. 476 (1957). Brennan, 7-2. (one of the seven dissenting in part).
A federal statute forbade mailing of "obscene, lewd, lasci-

vious, or filthy" publications. Roth was convicted of violating the statute and appealed, claiming a 1st Amendment right. The Supreme Court affirmed, holding obscenity, defined as a work appealing to prurient interest "utterly without redeeming social importance," not protected by the 1st Amendment; and holding the statute to be a proper exercise of the Article I, Section 8, Clause 7 postal power. [159]

122. *Saia v. New York,* 334 U.S. 588 (1948). Douglas, 5-4.
A New York ordinance forbade the use of sound trucks on public streets without a permit from the chief of police, who was given no standard to guide his discretion. Saia was a Jehovah's Witness who had been granted a permit to broadcast religious lectures in a fixed place in a public park on specified Sundays. When complaints were filed with the police chief and he continued broadcasting anyway, his license was revoked. The Supreme Court reversed the conviction of the user without a permit, on the ground that unfettered discretion was contrary to the freedom of speech guaranteed by the 1st and 14th Amendments because the ordinance permitted a prior restraint on his right to speak. [151]

123. *Scales v. United States,* 367 U.S. 203 (1961). Harlan, 6-3.
The membership clause of the Smith Act makes it a crime to belong to an organization advocating overthrow of the United States Government by force or violence. The district court charged the jury that Scales could not be convicted unless they found (1) Scales advocated action as soon as possible, (2) he was an "active" member of the Party and not merely a passive or technical member, and (3) he had knowledge of the Party's illegal advocacy and had a specific intent to bring about violent overthrow "as speedily as circumstances would permit." He was convicted, and the Supreme Court affirmed, against a challenge that the Smith Act was unconstitutional. But without the charge to the jury as given, the Act could not constitutionally make Scales' membership a crime. All elements, including activeness, knowledge, and intent, were necessary. [156]

124. *Schechter Poultry Corp. v. United States,* 295 U.S. 495 (1935). Hughes, C.J., U.
The company was convicted of violating the Live Poultry Code, which was promulgated by a Presidential order pursuant to the National Industrial Recovery Act. The Act provided that if an industry did not establish its own code of prices and fair competition, the President could establish one. The Supreme Court held the NIRA unconstitutional since it delegated far too much legislative power to the President; the Act set no standards, giving the President and private groups a blank check. [33]

129. *Sherbert v. Verner,* 374 U.S. 398 (1963). Brennan, 7-2.
Plaintiff, a Seventh Day Adventist, whose religion forbade her from working on Saturday, was discharged from her job. When she could find no work because all jobs required her working on Saturday, she filed a claim under the South Carolina Unemployment Compensation Act. She was denied benefits because she was capable of working but had refused to. The Supreme Court reversed the judgment, holding it to be a denial of her religious rights under the free exercise clause. [146]

130. *Slaughter-House Cases* (Butcher's Benevolent Assoc. v. The Crescent City Live-Stock Landing & Slaughter-House Co.), 83 U.S. (16 Wall.) 36 (1873). Miller, 5-4.
The 13th Amendment does not apply to business corporations and the 14th Amendment does not prevent a city from establishing a monopoly in which all butchers are required to do their slaughtering at one slaughter house, even though other houses are forced out of business. [203-4]

131. *Smith v. Allwright,* 321 U.S. 649 (1944). Reed, 8-1.
Smith, a Negro, brought suit because Texas election judges refused to let him vote in the Democratic party primary for Congress solely because of his race. The Supreme Court held that the Democratic party, when it forbade membership in order to prevent people from voting, was an instrumentality of the state and was prohibited from denying the vote by the 15th Amendment. The party primary was an essential part of choosing national officials, and the whole structure of the party primary, including the right of the people of the party to determine who can vote, was established by state laws. [226-7]

132. *Sweatt v. Painter,* 399 U.S. 629 (1950). Vinson, C.J., U.
Texas law prohibited the University of Texas law school from accepting Negroes. The state built a Negro law school which was far inferior to the law school at the University, in terms of physical facilities, library, professors, and student body. The Supreme Court held that the denial of admission was unconstitutional under the equal protection clause since the Negro school was far from equal. [216]

133. *Swift & Co. v. United States*, 196 U.S. 375 (1905). Holmes, U.
A number of companies and individuals were charged with violation of the Sherman Antitrust Act because, among other things, they constituted a substantial proportion of fresh meat dealers in the United States and had agreed to fix prices and to get less than legal rates from railroads in order to hurt competitors. The companies argued that these

were attempts to create monopolies within a single state. Even so, said the Supreme Court, in effect overruling *United States v. E.C. Knight,* the monopoly was within the scope of the Sherman Act since its aim was to fix interstate prices. Because the meat sales and shipments were between citizens and companies of different states, the application of the Sherman Act in these circumstances was within the commerce power. [54]

134. *Takahashi v. Fish & Game Commission,* 334 U.S. 410 (1948). Black, 7-2.
Takahashi was ineligible for United States citizenship because he was Japanese, and Congress did not allow Japanese to apply for citizenship. California denied him a commercial fishing license. The state defended on the ground that it could use the federal discrimination as grounds to prevent Takahashi from fishing. The Supreme Court denied the power, holding the refusal to issue the license unconstitutional under the equal protection clause. The fact that Takahashi was allowed by Congress to live in the United States, even though as an alien, shows that it was intended he should live on an equal footing with citizens, as guaranteed by the 14th Amendment (which speaks of persons and not citizens). *Terrace v. Thompson* was held to be a very special case, since the states were assumed to have a special interest in controlling the disposition of land. [221]

135. *Terrace v. Thompson,* 263 U.S. 197 (1923). Butler, 6-2.
Terrace wanted to lease land to a Japanese alien. Washington State law made this a crime, because the alien had not declared his intention to become a citizen. Under federal law he could not become a citizen. Terrace sued the attorney general, Thompson, to prevent him from prosecuting, asserting that he was denied due process and equal protection of the law. The Supreme Court refused to enjoin Thompson, since the state law was held to make a reasonable distinction between those who declared their intention to become citizens and those who did not. The discrimination which resulted in this case was based on federal law, which was not unconstitutional since Congress has complete, unreviewable authority in this area. (The present immigration law provides that no one can be excluded because of race or religion.) [221]

136. *Terry v. Adams,* 345 U.S. 461 (1953). Black, 8-1.
The Jaybird Democratic Association ran candidates in a Texas primary in May; the winner in the county went on to run in the Democratic primary, and the winner to run in the November elections. Negroes were barred by the Jaybird party from participating. The party had no official connection with the Democratic party, did not conduct primaries

under state law. But winners of the pre-primary always won the final election. The Supreme Court held the discrimination to be a violation of the 15th Amendment, finding the party to be an instrumentality of the state. [227]

137. *Testa v. Katt,* 330 U.S. 386 (1947). Black, U.
The Emergency Price Control Act, a federal law, allowed any person charged more than fixed prices on goods to sue "in any court of competent jurisdiction." The plaintiff sued in a Rhode Island state court, claiming that the defendant overcharged him for an automobile. The court dismissed the suit on the ground that the law was penal in nature and since it was a statute of a separate sovereign, the state did not have to enforce it. The Supreme Court reversed, holding that Article 6, the supremacy clause, makes federal law supreme and that the states are not independent sovereigns in this regard; they are subject to federal law and when Congress says state courts have jurisdiction to hear a case such as this, it is federal policy that they hear the case and render a judgment. [126]

138. *Thomas v. Collins,* 323 U.S. 516 (1945). Rutledge, 5-4.
Thomas addressed a mass union meeting in Texas without first obtaining an organizer's card as required by state law for those intending to solicit members. The state issued a restraining order the afternoon of the speech, but Thomas went ahead and delivered it, asking all who were not members to join the local and specifically solicited a particular person. He was arrested and held in contempt for violating the restraining order. His conviction was reversed by the Supreme Court because the Texas statute was an unconstitutional restraint on the freedom of speech. There was no clear and present danger of a serious harm to the state. The meeting was entirely orderly and Thomas did not himself accept union dues or registration fees. [162]

139. *Thornhill v. Alabama,* 310 U.S. 88 (1940). Murphy 8-1.
An Alabama statute prohibited picketing a place of business with the intent of persuading others not to do business with or work for the company. Thornhill was convicted of picketing in front of an industrial plant. The Supreme Court ruled that the statute violated the 1st and 14th Amendments, because it interfered with the freedom of a person to discuss openly matters of labor unions, a topic of wide public concern. The Court announced that it would examine such a statute "on its face"; the mere fact that Thornhill could have urged others not to deal with the Company on a place other than a public street and that there was a *possibility* of violence was not sufficient to make the statute constitutional. [148, 149]

140. *Torcaso v. Watkins,* 367 U.S. 488 (1961). Black, U.
The governor of Maryland appointed the plaintiff to the office of notary public. Before he was entitled to assume his office, he was required by the state law to take an oath, swearing his belief in God. This he refused to do and the Supreme Court struck down the law when he appealed from his rejection from the office. The law was held to be contrary to the 1st Amendment as made applicable to the states by the 14th. [127]

141. *Trop v. Dulles,* 356 U.S. 86 (1958). Warren, C.J., 5-4.
Trop deserted the Army in Morocco in 1944. He was a native-born citizen and as a result of a court-martial lost his citizenship as a penalty under the Nationality Act of 1940. A majority thought such a statute unconstitutional as applied to Trop insofar as he had not in any way become involved with a foreign nation. Four of the majority thought the sentence also unconstitutional because cruel and unusual. [190]

142. *Truax v. Raich,* 239 U.S. 33 (1915). Hughes, 8-1.
An Arizona law required all businesses hiring more than five workers to make sure that 80 percent of them were native-born citizens or qualified voters. Raich was an Austrian citizen, admitted to the United States under federal law, who lost his job because his employer feared the consequences of violating the law. The Supreme Court ruled that the law violated the equal protection clause because the Arizona Act discriminated between aliens and citizens with respect to employment. The equal protection clause speaks of persons and not citizens, and aliens cannot thus be denied the right to earn a living. [221]

143. *Tumey v. Ohio,* 273 U.S. 510 (1927). Taft, C.J., U.
Mayors of cities and towns in Ohio were authorized to hear cases involving violations of the state's liquor laws and received a percentage of the fine as fee. Tumey was brought before a mayor who fined him $100. (The mayor received $12 which he would not have had Tumey not been convicted.) Tumey appealed to the Supreme Court, which reversed the conviction, holding the mayor's obvious bias enough to make the statute unconstitutional as a deprivation of liberty (Tumey was ordered to jail until he paid) and property without due process of law. No matter how strong the evidence against an accused, an impartial judge is always a constitutional necessity. [179]

144. *Two Guys from Harrison, Inc. v. McGinley,* 366 U.S. 582 (1961). Warren, C.J., 8-1.
A large discount department store stayed open on Sundays

in violation of Pennsylvania law. It sought an injunction to restrain enforcement of the law. The district court refused to pass on the constitutionality of the statute on the ground that the meaning of the law was unsettled in Pennsylvania, that there was no imminent threat of prosecution. On a direct appeal to the Supreme Court (there was no Court of Appeals review because under federal law a suit seeking injunction against a state official in federal court goes directly to the Supreme Court on appeal), it was held that the law is not one respecting an establishment or religion and is not unconstitutional. [147]

145. *United Public Workers v. Mitchell*, 330 U.S. 75 (1947). Reed, 4-3.
The Hatch Act forbade federal employees from taking part in certain political activities. Poole, a roller in the United States Mint, was a ward executive committeeman and had worked at the polls on election day. The Supreme Court held that the Hatch Act was constitutional, and did not violate Poole's rights under the 9th and 10th Amendments since the regulation was entirely reasonable in promoting efficiency in the government. [95]

146. *United States v. Causby*, 328 U.S. 256 (1946). Douglas, 6-2.
Military airplanes flew very low over a chicken farm in order to land at and take off from an adjacent municipal airport which the United States Government leased. The noise so disrupted the farm life that it caused the property to become useless as a chicken farm. The Supreme Court held that there was a taking of property within the meaning of the 5th Amendment, for which just compensation was required. [208]

147. *United States v. Classic*, 313 U.S. 299 (1941). Stone, C.J., 5-3.
The federal criminal code makes interference with constitutional rights a crime. A Louisiana commissioner of elections was convicted of changing the votes in a party primary for a Congressional Representative. The Court upheld the conviction, saying that the right to vote for a Representative includes the right to have the vote counted and that an interference with that right, by deliberately changing the vote, was an interference with the constitutional right to vote. This was the first case in which the Court recognized the party primary as an election protected by the Constitution (the Louisiana primary was paid for by public funds and was regulated by state laws). [226]

148. *United States v. Cohen Grocery Co.*, 255 U.S. 81 (1921). White, C.J., 8-0.

The company was a sugar dealer and was indicted for violation of a wartime act penalizing the charging of "any unreasonable rate or charge in handling or dealing in or with any necessaries." The lower court dismissed the indictment, and the Supreme Court affirmed, holding that the Act set up no ascertainable standard of guilt and was therefore a violation of due process (5th Amendment) and of a person's right to be informed of the nature of the accusation against him (6th Amendment) and that the state of war did not suspend these amendments. [185]

149. *United States v. Curtiss-Wright Export Corp.*, 299 U.S. 304 (1936). Sutherland, 7-1.
Congress empowered the President to proclaim sale of arms in the United States to countries at war a crime if he found that the prohibition would tend to lead toward peace between those engaged in the fighting. Curtiss-Wright Export Corp. sold weapons to Bolivia, which was engaged in war; the President had previously forbidden such sales by proclamation. The company defended on the ground that the law was an unconstititional delegation of power, but the Supreme Court upheld the law. Noting that the law related to the field of foreign relations, over which the President has exclusive power, the Court held that Congress and the President could lawfully team up in the delicate area of international relations—the Congress declaring the prohibition *if* the President declares the interest of the United States. The President has the power to declare the one, the Congress to declare the other. [86]

150. *United States v. F. W. Darby Lumber Co.*, 312 U.S. 100 (1941). Stone, C.J., U.
Convicted of a violation of the National Labor Relations Act, Darby appealed to the Supreme Court, claiming that the Act was unconstitutional, since Congress did not have power to regulate prices and hours of manufacturers within a state. The Supreme Court held that the interstate commerce power included the power to so regulate those businesses which were interstate. The Darby Lumber Company sold finished lumber across state lines and this was enough to make the business interstate in character. This case overruled *Hammer v. Dagenhart.* [194]

151. *United States v. E.C. Knight Co.* 156 U.S. 1 (1895). Fuller, C.J., 8-1.
The company was charged under the Sherman Antitrust Act of attempting to help control the price of sugar by turning over its property, including factories, along with the property of four other companies, to the American Sugar Refining Company, in return for stock, so that Sugar Refining could control sugar production. The Court held that this

combination did not violate the Sherman Act, since the *manufacturer* of a product, with intent later to ship out of state, does not put the sugar into interstate commerce. The companies were not attempting to control interstate commerce, but merely trying to make more money from manufacturing. This distinction was difficult to maintain and the case was overruled—see *Swift v. United States, NLRB v. Jones & Laughlin*, and *United States v. F. W. Darby Lumber Company*. [54]

152. *United States v. Hudson and Goodwin*, 11 U.S. (7 Cr.) 32 (1812). Johnson, U.
The courts of the United States have no common law jurisdiction in criminal matters; that is, they cannot convict a person of an act unless the Congress first makes "the act a crime, affix[es] a punishment to it," and says which courts have jurisdiction to hear the case. The defendants here had claimed that President Jefferson and Congress had made a secret deal with Napoleon, planning to give him $2,000,000 in return for his making a treaty with Spain. There was no Congressional statute against "libel" of the President (and given the 1st Amendment, such a statute might have been recognized as unconstitutional even then, see *New York Times v. Sullivan*); therefore the defendants committed no crime and the court could not convict them by inventing a crime. [185]

153. *United States v. Lovett*, 328 U.S. 303 (1946). Black, 8-0.
Three government officers, Lovett, Watson, and Dodd, had their salaries revoked by Congress, even though the government agencies for which they worked were satisfied with their performance. Congress provided that they could not be paid unless the President reappointed them to their jobs and the Senate consented. The three sued for their salaries, and the Supreme Court awarded it to them, holding that the law taking away their salaries was a bill of attainder. Their salaries had been legislated away because they, among others, had been called "unrepresentative, crackpot, radical bureaucrats" by a Congressman. He also branded them as members of "Communist front organizations." To refuse to appropriate money for their salaries was a punishment without a court trial, which is the essence of the prohibition against bills of attainder. [77]

154. *United States v. Nice*, 241 U.S. 591 (1916). Van Devanter, U.
An Act of Congress forbade the sale of liquor to Indians. Nice sold liquor to a member of the Sioux tribe who was under charge of a United States Indian agent. The United States held the title to the land on which he lived in trust. The lower court dismissed Nice's indictment because it held

Congress to have surpassed its power. The Supreme Court reinstated the indictment, holding that Congress had the power to regulate commerce with Indians still in a tribal status. [60]

155. *United States v. Price*, 383 U.S. 787 (1966). Fortas, U.
Private citizens were convicted of violating a federal statute which provided penalties for anyone who deprived a person of constitutional rights. The act was murder, which is a deprivation of the right to life, to travel, to trial, and to sundry others. The indictments were dismissed in the lower court on the grounds that a federal law based on section 5 of the 14th Amendment could only be used against state officials. The Supreme Court reversed, saying that since it was alleged the individuals here acted in concert with the police in denying rights, they acted under "color of state law," and this was sufficient state action for the federal law to be applicable. [224]

156. *United States v. Provoo*, 350 U.S. 857 (1955). Per curiam.
This was a prosecution for treason. Provoo worked for the Japanese as a soldier. The government deliberately brought trial in New York, where venue was questionable, but justified its actions on the grounds that there was governmental advantage to a New York federal court trial. The trial was delayed from 1949 to 1955, while the defendant remained in prison with no chance to interview possible witnesses, many of whom died during that time. A habeas corpus petition was granted: the delay was a denial of the right to a speedy trial under the 6th Amendment. [181]

157. *United States v. Rumely*, 345 U.S. 41 (1953). Frankfurter, 7-0.
Rumely was secretary of an organization which sold political books. He refused to tell Congress the names of those who made bulk purchases, when he was questioned in connection with lobbying activities, and was convicted under a federal law making such refusals a crime. The Supreme Court reversed, holding that the committee was authorized only to investigate lobbying activities, that the sale of books to the general public was not lobbying since it was not a direct appeal to members of Congress. The Court thus avoided the more serious question whether an attempt by Congress to inquire into efforts of private individuals to influence public thinking by the distribution of books and periodicals would be constitutional. [44, 168]

158. *United States v. Von's Grocery Co.*, 384 U.S. 270 (1966).
Black, 6-2.
Von's was the third largest retail grocery chain in Los An-

geles, and Shopping Bag Food Stores was the sixth. The Clayton Act prohibits mergers which would substantially tend to lessen competition, but in holding the merger illegal the Supreme Court concentrated on the fact that the small groceries were being forced out of business in the area and that the Sherman and Clayton Acts were enacted in order to prevent the concentration of economic power. [55]

159. *United States v. Women's Sportswear Manufacturers' Assoc.,* 336 U.S. 460 (1949). Jackson, U.
The company sold 80 percent of its production in interstate commerce. It signed a contract to employ only union stitchers who were also members of a particular trade association. The Supreme Court held the agreement a violation of the Sherman Act, since its effect was to restrain interstate commerce, restrict competition, prices, and markets. [55]

160. *Village of Euclid v. Ambler Realty Co.,* 272 U.S. 365 (1926). Sutherland, 6-3.
The Ambler Realty Company owned land which it was going to save for industrial development. The Village of Euclid passed a zoning ordinance, which restricted the use of the land to residential purposes. The company protested the ordinance, on the grounds that it was a taking of property without due process of law. The Supreme Court upheld the law, declaring that the police power of the state could "abate a nuisance," and that included the power to zone private land for the public good. [209]

161. *Watkins v. United States,* 354 U.S. 178 (1957). Warren, C.J., 6-1.
Watkins was called to testify as a witness before a House Un-American Activities subcommittee, which was investigating people alleged to be members of the Communist Party. Watkins refused to answer questions about other people he thought had left the Party, because he thought the questions were irrelevant to the subcommittee's business. He was indicted and convicted for contempt of Congress; the Supreme Court reversed. The subcommittee had given him no reason to believe the questions were pertinent to its investigation, and a witness can refuse to answer nonpertinent questions. Congress does not have the power to "expose for the sake of exposure" and the witness has the right not to speak. The conviction was reversed because it violated 5th Amendment due process. [32]

162. *Weeks v. United States,* 232 U.S. 383 (1914). Day, U.
Weeks was suspected of sending lottery tickets through the mail, a federal crime. He was arrested without a warrant, and police officers illegally searched his home, finding in-

criminating papers which they turned over to the United
States marshal. Weeks was convicted. The Supreme Court
reversed, holding that evidence seized contrary to the 4th
Amendment cannot be used in federal trials. [170]

163. *Wesberry v. Sanders,* 376 U.S. 1 (1964), Black, 8-1.
Georgia voters asserted that within the state the districts for
the United States House of Representatives were not equal
in population size and that the relative weight of votes must
be the same in each district within the state to be constitutional. The Supreme Court agreed, resting not on the equal
protection clause but on Article 1, Section 2, Clause 1,
which says the "People" shall elect members of the House.
"As nearly as is practicable one man's vote in a congressional election is to be worth as much as another's." [35, 140]

164. *West Virginia State Board of Education v. Barnette,* 319
U.S. 624 (1943). Jackson, 6-3.
West Virginia required all schoolchildren to recite the
pledge of allegiance to the flag each day. When Jehovah's
Witnesses refused, because their religion forbade them from
taking oaths before images, the students were expelled from
school and their parents threatened with prosecution. The
West Virginia court upheld the law, but the Supreme Court
reversed, holding the law unconstitutional because it was an
interference with the freedom of religious exercise and of
speech. [145]

165. *Whitney v. California,* 274 U.S. 357 (1927). Sanford, U.
Miss Whitney belonged to the Communist Labor Party and
took part in the proceedings at one of its meetings. She was
convicted under the state criminal syndicalism act, making
unlawful any association with a group which advocates violence or unlawful acts as a means of effecting industrial or
political change. The Party debated many resolutions calling
for political action, but voted down a proposal to urge the
membership to vote for the Communist Labor Party at all
elections to show its political power. Miss Whitney denied
that she had any intention of violating any known law. The
Supreme Court affirmed the conviction, holding the law
constitutional even though it did restrict a right to speak
and associate which existed prior to the enactment of the
statute. [154]

166. *Wickard v. Filburn,* 317 U.S. 111 (1942). Jackson, U.
Filburn raised a small amount of wheat on his farm, in excess of the amount allowed under the Agricultural Adjustment Act. He used the excess entirely for his own consumption on the farm, for feeding livestock, making flour, and
for seeding. Filburn refused to pay the fine for growing too

much wheat and appealed his conviction. The Supreme Court upheld the fine, ruling that the interstate commerce power extends even to this situation. Consumption of wheat on the farm has a substantial effect on market prices, since it is in competition with wheat which is sold. If everyone did what Filburn did interstate commerce in wheat would be seriously affected. [54]

167. *Wolf v. Colorado,* 338 U.S. 25 (1949). Frankfurter, 6-3.
Wolf was convicted of a conspiracy in state court largely through admission of evidence at trial that would have been inadmissible in federal court because it was illegally seized. The Supreme Court affirmed the conviction. Recognizing that the illegal seizure was a violation of the 4th Amendment the Court nevertheless refused to exclude the evidence. This case was overruled by *Mapp v. Ohio* when it became apparent that exclusion was the only method to enforce the "core" of the 4th Amendment and secure the right of privacy against arbitrary police invasion. [171]

168. *Wong Sun v. United States,* 371 U.S. 471 (1963). Brennan, 5-4.
Toy was illegally chased into his bedroom, handcuffed, and arrested. He confessed his crime to the federal narcotics officers and was convicted. The Supreme Court reversed the conviction because the verbal confession, a result of the illegal arrest and search, was illegal evidence and its use in a federal trial would be unconstitutional under the 4th Amendment. [170]

169. *Worcester v. Georgia,* 31 U.S. (6 Pet.) 515 (1832). Marshall, C.J., 6-1.
A Vermont missionary resided by authority of the President in territory granted by the United States to the Cherokees in Georgia. That state convicted him for living within the territory without a license or permit from the governor, a state crime. The Supreme Court upheld the treaties giving the land to the Cherokees; therefore, the territory was not within the jurisdiction of Georgia, and the conviction was unlawful. It was this case and related ones which led President Jackson supposedly to say "John Marshall has made his decision; now let him enforce it." The treaties were ignored and the Cherokees eventually were forced off their Georgia reservations. [25]

170. *Yates v. United States,* 354 U.S. 298 (1957). Harlan, 6-1 (two of the six concurred in part and dissented in part).
Yates and thirteen others were convicted of violating the Smith Act, which proscribes the conspiracy to advocate the overthrow of the government by force. The evidence

showed they were members of the Communist Party, that they conspired to publish articles, run schools for the indoctrination of teachers who would advocate, etc. The Supreme Court reversed the convictions, ordering indictments against five to be dismissed for lack of evidence and new trials for the other nine. Narrowing *Dennis v. United States*, the Court ruled that the Smith Act does not prohibit advocacy and teaching of forcible overthrow as an abstract principle; it prohibits advocacy only when it is a direct incitement to action, implying that a rule against advocacy in the abstract might be unconstitutional. Since the jury could not determine this difference from the judge's instructions, there was error and new trials were necessary. [156]

171. *Yick Wo v. Hopkins*, 118 U.S. 356 (1886). Matthews, U.
The equal protection clause applies even to aliens who are discriminated against by city administrative officials, who in this case gave licenses to non-Chinese launderers, but denied permits to Chinese aliens. The officials claimed the Chinese laundries were fire hazards, but their buildings were substantially the same as those of people who had been granted licenses. Convictions for running a laundry without a license were reversed. [212]

172. *Youngstown Sheet & Tube Co. v. Sawyer* (The Steel Seizure Case), 343 U.S. 579 (1952). Black, 6-3.
After the failure of the company and the union to settle their differences, the President seized the mills and ordered the workers back to their jobs, fearing that the stoppage of work would endanger the war effort in Korea. The Supreme Court ruled that the seizure was unconstitutional, not being within the "executive power" of the President, distinguishing this case from those in which the President seized private property under authority from Congress. [86]

173. *Zorach v. Clauson*, 343 U.S. 306 (1952). Douglas, 6-3.
New York allowed its schoolchildren to go outside the school for religious instruction upon the written request of their parents. The "released time" program did not require any public expenditures. The Supreme Court held the law constitutional, not a violation of the free exercise or establishment clauses of the 1st Amendment. No one was forced to take religious instruction or condemned or ridiculed because he did not wish to be released from school. [143]

RECENT CASES

174. *Keyishian v. Board of Regents*, 385 U.S. 589—(1967). Brennan, 5-4.
The New York Education law in part provided that "a person employed as superintendent of schools, teacher or em-

ployee in the public schools, in any city or school district of the state, shall be removed from such position for the utterance of any treasonable or seditious word or words or the doing of any treasonable or seditious act or acts while holding such position." Teachers at the State University of New York were dismissed when they failed to comply with procedural requirements, and they joined others in a suit to have the law declared unconstitutional. The Supreme Court agreed and struck down the laws as vague and overboard. State employment, the Court held, cannot be conditioned on a person's agreement not to exercise his constitutional rights, such as belonging to an organization, nor can he be scared away from joining by a vaguely-worded statute's threat of removal. [165, 166]

175. *Sheppard v. Maxwell*, 384 U.S. 333 (1966). Clark, 8-1.
Sheppard was convicted of second-degree murder. In the five months preceding the trial the community was subject to a barrage of newspaper stories and editorials accusing him of the crime and pointing to damaging evidence that was never later introduced at trial. The trial itself had a "carnival atmosphere," and reporters had easy access to the jury. The jury read and heard commentary highly prejudicial to the defendant. The chief prosecutor and the trial judge were involved in an election campaign in which the handling and outcome of the trial played an important part. The Supreme Court reversed the conviction. The circumstances of the trial denied the defendant his right to an impartial jury, guaranteed by the 6th Amendment as made applicable to the states by the 14th. [183]

176. *Adderley v. Florida*, 385 U.S. 39 (1967). Black, 5-4.
Two hundred Florida students marched onto jailhouse grounds to protest the jailing of other students and the state's policy of segregating the races in the jails. The sheriff gave the students 10 minutes to leave and arrested them when they failed to go. The Supreme Court affirmed their conviction under the state's "malicious trepass" statute, distinguishing *Cox v. Louisiana* because here the students were in fact "near" the jailhouse. [164]

177. *Afroyim v. Rusk*, 387 U.S. 253 (1967). Black, 5-4.
Afroyim, having lived in Israel for 10 years, applied to the State Department for renewal of his passport. The Department declared he had forfeited his citizenship because he had voted in a local Israeli election two years before. The Court declared that Congress (under whose authority the Department had acted) did not have the power to cause such a forfeiture. [60-61]

APPENDIX

THE CONSTITUTION OF THE
UNITED STATES OF AMERICA

WE THE PEOPLE of the United States, in Order to form a more perfect Union, establish Justice, insure domestic Tranquility, provide for the common defence, promote the general Welfare, and secure the Blessings of Liberty to ourselves and our Posterity, do ordain and establish this CONSTITUTION for the United States of America.

ARTICLE I

Section 1. All legislative Powers herein granted shall be vested in a Congress of the United States, which shall consist of a Senate and House of Representatives.

Section 2. The House of Representatives shall be composed of Members chosen every second Year by the People of the several States, and the Electors in each State shall have the Qualifications requisite for Electors of the most numerous Branch of the State Legislature.

No Person shall be a Representative who shall not have attained to the Age of twenty-five Years, and been seven Years a Citizen of the United States, and who shall not, when elected, be an Inhabitant of the State in which he shall be chosen.

[Representatives and direct Taxes shall be apportioned among the several States which may be included within this Union, according to their respective Numbers, which shall be determined by adding to the whole Number of free Persons, including those bound to Service for a Term of Years, and excluding Indians not taxed, three fifths of all other Persons.] The actual Enumeration

Note: The Constitution and all amendments are given here in their original form. Items which have since been amended or superseded are bracketed.

298

shall be made within three Years after the first Meeting of the Congress of the United States, and within every subsequent Term of ten Years, in such Manner as they shall by Law direct. The Number of Representatives shall not exceed one for every thirty Thousand, but each State shall have at Least one Representative; and until such enumeration shall be made, the State of New Hampshire shall be entitled to chuse three, Massachusetts eight, Rhode-Island and Providence Plantations one, Connecticut five, New York six, New Jersey four, Pennsylvania eight, Delaware one, Maryland six, Virginia ten, North Carolina five, South Carolina five, and Georgia three.

When vacancies happen in the Representation from any State, the Executive Authority thereof shall issue Writs of Election to fill such Vacancies.

The House of Representatives shall chuse their Speaker and other officers; and shall have the sole Power of Impeachment.

Section 3. The Senate of the United States shall be composed of two Senators from each State, [chosen by the Legislature thereof,] for six Years; and each Senator shall have one Vote.

Immediately after they shall be assembled in Consequence of the first Election, they shall be divided as equally as may be into three Classes. The Seats of the Senators of the first Class shall be vacated at the Expiration of the second Year, of the second Class at the Expiration of the fourth Year, and of the third Class at the Expiration of the sixth Year, so that one-third may be chosen every second Year; [and if Vacancies happen by Resignation, or otherwise, during the Recess of the Legislature of any State, the Executive thereof may make temporary Appointments until the next Meeting of the Legislature, which shall then fill such Vacancies.]

No Person shall be a Senator who shall not have attained to the Age of thirty Years, and been nine Years a Citizen of the United States, and who shall not, when elected, be an Inhabitant of that State for which he shall be chosen.

The Vice President of the United States shall be President of the Senate, but shall have no Vote, unless they be equally divided.

The Senate shall chuse their other Officers, and also a President pro tempore, in the absence of the Vice President, or when he shall exercise the Office of President of the United States.

The Senate shall have the sole Power to try all Impeachments. When sitting for that Purpose, they shall be on Oath or Affirmation. When the President of the United States is tried, the Chief Justice shall preside: And no Person shall be convicted without the Concurrence of two thirds of the Members present.

Judgment in Cases of Impeachment shall not extend further than to removal from Office, and disqualification to hold and enjoy any Office of honor, Trust or Profit under the United States: but the Party convicted shall nevertheless be liable and subject to Indictment, Trial, Judgment and Punishment, according to Law.

Section 4. The Times, Places and Manner of holding Elections for Senators and Representatives, shall be prescribed in each State by the Legislature thereof; but the Congress may at any time by Law make or alter such Regulations, except as to the Places of chusing Senators.

The Congress shall assemble at least once in every Year, and such Meeting shall [be on the first Monday in December,] unless they shall by Law appoint a different Day.

Section 5. Each House shall be the Judge of the Elections, Returns and Qualifications of its own Members, and a Majority of each shall constitute a Quorum to do Business; but a smaller number may adjourn from day to day, and may be authorized to compel the Attendance of absent Members, in such Manner, and under such Penalties as each House may provide.

Each House may determine the Rules of its Proceedings, punish its Members for disorderly Behavior, and, with the Concurrence of two thirds, expel a Member.

Each House shall keep a Journal of its Proceedings, and from time to time publish the same, excepting such Parts as may in their Judgment require Secrecy; and the Yeas and Nays of the Members of either House on any question shall, at the Desire of one fifth of those Present, be entered on the Journal.

Neither House, during the Session of Congress, shall, without the Consent of the other, adjourn for more than three days, nor to any other Place than that in which the two Houses shall be sitting.

Section 6. The Senators and Representatives shall receive a Compensation for their Services, to be ascertained by Law, and paid out of the Treasury of the United States. They shall in all Cases, except Treason, Felony and Breach of the Peace, be privileged from Arrest during their Attendance at the Session of their respective Houses, and in going to and returning from the same; and for any Speech or Debate in either House, they shall not be questioned in any other Place.

No Senator or Representative shall, during the Time for which he was elected, be appointed to any civil Office under the Authority of the United States, which shall have been created, or the Emoluments whereof shall have been encreased during such time; and no Person holding any Office under the United States, shall be a Member of either House during his Continuance in Office.

Section 7. All Bills for raising Revenue shall originate in the

House of Representatives; but the Senate may propose or concur with Amendments as on other Bills.

Every Bill which shall have passed the House of Representatives and the Senate, shall, before it becomes a Law, be presented to the President of the United States; If he approve he shall sign it, but if not he shall return it, with his Objections to that House in which it shall have originated, who shall enter the Objections at large on their Journal, and proceed to reconsider it. If after such Reconsideration two thirds of that House shall agree to pass the Bill, it shall be sent, together with the Objections, to the other House, by which it shall likewise be reconsidered, and if approved by two thirds of that House, it shall become a Law. But in all such Cases the Votes of both Houses shall be determined by Yeas and Nays, and the Names of the Persons voting for and against the Bill shall be entered on the Journal of each House respectively. If any Bill shall not be returned by the President within ten Days (Sundays excepted) after it shall have been presented to him, the Same shall be a Law, in like Manner as if he had signed it, unless the Congress by their Adjournment prevent its Return, in which Case it shall not be a Law.

Every Order, Resolution, or Vote to which the Concurrence of the Senate and House of Representatives may be necessary (except on a question of Adjournment) shall be presented to the President of the United States; and before the Same shall take Effect, shall be approved by him, or being disapproved by him, shall be repassed by two thirds of the Senate and House of Representatives, according to the Rules and Limitations prescribed in the Case of a Bill.

Section 8. The Congress shall have Power To lay and collect Taxes, Duties, Imposts and Excises, to pay the Debts and provide for the common Defence and general Welfare of the United States; but all Duties, Imposts and Excises shall be uniform throughout the United States;

To borrow money on the credit of the United States;

To regulate Commerce with foreign Nations, and among the several States, and with the Indian Tribes;

To establish a uniform Rule of Naturalization, and uniform Laws on the subject of Bankruptcies throughout the United States;

To coin Money, regulate the Value thereof, and of foreign Coin, and fix the Standard of Weights and Measures;

To provide for the Punishment of counterfeiting the Securities and current Coin of the United States;

To establish Post Offices and post Roads;

To promote the Progress of Science and useful Arts, by securing for limited Times to Authors and Inventors the exclusive Right to their respective Writings and Discoveries;

To constitute Tribunals inferior to the supreme Court;

To define and punish Piracies and Felonies committed on the high Seas, and Offenses against the Law of Nations;

To declare War, grant Letters of Marque and Reprisal, and make Rules concerning Captures on Land and Water;

To raise and support Armies, but no Appropriation of Money to that Use shall be for a longer Term than two Years;

To provide and maintain a Navy;

To make Rules for the Government and Regulation of the land and naval Forces;

To provide for calling forth the Militia to execute the Laws of the Union, suppress Insurrections and repel Invasions;

To provide for organizing, arming, and disciplining the Militia, and for governing such Part of them as may be employed in the Service of the United States, reserving to the States respectively, the Appointment of the Officers, and the Authority of training the Militia according to the discipline prescribed by Congress;

To exercise exclusive Legislation in all Cases whatsoever, over such District (not exceeding ten Miles square) as may, by Cession of particular States, and the acceptance of Congress, become the Seat of the Government of the United States, and to exercise like Authority over all Places purchased by the Consent of the Legislature of the State in which the Same shall be, for the Erection of Forts, Magazines, Arsenals, dock-Yards, and other needful Buildings;—And

To make all Laws which shall be necessary and proper for carrying into Execution the foregoing Powers, and all other Powers vested by this Constitution in the Government of the United States, or in any Department or Officer thereof.

Section 9. The Migration or Importation of such Persons as any of the States now existing shall think proper to admit, shall not be prohibited by the Congress prior to the Year one thousand eight hundred and eight, but a tax or duty may be imposed on such Importation, not exceeding ten dollars for each Person.

The privilege of the Writ of Habeas Corpus shall not be suspended, unless when in Cases of Rebellion or Invasion the public Safety may require it.

No Bill of Attainder or ex post facto Law shall be passed.

No capitation, or other direct, Tax shall be laid, unless in Proportion to the Census or Enumeration herein before directed to be taken.

No Tax or Duty shall be laid on Articles exported from any State.

No Preference shall be given by any Regulation of Commerce or Revenue to the Ports of one State over those of another: nor shall Vessels bound to, or from, one State, be obliged to enter, clear, or pay Duties in another.

No Money shall be drawn from the Treasury, but in Consequence of Appropriations made by law; and a regular Statement and Account of the Receipts and Expenditures of all public Money shall be published from time to time.

No Title of Nobility shall be granted by the United States: And no Person holding any Office of Profit or Trust under them, shall, without the Consent of the Congress, accept of any present, Emolument, Office, or Title, of any kind whatever, from any King, Prince, or foreign State.

Section 10. No State shall enter into any Treaty, Alliance, or Confederation; grant Letters of Marque and Reprisal; coin Money; emit Bills of Credit; make any Thing but gold and silver Coin a Tender in Payment of Debts; pass any Bill of Attainder, ex post facto Law, or Law impairing the Obligation of Contracts, or grant any Title of Nobility.

No State shall, without the Consent of the Congress, lay any Imposts or Duties on Imports or Exports, except what may be absolutely necessary for executing its inspection Laws: and the net Produce of all Duties and Imposts, laid by any State on Imports or Exports, shall be for the Use of the Treasury of the United States; and all such Laws shall be subject to the Revision and Control of the Congress.

No State shall, without the Consent of Congress, lay any duty of Tonnage, keep Troops, or Ships of War in time of Peace, enter into any Agreement or Compact with another State, or with a foreign Power, or engage in War, unless actually invaded, or in such imminent Danger as will not admit of delay.

ARTICLE II

Section 1. The executive Power shall be vested in a President of the United States of America. He shall hold his Office during the Term of four Years, and, together with the Vice-President, chosen for the same Term, be elected, as follows.

Each State shall appoint, in such Manner as the Legislature thereof may direct, a Number of Electors, equal to the whole Number of Senators and Representatives to which the State may be entitled in the Congress: but no Senator or Representative, or Persons holding an Office of Trust or Profit under the United States, shall be appointed an Elector.

[The Electors shall meet in their respective States, and vote by Ballot for two persons, of whom one at least shall not be an Inhabitant of the same State with themselves. And they shall make a List of all the Persons voted for, and of the Number of Votes for each; which List they shall sign and certify, and transmit sealed to the Seat of the Government of the United States, directed to the President of the Senate. The President of the Senate shall, in the Presence of the Senate and House of Representatives, open all the Certificates, and the Votes shall then be counted. The

Person having the greatest number of Votes shall be the President, if such Number be a Majority of the whole Number of Electors appointed; and if there be more than one who have such Majority, and have an equal Number of Votes, then the House of Representatives shall immediately chuse by Ballot one of them for President; and if no Person have a Majority, then from the five highest on the List the said House shall in like Manner chuse the President. But in chusing the President, the Votes shall be taken by States, the Representation from each State having one Vote; A quorum for this Purpose shall consist of a Member or Members from two-thirds of the States, and a Majority of all the States shall be necessary to a Choice. In every Case, after the Choice of the President, the Person having the greatest Number of Votes of the Electors shall be the Vice President. But if there should remain two or more who have equal Votes, the Senate shall chuse from them by Ballot the Vice-President.]

The Congress may determine the Time of chusing the Electors, and the Day on which they shall give their Votes; which Day shall be the same throughout the United States.

No person except a natural born Citizen, or a Citizen of the United States, at the time of the Adoption of this Constitution, shall be eligible to the Office of President; neither shall any Person be eligible to that Office who shall not have attained to the Age of thirty-five Years, and been fourteen Years a Resident within the United States.

In Case of the Removal of the President from Office, or of his Death, Resignation, or Inability to discharge the Powers and Duties of the said Office, the same shall devolve on the Vice President, and the Congress may by Law provide for the Case of [Removal,] Death, Resignation [or inability, both] of the President [and Vice President,] declaring what Officer shall then act as President, and such Officer shall act accordingly, until [the Disability be removed, or] a President shall be elected.

The President shall, at stated Times, receive for his Services, a Compensation, which shall neither be encreased nor diminished during the Period for which he shall have been elected, and he shall not receive within that Period any other Emolument from the United States, or any of them.

Before he enter on the Execution of his Office, he shall take the following Oath or Affirmation:—"I do solemnly swear (or affirm) that I will faithfully execute the Office of President of the United States, and will to the best of my Ability, preserve, protect and defend the Constitution of the United States."

Section 2. The President shall be Commander in Chief of the Army and Navy of the United States, and of the Militia of the several States, when called into the actual Service of the United States; he may require the Opinion in writing, of the principal Officer in each of the executive Departments, upon any subject relating to the Duties of their respective Offices, and he shall have Power to Grant Reprieves and Pardons for Offenses against the United States, except in Cases of Impeachment.

He shall have Power, by and with the Advice and Consent of the Senate, to make Treaties, provided two-thirds of the Senators present concur; and he shall nominate, and by and with the Advice and Consent of the Senate, shall appoint Ambassadors, other public Ministers and Consuls, Judges of the supreme Court, and all other Officers of the United States, whose Appointments are not herein otherwise provided for, and which shall be established by Law: but the Congress may by Law vest the Appointment of such inferior Officers, as they think proper, in the President alone, in the Courts of Law, or in the Heads of Departments.

The President shall have Power to fill up all Vacancies that may happen during the Recess of the Senate, by granting Commissions which shall expire at the End of their next Session.

Section 3. He shall from time to time give to the Congress Information of the State of the Union, and recommend to their Consideration such Measures as he shall judge necessary and expedient; he may, on extraordinary Occasions, convene both Houses, or either of them, and in Case of Disagreement between them, with Respect to the Time of Adjournment, he may adjourn them to such Time as he shall think proper; he shall receive Ambassadors and other public Ministers; he shall take Care that the Laws be faithfully executed, and shall Commission all the Officers of the United States.

Section 4. The President, Vice President and all civil Officers of the United States, shall be removed from Office on Impeachment for, and Conviction of, Treason, Bribery, or other high Crimes and Misdemeanors.

ARTICLE III

Section 1. The judicial Power of the United States, shall be vested in one Supreme Court, and in such inferior Courts as the Congress may from time to time ordain and establish. The Judges, both of the supreme and inferior Courts, shall hold their Offices during good behaviour, and shall, at stated Times, receive for their services a Compensation which shall not be diminished during their Continuance in Office.

Section 2. The judicial Power shall extend to all Cases, in Law and Equity, arising under this Constitution, the Laws of the United States, and Treaties made, or which shall be made, under their Authority; to all Cases affecting Ambassadors, other public Ministers and Consuls;—to all Cases of admiralty and maritime Jurisdiction;—to Controversies to which the United States shall be a Party;—to Controversies between two or more States: [—between a State and Citizens of another state;—] between Citizens of different States;—between Citizens of the same State claiming Lands under Grants of different States, and between a State, or the Citizens thereof, and foreign States, Citizens or Subjects.

In all Cases affecting Ambassadors, other public Ministers and Consuls, and those in which a State shall be Party, the supreme Court shall have original Jurisdiction. In all the other Cases before mentioned, the supreme Court shall have appellate Jurisdiction, both as to Law and Fact, with such Exceptions, and under such Regulations as the Congress shall make.

The trial of all Crimes, except in Cases of Impeachment, shall be by Jury; and such Trial shall be held in the State where the said Crimes shall have been committed; but when not committed within any state, the Trial shall be at such Place or Places as the Congress may by Law have directed.

Section 3. Treason against the United States, shall consist only in levying War against them; or in adhering to their Enemies, giving them Aid and Comfort. No Person shall be convicted of Treason unless on the Testimony of two Witnesses to the same overt Act, or on Confession in open Court.

The Congress shall have power to declare the Punishment of Treason, but no Attainder of Treason shall work Corruption of Blood, or Forfeiture except during the Life of the Person attained.

ARTICLE IV

Section 1. Full Faith and Credit shall be given in each State to the public Acts, Records, and judicial Proceedings of every other State. And the Congress may by general Laws prescribe the Manner in which such Acts, Records and Proceedings shall be proved, and the Effect thereof.

Section 2. The Citizens of each State shall be entitled to all Privileges and Immunities of Citizens in the several States.

A Person charged in any State with Treason, Felony, or other Crime, who shall flee from Justice, and be found in another State, shall on demand of the executive Authority of the State from which he fled, be delivered up, to be removed to the State having Jurisdiction of the Crime.

[No Person held to Service or Labour in one State, under the Laws thereof, escaping into another, shall, in Consequence of any Law or Regulation therein, be discharged from such Service or Labour, but shall be delivered up on Claim of the Party to whom such Service or Labour may be due.]

Section 3. New States may be admitted by the Congress into this Union; but no new State shall be formed or erected within the Jurisdiction of any other State; nor any State be formed by the Junction of two or more States, or parts of States, without the Consent of the Legislatures of the States concerned as well as of the Congress.

The Congress shall have Power to dispose of and make all needful Rules and Regulations respecting the Territory or other Property belonging to the United States; and nothing in this Constitution shall be so construed as to Prejudice any Claims of the United States, or of any particular State.

Section 4. The United States shall guarantee to every State in this Union a Republican Form of Government, and shall protect each of them against Invasion; and on Application of the Legislature, or of the Executive (when the Legislature cannot be convened) against domestic Violence.

ARTICLE V

The Congress, whenever two-thirds of both Houses shall deem it necessary, shall propose Amendments to this Constitution, or, on the Application of the Legislatures of two-thirds of the several States, shall call a Convention for proposing Amendments, which, in either Case, shall be valid to all Intents and Purposes, as part of this Constitution, when ratified by the Legislature of three-fourths of the several States, or by Conventions in three-fourths thereof, as the one or the other Mode of Ratification may be proposed by the Congress: Provided that no Amendment which may be made prior to the Year One thousand eight hundred and eight shall in any Manner affect the first and fourth Clauses in the Ninth Section of the first Article; and that no State, without its Consent, shall be deprived of its equal Suffrage in the Senate.

ARTICLE VI

All Debts contracted and Engagements entered into, before the Adoption of this Constitution, shall be as valid against the United States under this Constitution, as under the Confederation.

This Constitution, and the Laws of the United States which shall be made in Pursuance thereof; and all Treaties made, or which shall be made, under the Authority of the United States, shall be the supreme Law of the Land; and the Judges in every State shall be bound thereby, any Thing in the Constitution or Laws of any State to the Contrary notwithstanding.

The Senators and Representatives before mentioned, and the Members of the several State Legislatures, and all executive and judicial Officers, both of the United States and of the several States, shall be bound by Oath or Affirmation, to support this

Constitution; but no religious Test shall ever be required as a Qualification to any Office or public Trust under the United States.

ARTICLE VII

The Ratification of the Conventions of nine States shall be sufficient for the Establishment of this Constitution between the States so ratifying the Same.

DONE in Convention by the Unanimous Consent of the States present the Seventeenth Day of September in the Year of our Lord one thousand seven hundred and Eighty seven and of the Independence of the United States of America the Twelfth. In Witness whereof We have hereunto subscribed our Names.

Go WASHINGTON
Presidt and deputy from Virginia

New Hampshire

JOHN LANGDON
NICHOLAS GILMAN

Massachusetts

NATHANIEL GORHAM
RUFUS KING

Connecticut

WM SAML JOHNSON
ROGER SHERMAN

New York

ALEXANDER HAMILTON

New Jersey

WIL: LIVINGSTON
DAVID BREARLEY.
WM PATTERSON
JONA: DAYTON

Pennsylvania

B. FRANKLIN
ROBT. MORRIS

THOS. FITZSIMONS
JAMES WILSON
THOMAS MIFFLIN
GEO. CLYMER
JARED INGERSOLL
GOUV MORRIS

Delaware

GEO: READ
JOHN DICKINSON
JACO: BROOM
GUNNING BEDFORD jun
RICHARD BASSETT

Maryland

JAMES MCHENRY
DANL CARROL
DAN: of ST THOS JENIFER

Virginia

JOHN BLAIR
JAMES MADISON Jr.

North Carolina

WM BLOUNT
HU WILLIAMSON
RICHD DOBBS SPAIGHT

South Carolina	*Georgia*

J. RUTLEDGE
CHARLES PINCKNEY
CHARLES COTESWORTH PINCKNEY
PIERCE BUTLER.

WILLIAM FEW
ABR BALDWIN

Attest:
WILLIAM JACKSON, *Secretary.*

ARTICLES IN ADDITION TO, AND AMENDMENT OF, THE CONSTITUTION OF THE UNITED STATES OF AMERICA, PROPOSED BY CONGRESS, AND RATIFIED BY THE LEGISLATURES OF THE SEVERAL STATES, PURSUANT TO THE FIFTH ARTICLE OF THE ORIGINAL CONSTITUTION.

AMENDMENT I

Congress shall make no law respecting an establishment of religion, or prohibiting the free exercise thereof; or abridging the freedom of speech, or of the press; or the right of the people peaceably to assemble, and to petition the Government for a redress of grievances.

AMENDMENT II

A well regulated Militia, being necessary to the security of a free State, the right of the people to keep and bear Arms, shall not be infringed.

AMENDMENT III

No Soldier shall, in time of peace be quartered in any house, without the consent of the Owner, nor in time of war, but in a manner to be prescribed by law.

AMENDMENT IV

The right of the people to be secure in their persons, houses, papers, and effects, against unreasonable searches and seizures, shall not be violated, and no Warrants shall issue, but upon probable cause, supported by Oath or affirmation, and particularly describing the place to be searched, and the persons or things to be seized.

AMENDMENT V

No person shall be held to answer for a capital, or otherwise infamous crime, unless on a presentment or indictment of a Grand Jury, except in cases arising in the land or naval forces, or in the Militia, when in actual service in time of War or public danger; nor shall any person be subject for the same offence to be twice put in jeopardy of life or limb; nor shall be compelled in any criminal case to be a witness against himself, nor be deprived of life, liberty, or property, without due process of law; nor shall private property be taken for public use, without just compensation.

AMENDMENT VI

In all criminal prosecutions, the accused shall enjoy the right to a speedy and public trial, by an impartial jury of the State and district wherein the crime shall have been committed, which district shall have been previously ascertained by law, and to be informed of the nature and cause of the accusation; to be confronted with the witnesses against him; to have compulsory process for obtaining witnesses in his favor, and to have the Assistance of Counsel for his defence.

AMENDMENT VII

In suits at common law, where the value in controversy shall exceed twenty dollars, the right of trial by jury shall be preserved, and no fact tried by a jury, shall be otherwise reexamined in any Court of the United States, than according to the rules of the common law.

AMENDMENT VIII

Excessive bail shall not be required, nor excessive fines imposed, nor cruel and unusual punishments inflicted.

AMENDMENT IX

The enumeration in the Constitution, of certain rights, shall not be construed to deny or disparage others retained by the people.

AMENDMENT X

The powers not delegated to the United States by the Constitution, nor prohibited by it to the States, are reserved to the States respectively, or to the people.

AMENDMENT XI

The Judicial power of the United States shall not be construed to extend to any suit in law or equity, commenced or prosecuted against one of the United States by Citizens of another State, or by Citizens or Subjects of any Foreign State.

AMENDMENT XII

The Electors shall meet in their respective states and vote by ballot for President and Vice-President, one of whom, at least, shall not be an inhabitant of the same state with themselves; they shall name in their ballots the person voted for as President, and in distinct ballots the person voted for as Vice-President, and they shall make distinct lists of all persons voted for as President, and of all persons voted for as Vice-President, and of the number of votes for each, which lists they shall sign and certify, and transmit sealed to the seat of the government of the United States, directed to the President of the Senate;—The President of the Senate shall, in the presence of the Senate and House of Representatives, open all the certificates and the votes shall then be counted;—The person having the greatest number of votes for President, shall be the President, if such number be a majority of the whole number of Electors appointed; and if no person have such majority, then from the persons having the highest numbers not exceeding three on the list of those voted for as President, the House of Representatives shall choose immediately, by ballot, the President. But in choosing the President, the votes shall be taken by states, the representation from each state having one vote; a quorum for this purpose shall consist of a member or members from two-thirds of the states, and a majority of all the states shall be necessary to a choice. [And if the House of Representatives shall not choose a President whenever the right of choice shall devolve upon them, before the fourth day of March next following, then the Vice-President shall act as President, as in the case of the death or other constitutional disability of the President.—] The person having the greatest number of votes as Vice-President, shall be the Vice-President, if such number be a majority of the whole number of Electors appointed, and if no person have a majority, then from the two highest numbers on the list, the Senate shall choose the Vice-President; a quorum for the purpose shall consist of two-thirds of the whole number of Senators, and a majority of the whole number shall be necessary to a choice. But no person constitutionally ineligible to the office of President shall be eligible to that of Vice-President of the United States.

AMENDMENT XIII

Section 1. Neither slavery nor involuntary servitude, except as a punishment for crime whereof the party shall have been duly convicted, shall exist within the United States, or any place subject to their jurisdiction.

Section 2. Congress shall have power to enforce this article by appropriate legislation.

AMENDMENT XIV

Section 1. All persons born or naturalized in the United States, and subject to the jurisdiction thereof, are citizens of the United States and of the State wherein they reside. No State shall make or enforce any law which shall abridge the privileges or immunities of citizens of the United States; nor shall any State deprive any person of life, liberty, or property, without due process of law; nor deny to any person within its jurisdiction the equal protection of the laws.

Section 2. Representatives shall be apportioned among the several States according to their respective numbers, counting the whole number of persons in each State, excluding Indians not taxed. But when the right to vote at any election for the choice of electors for President and Vice-President of the United States, Representatives in Congress, the Executive and Judicial officers of a State, or the members of the Legislature thereof, is denied to any of the male inhabitants of such State, being twenty-one years of age, and citizens of the United States, or in any way abridged, except for participation in rebellion, or other crime, the basis of representation therein shall be reduced in the proportion which the number of such male citizens shall bear to the whole number of male citizens twenty-one years of age in such State.

Section 3. No person shall be a Senator or Representative in Congress, or elector of President and Vice-President, or hold any office, civil or military, under the United States, or under any State, who, having previously taken an oath, as a member of Congress, or as an officer of the United States, or as a member of any State legislature, or as an executive or judicial officer of any State, to support the Constitution of the United States, shall have engaged in insurrection or rebellion against the same, or given aid or comfort to the enemies thereof. But Congress may by a vote of two-thirds of each House, remove such disability.

Section 4. The validity of the public debt of the United States, authorized by law, including debts incurred for payment of pensions and bounties for services in suppressing insurrection or rebellion, shall not be questioned. But neither the United States nor any State shall assume or pay any debt or obligation incurred in aid of insurrection or rebellion against the United States, or any claim for the loss or emancipation of any slave; but all such debts, obligations and claims shall be held illegal and void.

Section 5. The Congress shall have power to enforce, by appropriate legislation, the provisions of this article.

AMENDMENT XV

Section 1. The right of citizens of the United States to vote shall not be denied or abridged by the United States or by any State on account of race, color, or previous condition of servitude.

Section 2. The Congress shall have power to enforce this article by appropriate legislation.

AMENDMENT XVI

The Congress shall have power to lay and collect taxes on incomes, from whatever source derived, without apportionment among the several States, and without regard to any census or enumeration.

AMENDMENT XVII

The Senate of the United States shall be composed of two Senators from each State, elected by the people thereof, for six years; and each Senator shall have one vote. The electors in each State shall have the qualifications requisite for electors of the most numerous branch of the State legislatures.

When vacancies happen in the representation of any State in the Senate, the executive authority of such State shall issue writs of election to fill such vacancies; *Provided,* That the legislature of any State may empower the executive thereof to make temporary appointments until the people fill the vacancies by election as the legislature may direct.

This amendment shall not be so construed as to affect the election or term of any Senator chosen before it becomes valid as part of the Constitution.

AMENDMENT XVIII

[Section 1. After one year from the ratification of this article the manufacture, sale, or transportation of intoxicating liquors within, the importation thereof into, or the exportation thereof from the United States and all territory subject to the jurisdiction thereof for beverage purposes is hereby prohibited.

[Section 2. The Congress and the several States shall have concurrent power to enforce this article by appropriate legislation.

[Section 3. This article shall be inoperative unless it shall have been ratified as an amendment to the Constitution by the legislatures of the several States, as provided in the Constitution, within seven years from the date of the submission hereof to the States by the Congress.]

AMENDMENT XIX

The right of citizens of the United States to vote shall not be denied or abridged by the United States or by any State on account of sex.

Congress shall have power to enforce this article by appropriate legislation.

AMENDMENT XX

Section 1. The terms of the President and Vice President shall end at noon on the 20th day of January, and the terms of Senators and Representatives at noon on the 3d day of January, of the years in which such terms would have ended if this article had not been ratified; and the terms of their successors shall then begin.

Section 2. The Congress shall assemble at least once in every year, and such meeting shall begin at noon on the 3d day of January, unless they shall by law appoint a different day.

Section 3. If, at the time fixed for the beginning of the term of the President, the President elect shall have died, the Vice President elect shall become President. If a President shall not have been chosen before the time fixed for the beginning of his term, or if the President elect shall have failed to quality, then the Vice President elect shall act as President until a President shall have qualified; and the Congress may by law provide for the case wherein neither a President elect nor a Vice President elect shall have qualified, declaring who shall then act as President, or the manner in which one who is to act shall be selected, and such person shall act accordingly until a President or Vice President shall have qualified.

Section 4. The Congress may by law provide for the case of the death of any of the persons from whom the House of Representatives may choose a President whenever the right of choice shall have devolved upon them, and for the case of the death of any of the persons from whom the Senate may choose a Vice President whenever the right of choice shall have devolved upon them.

Section 5. Sections 1 and 2 shall take effect on the 15th day of October following the ratification of this article.

Section 6. This article shall be inoperative unless it shall have been ratified as an amendment to the Constitution by the legislatures of three-fourths of the several States within seven years from the date of its submission.

AMENDMENT XXI

Section 1. The eighteenth article of amendment to the Constitution of the United States is hereby repealed.

Section 2. The transportation or importation into any State, Territory, or possession of the United States for delivery or use therein of intoxicating liquors, in violation of the laws thereof, is hereby prohibited.

Section 3. This article shall be inoperative unless it shall have been ratified as an amendment to the Constitution by conventions in the several States, as provided in the Constitution, within seven years from the date of the submission thereof to the States by the Congress.

Note: Amendment XXI was not ratified by state legislatures, but by state conventions summoned by Congress.

AMENDMENT XXII

Section 1. No person shall be elected to the office of the President more than twice, and no person who has held the office of President, or acted as President, for more than two years of a term to which some other person was elected President shall be elected to the office of the President more than once. But this Article shall not apply to any person holding the office of President when this Article was proposed by the Congress, and shall not prevent any person who may be holding the office of President, or acting as President, during the term within which this Article becomes operative from holding the office of President or acting as President during the remainder of such term.

Section 2. This article shall be inoperative unless it shall have been ratified as an amendment to the Constitution by the legislatures of three-fourths of the several States within seven years from the date of its submission to the States by the Congress.

AMENDMENT XXIII

Section 1. The District constituting the seat of Government of the United States shall appoint in such manner as the Congress may direct:

A number of electors of President and Vice President equal to the whole number of Senators and Representatives in Congress to which the District would be entitled if it were a State, but in no event more than the least populous State; they shall be in addition to those appointed by the States, but they shall be considered, for the purposes of the election of President and Vice President, to be electors appointed by a State; and they shall meet in the District and perform such duties as provided by the twelfth article of amendment.

Section 2. The Congress shall have power to enforce this article by appropriate legislation.

AMENDMENT XXIV

Section 1. The right of citizens of the United States to vote in any primary or other election for President or Vice President, for electors for President or Vice President, or for Senator or Representative in Congress, shall not be denied or abridged by the United States or any State by reason of failure to pay any poll tax or other tax.

Section 2. The Congress shall have power to enforce this article by appropriate legislation.

AMENDMENT XXV

Section 1. In the case of the removal of the President from office or his death or resignation, the Vice President shall become President.

Section 2. Whenever there is a vacancy in the office of the Vice President, the President shall nominate a Vice President who shall take the office upon confirmation by a majority vote of both houses of Congress.

Section 3. Whenever the President transmits to the President pro tempore of the Senate and the Speaker of the House of Representatives his written declaration that he is unable to discharge the powers and duties of his office, and until he transmits to them a written declaration to the contrary, such powers and duties shall be discharged by the Vice President as Acting President.

Section 4. Whenever the Vice President and a majority of either the principal officers of the executive departments, or of such other body as Congress may by law provide, transmit to the President pro tempore of the Senate and the Speaker of the House of Representatives their written declaration that the President is unable to discharge the powers and duties of his office, the Vice President shall immediately assume the powers and duties of the office as Acting President.

Thereafter, when the President transmits to the President pro tempore of the Senate and the Speaker of the House of Representatives his written declaration that no inability exists, he shall resume the powers and duties of his office unless the Vice President and a majority of either the principal officer of the executive department, or of such other body as Congress may by law provide, transmit within four days to the President pro tempore of the Senate and the Speaker of the House of Representatives their written declaration that the President is unable to discharge the powers and duties of his office. Thereupon Congress shall decide the issue, assembling within 48 hours for that purpose if not in session. If the Congress, within 21 days after receipt of the latter written declaration, or, if Congress is not in session, within 21 days after Congress is required to assemble, determines by two-thirds vote of both houses that the President is unable to discharge the powers and duties of his office, the Vice President shall continue to discharge the same as Acting President; otherwise, the President shall resume the power and duties of his office.

INDEX